D1357804

DAY HIKES AROUND
Missoula
MONTANA

INCLUDING THE BITTERROOTS
AND THE SEELEY-SWAN VALLEY

Robert Stone

4th EDITION

Day Hike Books, Inc.
RED LODGE, MONTANA

Published by Day Hike Books, Inc.
P.O. Box 865
Red Lodge, Montana 59068
www.dayhikebooks.com

Distributed by The Globe Pequot Press
246 Goose Lane
P.O. Box 480
Guilford, CT 06437-0480
800-243-0495 (direct order) · 800-820-2329 (fax order)
www.globe-pequot.com

Cover photograph by Nelson Kenter
kenterphotography.com
Back cover photograph by Robert Stone
Layout and maps by Paula Doherty

The author has made every attempt to provide accurate information in this book. However, trail routes and features may change—please use common sense and forethought, and be mindful of your own capabilities. Let this book guide you, but be aware that each hiker assumes responsibility for their own safety. The author and publisher do not assume any responsibility for loss, damage, or injury caused through the use of this book.

Copyright © 2013 by Day Hike Books, Inc.
4th Edition
Printed in the United States of America
ISBN: 978-1-57342-066-2
Library of Congress Control Number: 2011920362

Cover photo:
Clark Fork River

Back cover photo:
Lake Como

Table of Contents

THE HIKES

NORTHEAST MISSOULA

Rattlesnake National Recreation Area
(including the Sawmill—Curry Trail System)

Mount Jumbo Recreation Area
East Missoula

North Hills • Rattlesnake Valley

MISSOULA

City of Missoula • Mount Sentinel
Pattee Canyon Recreation Area • South Hills

Blue Mountain Recreation Area

NORTHWEST MISSOULA

Frenchtown • Ninemile Valley

SOUTHWEST MISSOULA: HIGHWAY 12

Lolo to Lolo Pass
including the Fish Creek Drainage

Lolo Pass into Idaho

BITTERROOT VALLEY

ROCK CREEK DRAINAGE

BLACKFOOT RIVER RECREATIONAL CORRIDOR

SEELEY—SWAN VALLEY

Section Maps:

p. 14   Overall map of all hikes

16   Northeast Missoula • Hikes 1–21

34   Sawmill–Curry Trail System • Hikes 5–9

44   Lower Rattlesnake Valley • Hikes 11–21

70   City of Missoula • Hikes 22–36

78   Downtown Missoula

106   Blue Mountain Recreation Area • Hikes 37–43

134   Ninemile Valley • Hikes 46–50

140   Highway 12: Lolo to Lolo Pass and Idaho • Hikes 51–65

150   Lolo Trail and connecting hikes • Hikes 54–61

178   Bitterroot Valley • Hikes 66–85

212   City of Hamilton

242   Seeley–Swan Valley • Hikes 93–102

Suggested commercial maps for additional hiking:

U.S. Geological Survey topographic maps

Beartooth Publishing: Missoula–Hamilton–Lost Trail Pass

CGM Services: Missoula Bike Map

Missoulian Hike Bike Run

U.S. Forest Service: Lolo National Forest–Seeley Lake

U.S. Forest Service: Selway Bitterroot Wilderness

U.S. Forest Service: Flathead National Forest

U.S. Forest Service: Rattlesnake National Rec. Area and Wilderness

Hiking Missoula

Missoula is rich in character and diversity with a wide variety of museums, art galleries, boutiques, restaurants, a university, musical and cultural events, as well as being encircled by picturesque scenery and a huge network of hiking trails. The town was first settled in the 1860s. It grew rapidly as a mining and logging center with the arrival of the railroad. It is now the third largest city in Montana and an active university town. A beautiful historic commercial district with turn-of-the-century architecture lines the downtown streets. The historic residential district spreads outward to the university. The University of Montana, on the banks of the Clark Fork River, is located near the base of Mount Sentinel by the mouth of Hellgate Canyon.

Missoula sits at the hub of five merging valleys at an elevation of 3,200 feet. The town is surrounded by mountains—the Bitterroot Range to the south, the Mission Range to the north, the Blackfoot and Hellgate Ranges to the east, and the Missoula Range to the west. Three major rivers—the Bitterroot, the Blackfoot, and the Clark Fork—run through or are within a few miles of the city. A short distance in any direction leads to national forests and wilderness areas.

The two-million-acre Lolo National Forest surrounds Missoula. The national forest has an abundance of wildlife, including black bear, grizzly, moose, deer, big horn sheep, mountain goats, wolves, and elk. The forest also has 350,000 acres of winter elk range. The land is rich with ponderosa pine, lodgepole pine, Douglas fir, subalpine fir, and western larch. The Lolo National Forest provides access into four wilderness areas and a variety of recreational areas. Within four miles of town are the Pattee Canyon Recreation Area, the Blue Mountain Recreation Area, and the Rattlesnake National Recreation Area. Much of the area is set aside for preservation as wilderness.

Rattlesnake Creek, Missoula's watershed, flows southward into the city through Rattlesnake Canyon's narrow valley floor. The drainage is fed by more than fifty smaller creeks. Within this area are several trailheads and a network of interconnecting trails. The trails run from gulches to mountain ridges, through alpine and subalpine landscape. The glacially carved topography is home to 7,000-foot summits, hanging valleys, cirques, and more than 30 lakes.

To the south of Missoula, along Highway 93, is the Bitterroot Valley. The Bitterroot River carved this wide valley that sits at an elevation of 3,000 feet. The fertile valley is nestled between two mountain ranges—the Bitterroot Mountains and the Sapphire Mountains.

The dramatic Bitterroot Mountains line the west side of the valley. The Bitterroots straddle the Continental Divide and form the Montana–Idaho border. The northern end of the range runs through Montana's wettest areas, receiving more than 100 inches of moisture annually. The Bitterroot Range is known for its jagged 9,000-foot granite peaks and deep canyons. Creeks run down 14 major canyons, fed from the alpine lakes above. Precipitous canyon walls rise 5,000 feet from the valley floor in only three miles. The Bitterroot National Forest covers the range, encompassing 1.6 million acres. About half the forest is protected wilderness area. The Bitterroot Mountains have an extensive 1,600-mile trail system, including the Nez Perce Trail (route of the tragic flight in 1877) and the historic Lewis and Clark Trail.

To the east of the Bitterroot Valley are the molten slopes of the Sapphire Mountains. The remote Sapphire Range has 98,000 acres of designated wilderness, including the Welcome Creek Wilderness. With narrow canyons and steep ridges, the main artery of the Welcome Creek Wilderness is Rock Creek, a blue-ribbon trout fishing creek.

To the northeast of Missoula, along Highway 83, is the glacially carved Seeley-Swan Valley. This ten-mile wide corridor extends for eighty miles with two beautiful rivers—the Clearwater River flowing southward and the Swan River flowing northward. The valley is bordered to the west for thirty miles by the majestic snow-capped Mission Mountains. To the valley's east is the Swan Mountain Range, offering access into the Bob Marshall Wilderness, the Scapegoat Wilderness, and the Great Bear Wilderness. Along the valley and its bordering mountain ranges are hundreds of pristine lakes. With over 400 miles of hiking trails, dozens of campgrounds, resorts, guest ranches, and easy access to the back country, the Seeley-Swan Valley is a recreational haven.

The trailheads are located within a 105-mile radius of Missoula (although most are much closer). All hikes can be completed during the day. Many trails, of course, continue for miles, connecting to a network of trails across the mountains. A quick glance at the hikes' summaries will allow you to choose a hike that is appropriate to your ability and desire. An overall map on the next page identifies the general locations of the hikes and major access roads. Several other regional maps in this book (underlined in the table of contents), as well as maps for each hike, provide the essential details. Relevant commercial maps are listed under the hikes' statistics if you wish to explore more of the area. A good selection includes the Beartooth Publishing: Missoula/Hamilton/Lost Trail Pass map, the Lolo National Forest map, Selway-Bitterroot Wilderness map, Flathead National Forest map, Rattlesnake Wilderness map, and the U.S.G.S. topographic maps (all published by the U.S. Forest Service). CGM Services produces the Missoula Bike Map that details the best bike routes within the city. Pick up a copy of the Missoulian Hike Bike Run guide for a quick overview of the trails around the city.

Even though these trails are described as day hikes, some of the trails involve serious backcountry hiking. Reference the hiking statistics listed at the top of each page for an approximation of difficulty, and match the hikes to your ability. Hiking times are calculated for continuous hiking. Allow extra time for exploration. Feel free to hike farther than these day hike suggestions, but be sure to carry additional topographic maps and supplies. Use good judgement about your capabilities, and be prepared with adequate clothing and supplies.

The elevation for these hikes may be as high as 8,000 feet. Be aware that the increased elevation affects your stamina. Weather conditions undoubtedly change throughout the day and seasons. It is imperative to wear warm, layered clothing, especially when hiking up to higher elevations. Snacks, water, and a basic first aid kit are a must. Both black and grizzly bears inhabit the region, so wear a bear bell and hike in a group whenever possible. Some preparation and forethought will help ensure a safe, enjoyable, and memorable hike.

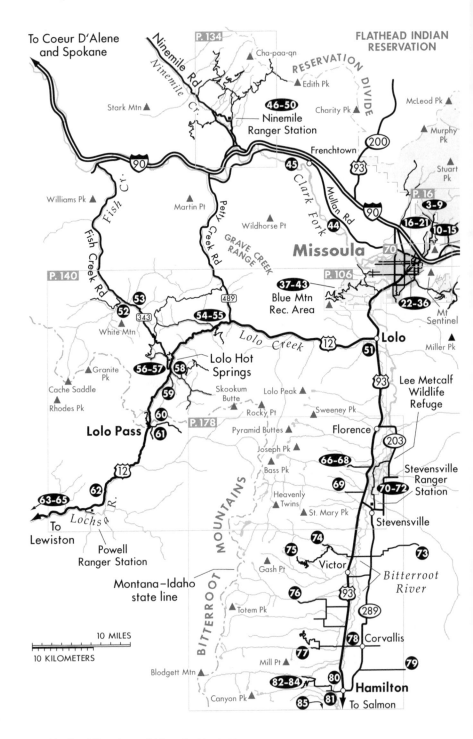

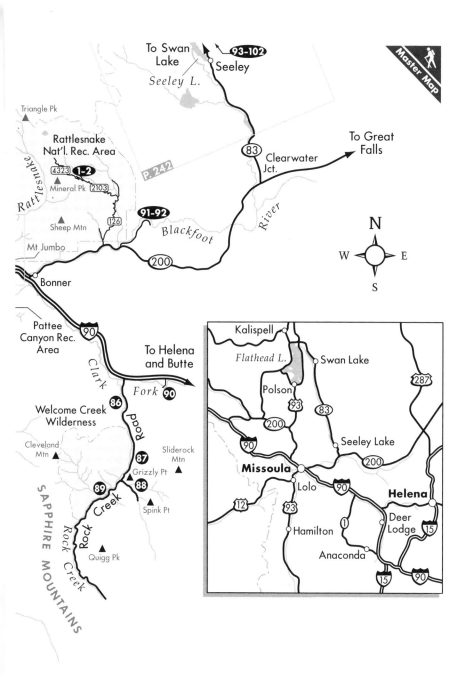

MAP of the HIKES

MISSOULA and VICINITY

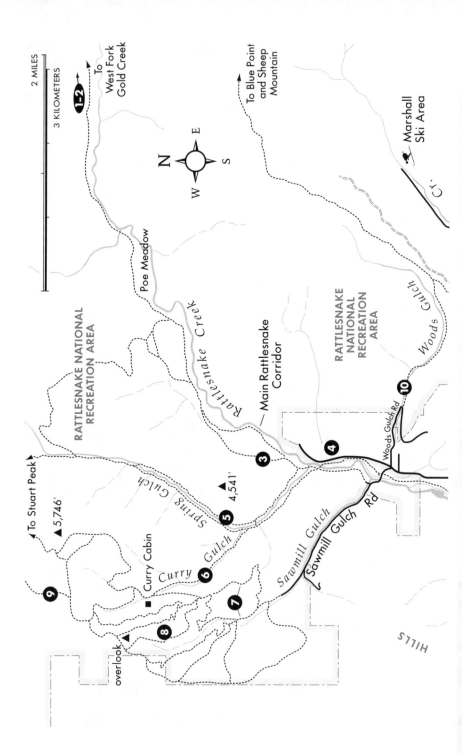

2 MILES

3 KILOMETERS

1-2

To West Fork Gold Creek

To Blue Point and Sheep Mountain

Marshall Ski Area

N E S W

Poe Meadow

Rattlesnake Creek

RATTLESNAKE NATIONAL RECREATION AREA

Main Rattlesnake Corridor

RATTLESNAKE NATIONAL RECREATION AREA

Woods Gulch

3

4

10

Woods Gulch Rd

To Stuart Peak

▲5,746'

▲4,541'

Spring Gulch

5

Curry Cabin

Curry Gulch

6

9

7

8

overlook

Sawmill Gulch

Sawmill Gulch Rd

HILLS

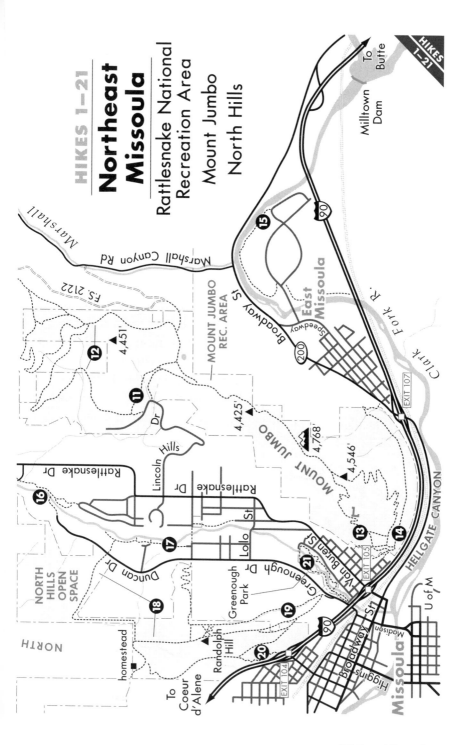

HIKES 1–21

Northeast Missoula

Rattlesnake National Recreation Area
Mount Jumbo
North Hills

1. Boulder Point and Boulder Lake
RATTLESNAKE NATIONAL RECREATION AREA

Hiking distance: 10 miles round trip
Hiking time: 6 hours
Elevation gain: 1,700 feet
Maps: U.S.G.S. Wapiti Lake
Beartooth Publishing: Missoula, Hamilton, Lost Trail Pass
U.S.F.S. Rattlesnake Nat'l. Recreation Area and Wilderness
Rattlesnake National Recreation Area and Wilderness map

Boulder Point is perched atop 7,293-foot cliffs in the Gold Creek area of the Upper Rattlesnake Wilderness. Boulder Point was the site of a fire lookout until 2003, when the Mineral/Primm Fire reduced it to a few charred remains. From this summit is a spectacular view of Boulder Lake, the Gold Creek drainage, and a view across the forested wilderness to the Mission Mountains. Past the point, the trail continues steeply down the cliffs to Boulder Lake. This 109-acre alpine lake is the largest among more than 30 lakes in the Rattlesnake Wilderness. The lake sits in a forested cirque and is the source of Gold Creek, a tributary of the Blackfoot River. The Boulder Lake Trail leads to both Boulder Point and Boulder Lake. En route, the trail winds through open meadows, lodgepole

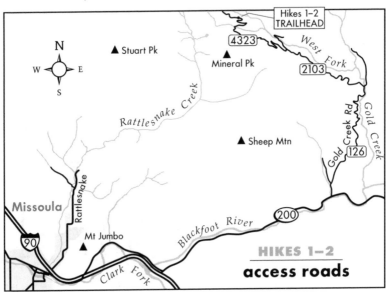

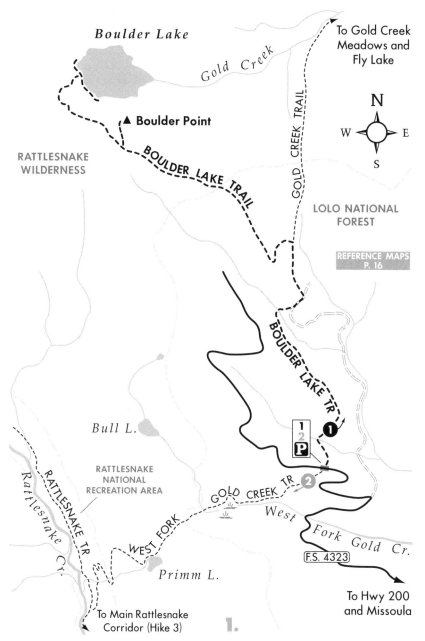

Boulder Lake

Gold Creek

To Gold Creek
Meadows and
Fly Lake

▲ **Boulder Point**

GOLD CREEK TRAIL

N
W ✦ E
S

**RATTLESNAKE
WILDERNESS**

BOULDER LAKE TRAIL

GOLD

**LOLO NATIONAL
FOREST**

REFERENCE MAPS
P. 16

BOULDER LAKE TR

Bull L.

**RATTLESNAKE
NATIONAL
RECREATION AREA**

1
2
P

❶

GOLD CREEK TR

❷

Rattlesnake Cr.

RATTLESNAKE TR

WEST FORK

West Fork Gold Cr.

F.S. 4323

Primm L.

To Main Rattlesnake
Corridor (Hike 3)

To Hwy 200
and Missoula

1.

Boulder Point and Boulder Lake
RATTLESNAKE NATIONAL RECREATION AREA

and alpine forests, burn areas from the Mineral/Primm Fire, and crosses two creeks.

To the trailhead

From Missoula, drive 4 miles east on I-90, and exit onto Highway 200 East (Exit 109). Continue 10.5 miles to signed Gold Creek Road (Forest Service Road 126). Turn left and drive 6 miles to posted Forest Service Road 2103. Veer left and go 5.1 miles to Forest Service Road 4323, signed for the West Fork Gold Creek Trailhead. Turn left and continue 5.5 miles to the signed trailhead. Park in the pullouts on either side of the road.

The hike

From the trailhead kiosk, head north, passing through a skeleton forest from the wildfire of 2003. Descend to a major fork of the West Fork of Gold Creek. Cross downfall logs over the creek, and head up the rock-dotted hill. Pass through flower-filled meadows with burned tree stumps and a young forest of pines and firs. At 1.7 miles, cross a second feeder stream on downfall logs. Continue to a defunct road at 2 miles. Veer left on the road, and walk 400 yards to a distinct cairn on the left. Go left on the trail, and enter a lodgepole pine forest. At 2.6 miles is a junction marked by a sign posted on a tree. The Gold Creek Trail continues straight ahead, leading to Gold Creek Meadows and Fly Lake.

For this hike, bear left, staying on the Boulder Lake Trail. Steadily ascend the mountain, gaining 600 feet over the next mile to the signed Rattlesnake Wilderness boundary. Continue climbing on the rocky path to the edge of the cliffs, with a near-vertical drop into the Gold Creek drainage. Follow the cliff edge less than a quarter mile to a signed fork. The main trail leads to the water's edge of Boulder Lake. For now, bear right and follow the spine of the mountain as the path fades in and out. The footpath ends at Boulder Point, offering a spectacular view of Boulder Lake 800 feet below. After savoring the expansive views, return to the junction.

To continue 1.2 miles to Boulder Lake, go to the right and gently descend northwest. Curve right and weave sharply down to the edge of the forested lake. Return by retracing your route. ∎

2. West Fork Gold Creek Trail to Primm Lake and Rattlesnake Creek

RATTLESNAKE NATIONAL RECREATION AREA

Hiking distance: 3.6 miles round trip to Primm Lake
6.6 miles round trip to Rattlesnake Creek
Hiking time: 2 hours to Primm Lake
4 hours to Rattlesnake Creek
Elevation gain: 200 feet to Primm Lake;
1,100 feet to Rattlesnake Creek

**map
page 22**

Maps: U.S.G.S. Wapiti Lake
Beartooth Publishing: Missoula, Hamilton, Lost Trail Pass
U.S.F.S. Rattlesnake Nat'l. Recreation Area and Wilderness
Rattlesnake National Recreation Area and Wilderness map

The glacially carved Rattlesnake Mountains form the northern backdrop of Missoula Valley. The headwaters of the West Fork Gold Creek begin at the northern base of 7,447-foot Mineral Peak in the upper Rattlesnake Wilderness. The West Fork Gold Creek Trail traverses the north slope of the creek drainage to Primm Lake. The tree-lined alpine lake rests in a scenic depression at the foot of Mineral Peak. From the lake, the trail zippers down the east wall of Rattlesnake Canyon to Rattlesnake Creek in a stunningly gorgeous setting of towering cliffs and giant larch trees.

To the trailhead

From Missoula, drive 4 miles east on I-90, and exit onto Highway 200 East (Exit 109). Continue 10.5 miles to signed Gold Creek Road (Forest Service Road 126). Turn left and drive 6 miles to posted Forest Service Road 2103. Veer left and go 5.1 miles to Forest Service Road 4323, signed for the West Fork Gold Creek Trailhead. Turn left and continue 5.5 miles to the signed trailhead. Park in the pullouts on either side of the road.

The hike

From the trailhead kiosk, take the signed West Fork Gold Creek Trail on the south side of the road. The footpath gently descends through an open landscape dotted with pines. The fire lookout atop Mineral Peak can be seen to the south. Gently lose elevation through a lodgepole pine forest on the northern slope of the West Fork Gold Creek Canyon. Weave through the quiet of the old forest. Skirt around the north side of a wetland meadow. Heading west, hop across the West Fork of Gold Creek. At 1.3 miles, enter the signed Rattlesnake Wilderness. Continue downhill, reaching the north end of Primm Lake at 1.8 miles. Follow the shoreline to the west side of the lake. This is a good turn-around spot for a 3.6-mile hike.

To extend the hike to Rattlesnake Creek, veer away from the Primm Lake area and begin the descent. Leave the Rattlesnake Wilderness 0.6 miles from the

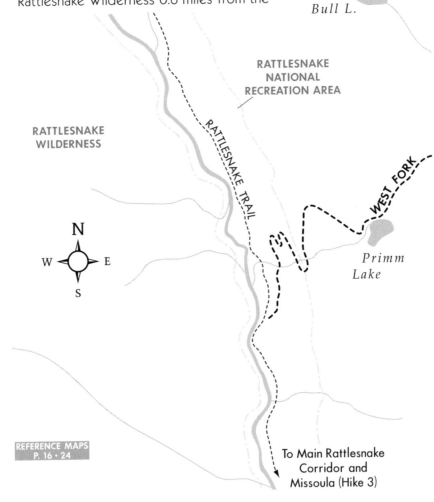

lake. Zigzag down the east Rattlesnake Canyon wall, losing 600 additional feet in elevation to the end of the trail at a junction with the Rattlesnake Trail and Rattlesnake Creek. The canyon bottom is lined with stands of giant larch trees and surrounded by towering cliffs. This is the turn-around point for a 6.6-mile hike.

This trail junction is located 11.6 miles north of the main corridor parking lot at the north end of Missoula (Hike 3). The trail to the main corridor parallels Rattlesnake Creek the entire distance. ■

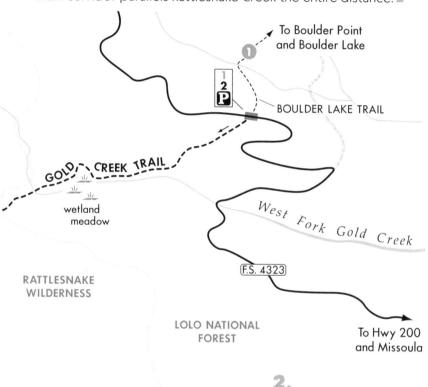

2.
West Fork
Gold Creek Trail
to Primm Lake and
Rattlesnake Creek
RATTLESNAKE NATIONAL
RECREATION AREA

3. Main Rattlesnake Corridor
RATTLESNAKE NATIONAL RECREATION AREA

Hiking distance: 6 miles round trip
Hiking time: 3 hours
Elevation gain: 400 feet
Maps: U.S.G.S. Northeast Missoula
   Beartooth Publishing: Missoula, Hamilton, Lost Trail Pass
   Rattlesnake Nat'l. Recreation Area and Wilderness map

**map
page 26**

The Rattlesnake National Recreation Area and Wilderness, part of the Lolo National Forest, encompasses 61,000 acres north of the Missoula city limits. The area offers many hiking options just a few miles from town. The recreation area contains 28,000 acres, while 33,000 acres are protected as wilderness. This spectacular area has sweeping mountains, hanging valleys, and lake-filled basins. Eight separate trailheads provide access to a web of interconnecting trails.

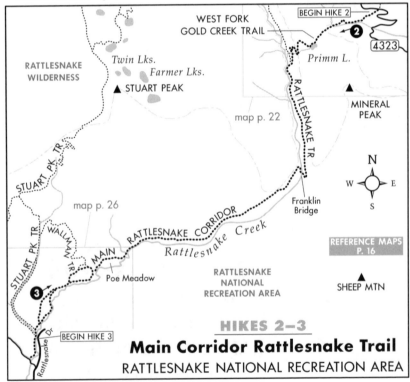

HIKES 2-3
Main Corridor Rattlesnake Trail
RATTLESNAKE NATIONAL RECREATION AREA

The main Rattlesnake corridor, an old logging and farm road, is a popular hiking, biking, and equestrian trail. This hike heads north up the main corridor of the glacially carved drainage. The path parallels Rattlesnake Creek through mountain meadows into protected pine forests, making two loops on the return. For extended hiking, the main trail continues up the Rattlesnake drainage to the lakes around Mosquito Peak, making a large loop back through Spring Gulch. The trail also links to the West Fork Gold Creek Trail 11.6 miles from the trailhead (Hike 2) and Boulder Lake (Hike 1). Dogs are allowed on the Main Rattlesnake Corridor for the first 1.7 miles (but not allowed from December 1—May 15.)

To the trailhead

From I-90 in Missoula, take the Van Buren Street exit and head 4.1 miles north to Sawmill Gulch Road on the left. (En route, Van Buren Street curves into Rattlesnake Drive.) Turn left, crossing over Rattlesnake Creek, and continue a quarter mile to the main trail parking lot on the right.

The hike

Walk up the gravel road past the trailhead sign, parallel to the west side of Rattlesnake Creek. Continue upstream beneath vertical multi-colored cliffs. At a half mile is a junction with the Stuart Peak Trail on the left (Hikes 5 and 6) and a bridge over Rattlesnake Creek on the right, which leads to a livestock trailhead on Rattlesnake Drive (Hike 4). Continue straight ahead on the wide main trail for another quarter mile, and take the smaller path to the right. This path stays close to the creek and reconnects with the main trail 1.7 miles from the trailhead. Continue following the main trail up canyon. At 2 miles, take the posted Wallman Trail to the left. Along the way are three trail forks. Take the right forks, rejoining the main trail. Return along the main trail, completing a double loop.

To extend the hike, the trail continues a half mile into Poe Meadow, then follows the creek 8.6 additional miles to the West Fork Gold Creek Trail—Hike 2. The main trail continues up the Rattlesnake Creek drainage to trail junctions leading to Boulder Lake and Mosquito Peak. ■

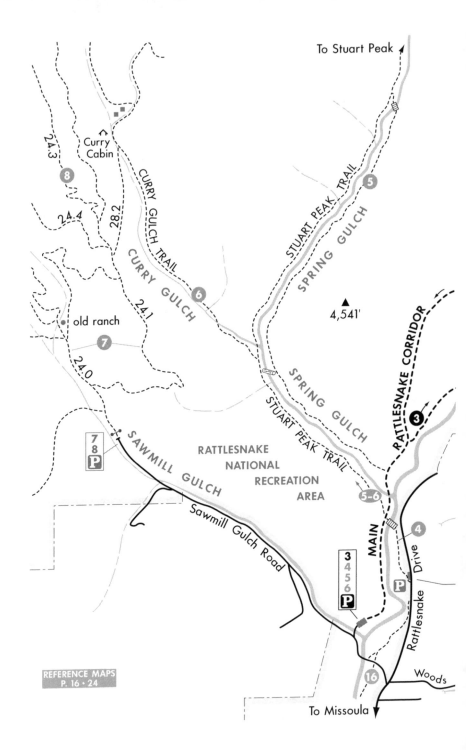

To Stuart Peak

24.3

8

Curry Cabin

24.4

28.2

CURRY GULCH TRAIL

CURRY GULCH

6

24.1

old ranch

7

24.0

5

STUART PEAK TRAIL

SPRING GULCH

▲ 4,541'

SPRING GULCH

STUART PEAK TRAIL

RATTLESNAKE CORRIDOR

3

RATTLESNAKE NATIONAL RECREATION AREA

5-6

MAIN

4

P

Rattlesnake Drive

7 8 P

SAWMILL GULCH

Sawmill Gulch Road

3 4 5 6 P

16

Woods

REFERENCE MAPS
P. 16 · 24

To Missoula

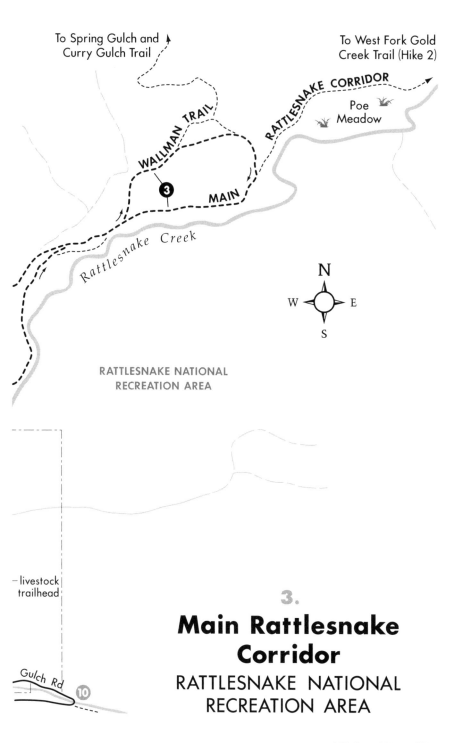

To Spring Gulch and
Curry Gulch Trail

To West Fork Gold
Creek Trail (Hike 2)

RATTLESNAKE CORRIDOR

Poe
Meadow

WALLMAN TRAIL

3

MAIN

Rattlesnake Creek

N
W · E
S

RATTLESNAKE NATIONAL
RECREATION AREA

–livestock
trailhead

Gulch Rd 10

3.
Main Rattlesnake
Corridor
RATTLESNAKE NATIONAL
RECREATION AREA

4. Basic Rattlesnake Loop
RATTLESNAKE NATIONAL RECREATION AREA

Hiking distance: 1.5-mile loop
Hiking time: 45 minutes
Elevation gain: level
Maps: U.S.G.S. Northeast Missoula
Beartooth Publishing: Missoula, Hamilton, Lost Trail Pass
Rattlesnake Nat'l. Recreation Area and Wilderness map

This short, but scenic hike is the most basic loop that can be hiked in the Rattlesnake National Recreation Area. It is a perfect introduction to the area. Rattlesnake Creek flows through the heart of this magnificent recreation and wilderness area on the north edge of Missoula. Snow-melt, high-mountain lakes, and springs feed the 23-mile cascading creek. This hike loops around both sides of the tumbling waterway. Along the way are rocky cliffs, grassland meadows, and a forest of ponderosa pines.

To the trailhead

From I-90 in Missoula, take the Van Buren Street exit. Head 4.1 miles north to Sawmill Gulch Road on the left. (En route, Van Buren Street curves into Rattlesnake Drive.) Turn left, crossing over Rattlesnake Creek, and continue a quarter mile to the main trailhead parking lot on the right.

The hike

Walk up the gravel road past the trailhead sign, parallel to the west side of Rattlesnake Creek. Continue upstream beneath vertical multi-colored cliffs on the left. At a half mile is a junction with the Stuart Peak Trail on the left (Hikes 5 and 6). The main Rattlesnake corridor continues straight ahead (Hike 3).

Bear right and cross the wood and steel bridge over Rattlesnake Creek. Weave a quarter mile through mixed shrubs and meadows to the livestock trailhead. Curve right, skirting the parking lot while overlooking the creek, until reaching Rattlesnake Drive. Walk 250 yards along the side of the road and pick up the trail again. Veer right on the forested footpath filled with the sound of the cascading creek. At 1.3 miles, the path reaches

Sawmill Gulch Road, directly across from the end of Hike 16. Bear right and cross the bridge over Rattlesnake Creek. Continue 0.2 miles back to the trailhead parking lot on the right. ■

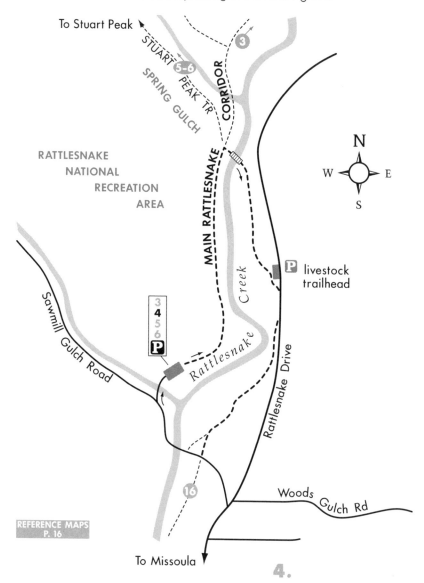

Basic Rattlesnake Loop
RATTLESNAKE NATIONAL RECREATION AREA

5. Stuart Peak Trail: Spring Gulch Loop
RATTLESNAKE NATIONAL RECREATION AREA

Hiking distance: 5.5-mile loop
Hiking time: 3 hours
Elevation gain: 450 feet
Maps: U.S.G.S. Northeast Missoula
　　　　Beartooth Publishing: Missoula, Hamilton, Lost Trail Pass
　　　　Rattlesnake Nat'l. Recreation Area and Wilderness map

Spring Gulch forms on the southwest flank of Stuart Peak and joins with Rattlesnake Creek at the south end of the Rattlesnake National Recreation Area just north of Missoula. The strenuous Stuart Peak Trail parallels Spring Creek seven miles, branching off the main Rattlesnake corridor to the wilderness boundary beneath 7,960-foot Stuart Peak. This easier loop hike climbs up Spring Gulch around both sides of Spring Creek on old cow paths and a farm lane. Remnants from century-old homesites, vacated in the 1930s, can be spotted in the main valley and Spring Gulch. Watch for building foundations and old apple orchards.

To the trailhead

From I-90 in Missoula, take the Van Buren Street exit and head 4.1 miles north to Sawmill Gulch Road on the left. (En route, Van Buren Street curves into Rattlesnake Drive.) Turn left, crossing over Rattlesnake Creek, and continue a quarter mile to the main trail parking lot on the right.

The hike

Hike north past the trailhead sign, parallel to the west side of Rattlesnake Creek on the main Rattlesnake corridor. Continue upstream beneath vertical, multi-colored cliffs. At a half mile is a junction with the Stuart Peak Trail on the left. To the right is a bridge crossing over Rattlesnake Creek to a livestock trailhead on Rattlesnake Drive. Take the narrower Stuart Peak Trail on the left, heading upstream on the south side of Spring Gulch. At the 1.3-mile marker is a log crossing to the right over Spring Gulch for a shorter 2.6-mile loop. Continue north up Spring Gulch, passing the Curry Gulch Trail on the left (Hike 6). At 2.7 miles, as Spring

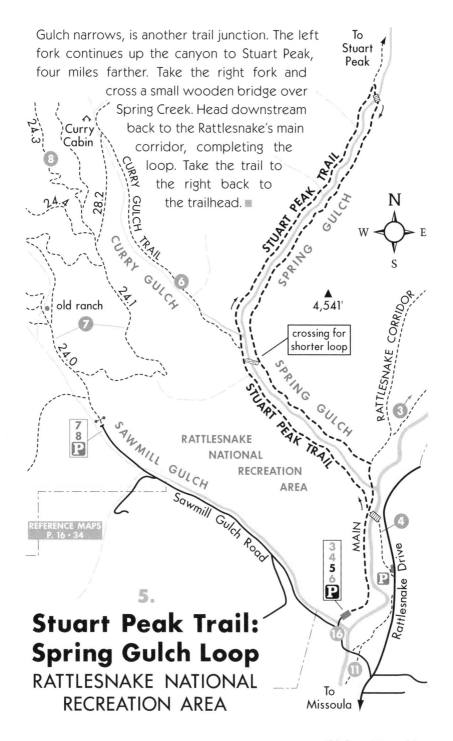

Gulch narrows, is another trail junction. The left fork continues up the canyon to Stuart Peak, four miles farther. Take the right fork and cross a small wooden bridge over Spring Creek. Head downstream back to the Rattlesnake's main corridor, completing the loop. Take the trail to the right back to the trailhead. ◼

To Stuart Peak

24.3

Curry Cabin

8

24.4

28.2

CURRY GULCH TRAIL

CURRY GULCH

24.1

old ranch

7

24.0

STUART PEAK TRAIL

SPRING GULCH

N
W ✦ E
S

▲ 4,541'

crossing for shorter loop

SPRING GULCH

STUART PEAK TRAIL

RATTLESNAKE CORRIDOR

3

7
8
P

SAWMILL GULCH

RATTLESNAKE
NATIONAL
RECREATION
AREA

REFERENCE MAPS
P. 16 · 34

Sawmill Gulch Road

MAIN

3
4
5
6
P

P

Rattlesnake Drive

16

11

5.
Stuart Peak Trail:
Spring Gulch Loop
RATTLESNAKE NATIONAL
RECREATION AREA

To Missoula

6. Curry Gulch Trail to Curry Cabin
RATTLESNAKE NATIONAL RECREATION AREA

Hiking distance: 4.8-mile loop
Hiking time: 2.5 hours
Elevation gain: 400 feet
Maps: U.S.G.S. Northeast Missoula
Beartooth Publishing: Missoula, Hamilton, Lost Trail Pass
Rattlesnake Nat'l. Recreation Area and Wilderness map

Sawmill Gulch and Curry Gulch are fertile mountain drainages in the southwest corner of the Rattlesnake National Recreation Area. The drainages lie within the 880-acre Sawmill–Curry Trail System. The network of trails, dating back to the 1880s, has been made by prospectors, settlers, and livestock. Additional logging roads were developed in the 1960s and 1970s, forming a mosaic of trails that cross through the area. This hike leads to Curry Cabin, a multi-room log cabin built in the late 1800s by Jacob Curry. At the site are two additional log structures—an earth-covered root cellar and an old shed. Several routes can be taken to reach Curry Cabin. This hike begins in the main Rattlesnake corridor and follows the most direct route up two spring-fed canyons—Spring Gulch and Curry Gulch. Dogs are not allowed.

To the trailhead

From I-90 in Missoula, take the Van Buren Street exit and head 4.1 miles north to Sawmill Gulch Road on the left. (En route, Van Buren Street curves into Rattlesnake Drive.) Turn left, crossing over Rattlesnake Creek, and continue a quarter mile to the main trail parking lot on the right.

The hike

Hike north past the trailhead sign, parallel to the west side of Rattlesnake Creek on the main Rattlesnake corridor. Continue upstream beneath vertical multi-colored cliffs. At a half mile is a junction with the Stuart Peak Trail on the left. To the right is a bridge crossing Rattlesnake Creek to a livestock trailhead on Rattlesnake Drive. Bear left up the forested draw along the left bank of Spring Gulch. At the 1.3-mile marker is a log crossing

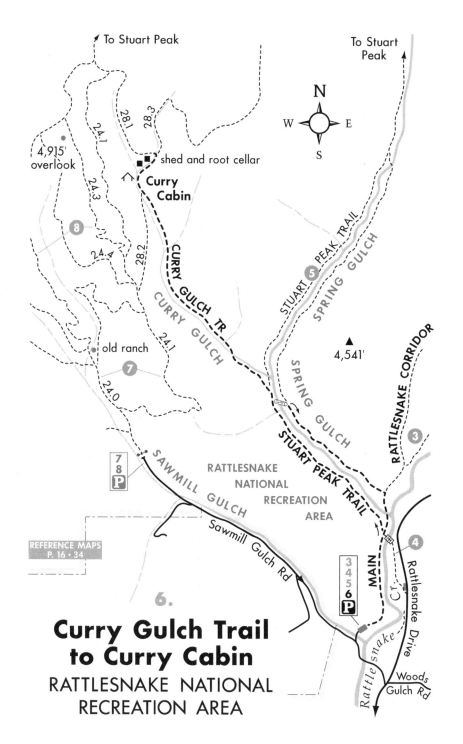

To Stuart Peak

To Stuart Peak

N
W — E
S

4,915' overlook

28.3
28.1
24.1
24.3
shed and root cellar
Curry Cabin

8

28.2

CURRY GULCH TR

CURRY GULCH

24.4

old ranch

24.1

7

24.0

STUART PEAK TRAIL

5

SPRING GULCH

SPRING GULCH

▲ 4,541'

RATTLESNAKE CORRIDOR

3

7 8 **P**

SAWMILL GULCH

RATTLESNAKE NATIONAL RECREATION AREA

STUART PEAK TRAIL

4

Rattlesnake Drive

REFERENCE MAPS
P. 16 • 34

Sawmill Gulch Rd

3 4 5 6 **P**

MAIN

Rattlesnake Cr.

6.

Curry Gulch Trail to Curry Cabin
RATTLESNAKE NATIONAL RECREATION AREA

Woods Gulch Rd

over Spring Gulch, which will be crossed on the return. For now, continue straight ahead about 100 yards north to the signed Curry Gulch Trail. To the right, the trail continues along Spring Gulch—Hike 5. Go to the left, winding through the dense forest while steadily climbing up the drainage. One mile up Curry Gulch is a signed junction. The left fork leads to Sawmill Gulch (Hike 7). Take the right fork 200 yards to the Curry Cabin. After exploring the structures, return along the same trail to the cut-across trail at the 1.3-mile marker. Cross the logs over Spring Gulch, and return to the right along the east side of the creek, heading downstream to the main Rattlesnake corridor. Go to the right, back to the trailhead. ■

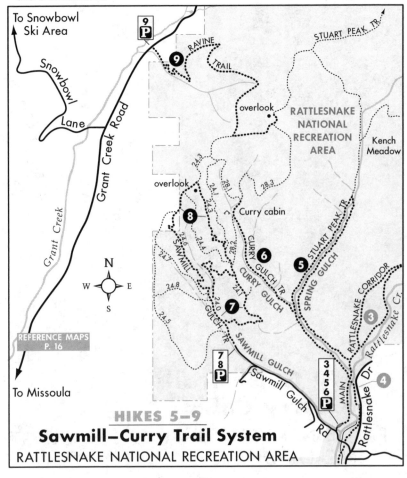

HIKES 5–9
Sawmill–Curry Trail System
RATTLESNAKE NATIONAL RECREATION AREA

7. Lower Sawmill Gulch Loop
RATTLESNAKE NATIONAL RECREATION AREA

Hiking distance: 2.6-mile loop
Hiking time: 1.5 hours
Elevation gain: 500 feet
Maps: U.S.G.S. Northeast Missoula · Sawmill—Curry Trail System map
Beartooth Publishing: Missoula, Hamilton, Lost Trail Pass

map
page 36

Sawmill Gulch, part of the Sawmill-Curry Trail System, is a more recent addition (acquired in 1986) to the Rattlesnake National Recreation Area. The trails are quieter and less frequented than the main Rattlesnake corridor. Many of these trails were originally made in the 1800s by prospectors, settlers, and livestock. This trail follows a large meadow, passing remnants of century-old ranch buildings, homesites, and abandoned orchards. The trails through Sawmill Gulch connect with Curry Gulch (Hike 6) and Spring Gulch (Hike 5) for extended hiking. Dogs are not allowed.

To the trailhead

From I-90 in Missoula, take the Van Buren Street exit and head 4.1 miles north to Sawmill Gulch Road on the left. (En route, Van Buren Street curves into Rattlesnake Drive.) Turn left, crossing over Rattlesnake Creek, and continue 1.4 miles to the road's end. (At 1.2 miles is a road fork—stay to the right.)

The hike

From the parking area, pass the gate at the end of the road. Hike north up the grassy draw rimmed with pines. Pass the posted junction with Trail 24.1 on the right, the return trail. For now, follow the eastern edge of the meadow to the junction with a sign posted on a tree for Trail 24.0. Detour 100 yards straight ahead to the remnants of the old ranch buildings with foundation slabs, rock walls, and old timber.

Return to the junction and continue up Trail 24.0. Traverse the slope behind the old ranch into a narrow draw. Follow the draw to a sharp right bend. Head uphill along the eastern cliff edge, overlooking Sawmill Gulch. Wind through the pine forest to a junction. The left fork climbs to a 4,915-foot overlook (Hike 8) and connects with the Stuart Peak Trail. For this hike, bear right and descend through the forest on Trail 24.1, completing the loop in Sawmill Gulch. Go to the left, returning back down to the trailhead. ■

To overlook and
Stuart Peak Trail

24.1

To Curry
Cabin

24.3

24.4

8

28.2

28.1

6

24.6

CURRY GULCH TRAIL

24.7

8

24.0

CURRY GULCH

24.8

old ranch

24.1

SAWMILL

RATTLESNAKE
NATIONAL
RECREATION AREA

24.1

N

W   E

S

24.0

GULCH

24.5

7
8
P

Sawmill

To
Rattlesnake
Drive and
Missoula

Gulch Road

7.
Sawmill Gulch Loop
RATTLESNAKE NATIONAL
RECREATION AREA

8. Upper Sawmill Gulch Loop to Overlook

RATTLESNAKE NATIONAL RECREATION AREA

Hiking distance: 3.8-mile loop
Hiking time: 2 hours
Elevation gain: 1,100 feet

map
page 39

Maps: U.S.G.S. Northeast Missoula · Sawmill—Curry Trail System map
Beartooth Publishing: Missoula, Hamilton, Lost Trail Pass

This loop hike winds along Sawmill Gulch and Curry Gulch through forested terrain. The trail extends the lower Hike 7 loop, heading up a ridge to a 4,915-foot overlook. From the overlook are far-reaching views north into the Rattlesnake Wilderness. Dogs are not allowed.

To the trailhead

From I-90 in Missoula, take the Van Buren Street exit and head 4.1 miles north to Sawmill Gulch Road on the left. (En route, Van Buren Street curves into Rattlesnake Drive.) Turn left, crossing over Rattlesnake Creek, and continue 1.4 miles to the road's end. (At 1.2 miles is a road fork—stay to the right.)

The hike

From the parking area, pass the gate at the end of the road. Hike north up the grassy draw rimmed with pines. Pass the posted junction with Trail 24.1 on the right. Follow the eastern edge of the meadow to the junction with a sign posted on a tree for Trail 24.0. Begin the loop straight ahead 100 yards to the remnants of old ranch buildings with foundation slabs, rock walls, and old timber on the right. Fifty yards past the old ranch is a junction. Bear right and quickly switchback left. Climb the hillside above Sawmill Gulch. Switchback to the right and curve up the ridge. Climb to panoramic views of Lolo Peak and the Bitterroot Range. At the north end of the ridge, make a horseshoe right bend and continue uphill. The trail soon levels out and opens to far-reaching vistas. A short distance ahead is a junction with Trail 24.4. The right fork returns for a shorter loop. Continue straight to the ridge and a posted junction with Trail 24.3. Straight ahead is the Curry Gulch Trail and the Stuart Peak Trail.

Go to the right on the footpath, skirting the 4,915-foot overlook at the summit. Steadily weave down the mountain while enjoying the spectacular views of the forested mountains and Sawmill Gulch. Pass Trail 24.1 on the left and Trail 24.4 on the right to Trail 24.0 on the right. Take Trail 24.0 and wend down the hill into a narrow, grassy draw. Curve left down the east slope of the draw into Sawmill Gulch. Skirt the back side of the old ranch ruins, and complete the loop 100 yards past the old ranch. Go to the left, returning back down to the trailhead. ■

9. Ravine Trail to Overlook
RATTLESNAKE NATIONAL RECREATION AREA

Hiking distance: 6.2 miles round trip
Hiking time: 3 hours
Elevation gain: 1,550 feet
Maps: U.S.G.S. Northeast Missoula
  Sawmill-Curry Trail System map
  Beartooth Publishing: Missoula, Hamilton, Lost Trail Pass

**map
page 41**

The Ravine Trail is a 2.8-mile trail that climbs into the Rattlesnake National Recreation Area from Grant Creek. Switchbacks weave up the mountain through ponderosa pine and Douglas fir, making the climb relatively easy. The trail ends at a junction with the Sawmill Trail in the Rattlesnake Trail System. The Ravine Trail is the shortest route to Stuart Peak and can be hiked as a shuttle, returning through Spring Gulch, Curry Gulch, or Sawmill Gulch (Hikes 5—8). This hike leads to an overlook on a knoll by rock outcroppings, then returns along the same route. The overlook offers glimpses of the Snowbowl Ski Area.

Dogs are allowed on the Ravine Trail, but not past the junction with Trail 24.1 (Sawmill Trail). Dogs are not allowed from December 1—February 28.

To the trailhead

From Reserve Street and I-90 (Exit 101), drive north on Grant Creek Road, the north extension of Reserve Street. Drive 4.6 miles to

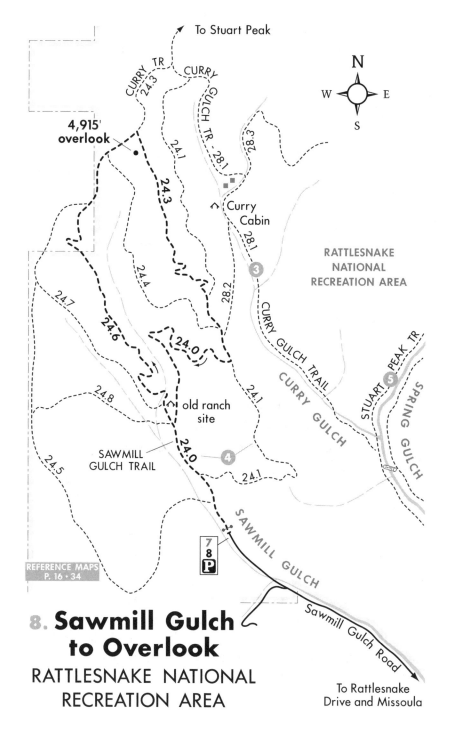

To Stuart Peak

N
W · E
S

CURRY TR 24.3

CURRY GULCH TR · 28.1

28.3

4,915' overlook

24.1

24.3

Curry Cabin

28.1

RATTLESNAKE
NATIONAL
RECREATION AREA

3

24.4

28.2

24.7

24.6

24.0

CURRY GULCH TRAIL

STUART PEAK TR.

5

SPRING GULCH

24.8

old ranch site

24.1

CURRY GULCH

SAWMILL
GULCH TRAIL

24.0

4

24.1

24.5

24.1

7
8
P

SAWMILL GULCH

REFERENCE MAPS
P. 16 · 34

Sawmill Gulch Road

8. Sawmill Gulch to Overlook
RATTLESNAKE NATIONAL RECREATION AREA

To Rattlesnake
Drive and Missoula

the posted Ravine Trail on the right. It is located 0.8 miles past the turnoff to Snowbowl Ski Resort. Turn right and park in the lot.

The hike

Pass the trailhead signage and enter the lush forest. Walk a quarter mile through a private land easement, then enter the Lolo National Forest. Head up the canyon, following the northeast side of the drainage. Zigzag up seven switchbacks, making the elevation gain gradual. Steadily climb through the dense Douglas fir and ponderosa pine forest, traversing the north canyon slope. Cross the drainage near its headwaters and continue up the south canyon wall. At 2.8 miles, the path ends at a T-junction with the Sawmill Trail (24.1). The right fork descends to Curry Gulch and Sawmill Gulch (Hikes 6—8). Bear left and continue uphill 0.3 miles to an overlook by a rock outcrop and a junction. This is our turnaround spot. To extend the hike, the trail continues to a junction with the Spring Gulch Trail (Hike 5) and on to Stuart Peak. Return by retracing your steps. ■

10. Woods Gulch: Sheep Mountain Trail

RATTLESNAKE NATIONAL RECREATION AREA

Hiking distance: 3 miles round trip
Hiking time: 1.5 hours
Elevation gain: 800 feet
Maps: U.S.G.S. Northeast Missoula · Missoulian Hike Bike Run guide
        U.S.F.S. Rattlesnake Nat'l. Recreation Area and Wilderness

map
page 43

Woods Gulch is a lush, streamside canyon along the southern end of Rattlesnake National Recreation Area. The 11-mile Sheep Mountain Trail ascends through Woods Gulch, following the stream-fed drainage in a ponderosa and lodgepole pine forest. This hike follows the first 1.5 miles of the trail, climbing to the ridge above Marshall Canyon. From the ridge are great views of Marshall Canyon, the Marshall Ski Area, and the surrounding

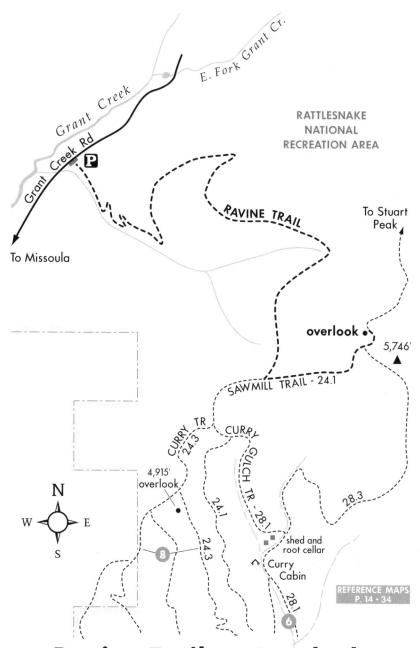

Grant Creek

E. Fork Grant Cr.

Grant Creek Rd

RATTLESNAKE
NATIONAL
RECREATION AREA

P

To Missoula

RAVINE TRAIL

To Stuart
Peak

overlook •

5,746'
▲

SAWMILL TRAIL - 24.1

CURRY TR 24.3

CURRY GULCH TR - 28.1

4,915'
overlook

N
W ◆ E
S

24.1

24.3

28.3

shed and
root cellar

Curry
Cabin

28.1

8

6

REFERENCE MAPS
P. 14 • 34

9. **Ravine Trail to Overlook**
RATTLESNAKE NATIONAL RECREATION AREA

mountains. The Sheep Mountain Trail connects with the extensive trail systems in the Rattlesnake National Recreation Area and Mount Jumbo Recreation Area.

To the trailhead

From I-90 in Missoula, take the Van Buren Street exit and head 4.1 miles north to Woods Gulch Road on the right. (En route, Van Buren Street curves into Rattlesnake Drive.) Turn right and continue 0.5 miles to the signed trailhead on the left. Park in the pullouts on the left.

The hike

Head east past the trail sign and up the forested gulch along the south side of the creek. At a quarter mile is the first of two consecutive creek crossings. Continue steadily uphill 1.5 miles to the top of Woods Gulch. At the ridge is a trail junction. The Sheep Mountain Trail continues along the ridge to the left to Blue Point at 5 miles and Sheep Mountain at 10 miles, following the border of the Rattlesnake National Recreation Area. The right fork connects with the Ridge Trail into the Mount Jumbo Recreation Area (Hikes 11 and 12). Both directions follow a gentle grade and are well-defined. After exploring in either direction, return back down Woods Gulch. ■

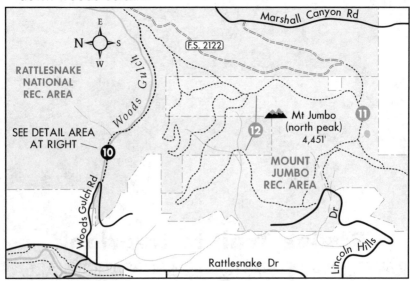

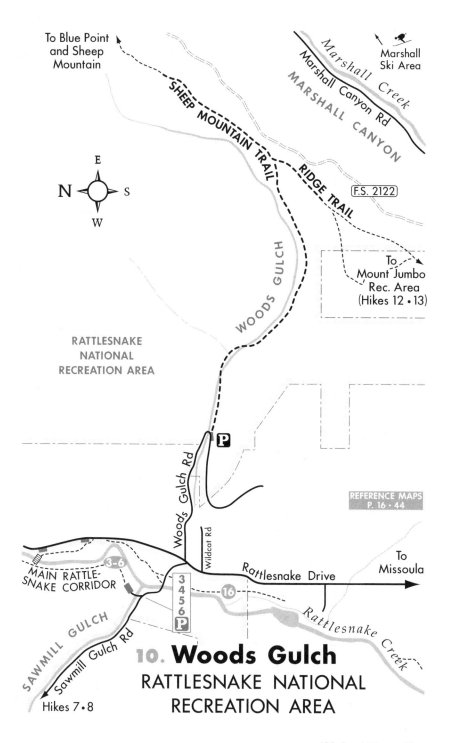

To Blue Point and Sheep Mountain

Marshall Ski Area

Marshall Creek

Marshall Canyon Rd

MARSHALL CANYON

SHEEP MOUNTAIN TRAIL

RIDGE TRAIL

F.S. 2122

WOODS GULCH

To Mount Jumbo Rec. Area (Hikes 12 • 13)

RATTLESNAKE NATIONAL RECREATION AREA

N E S W

P

Woods Gulch Rd

Wildcat Rd

REFERENCE MAPS P. 16 • 44

MAIN RATTLE-SNAKE CORRIDOR

3-6

To Missoula

Rattlesnake Drive

3 4 5 6 **P**

16

Rattlesnake Creek

SAWMILL GULCH

Sawmill Gulch Rd

Hikes 7 • 8

10. **Woods Gulch**
RATTLESNAKE NATIONAL RECREATION AREA

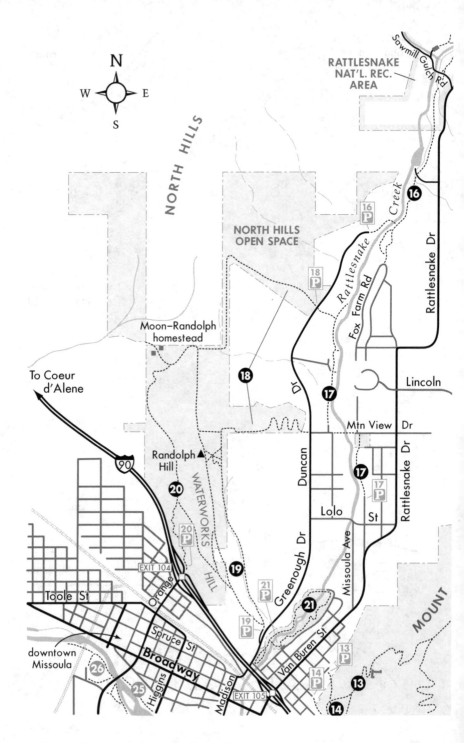

Lower Rattlesnake Valley
North Hills to Mount Jumbo

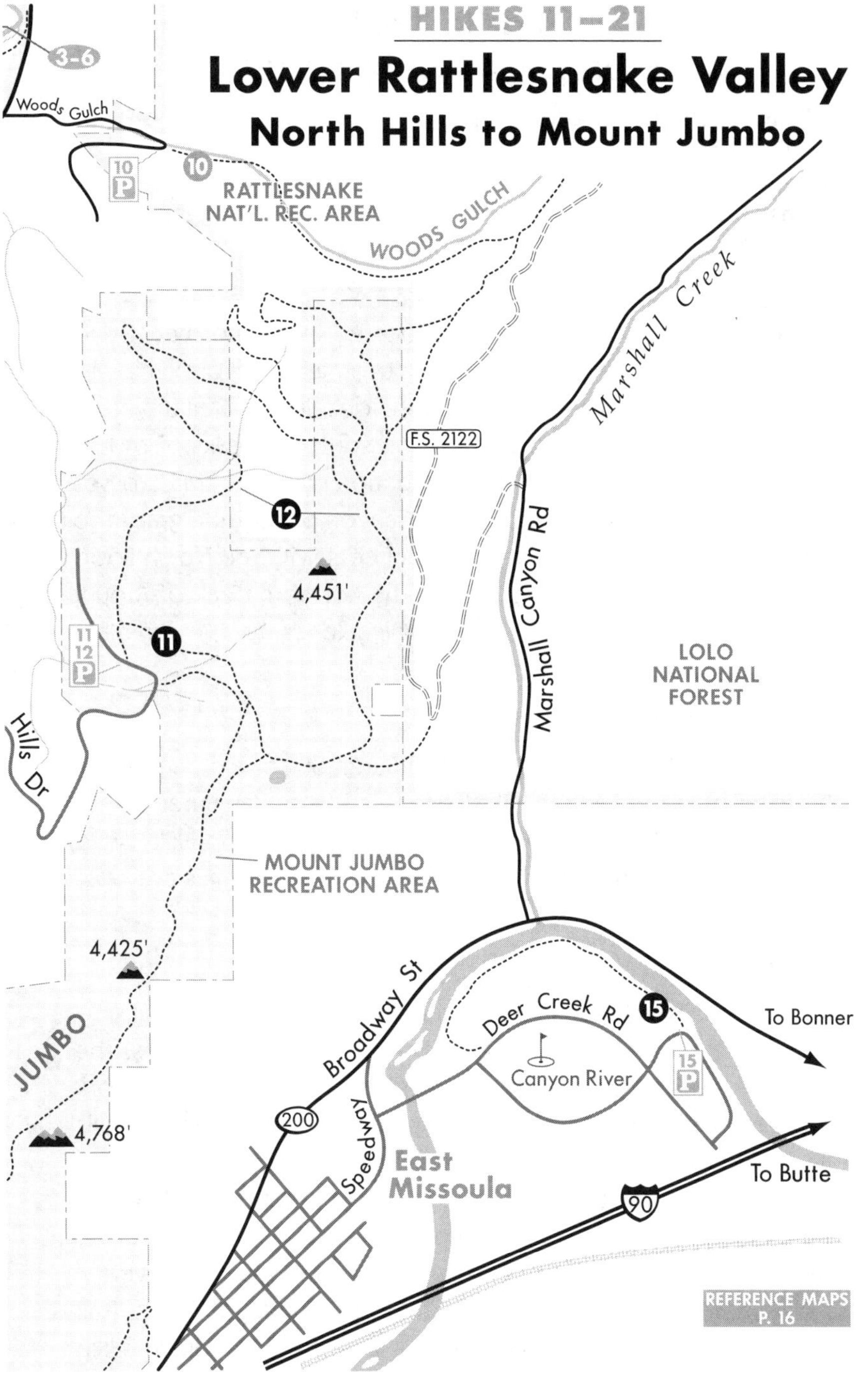

3-6

Woods Gulch

10
P

10

RATTLESNAKE
NAT'L. REC. AREA

WOODS GULCH

Marshall Creek

F.S. 2122

12

4,451'

11
12
P

11

Hills Dr

Marshall Canyon Rd

LOLO
NATIONAL
FOREST

MOUNT JUMBO
RECREATION AREA

4,425'

JUMBO

4,768'

Broadway St

Deer Creek Rd

15

To Bonner

Canyon River

15
P

Speedway

200

East
Missoula

90

To Butte

REFERENCE MAPS
P. 16

11. Saddle Trail
MOUNT JUMBO RECREATION AREA

Hiking distance: 3 miles round trip
Hiking time: 1.5 hours
Elevation gain: 300 feet
Maps: U.S.G.S. Northeast Missoula
       Mount Jumbo Area Recreation Plan map
       Beartooth Publishing: Missoula, Hamilton, Lost Trail Pass

Mount Jumbo Recreation Area is located at the northeast end of Missoula, offering several hiking trails in close proximity to the city and the university. The picturesque Saddle Trail traverses the saddle between the northern and southern peaks of Mount Jumbo, the centerpiece of the recreation area. The trail crosses from Rattlesnake Valley to Marshall Canyon on a gentle grade. To extend the hike, the Saddle Trail connects with the North Loop Trail (Hike 12), which loops around the northern peak of Mount Jumbo, and the Backbone Trail, which leads to the Loyola L (Hike 13).

To the trailhead

From I-90 in Missoula, take the Van Buren Street exit, and head 2.1 miles north to Lincoln Hills Drive. (En route, Van Buren Street curves into Rattlesnake Drive.) Turn right on Lincoln Hills Drive, and continue 1.5 miles to the signed trailhead. Parking is available on both sides of the road.

The hike

Pass the trailhead map and head north across the grassy hillside. At 0.1 mile is a junction just before reaching the utility lines. The left fork is the North Loop Trail (Hike 12). Take the right fork on the Saddle Trail. Head gently uphill, crossing the rolling hills and meadows. At the second pass, under the utility poles, is the Backbone Trail to the right, leading to the Loyola L (Hike 13). Continue on the Saddle Trail, curving left and heading east. Cross the rolling slopes through the tree-dotted meadow by a vernal pool. At 1.1 mile is a junction. To the left is the North Loop Trail (Hike 12), connecting to the Ridge Trail and Woods Gulch (Hike

10). Go right, traversing the hillside above the Clark Fork River and Hellgate Canyon, to the gated Mount Jumbo boundary and gate. Descend 0.2 miles to Forest Service Road 2122, which connects to Marshall Canyon. Return by retracing your steps. ■

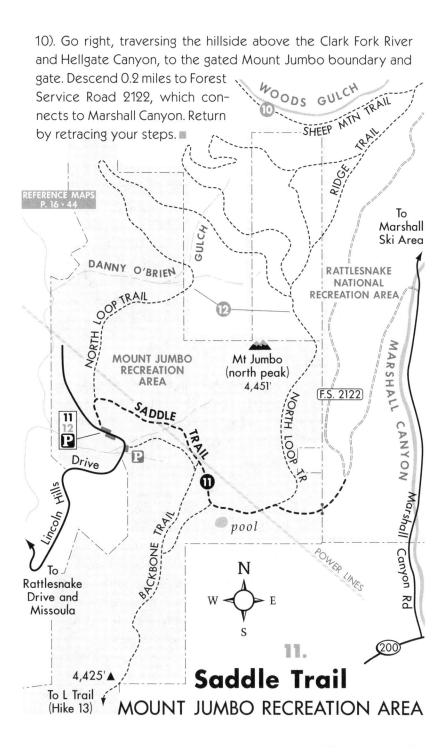

11.
Saddle Trail
MOUNT JUMBO RECREATION AREA

12. North Loop Trail
MOUNT JUMBO RECREATION AREA

Hiking distance: 5-mile loop
Hiking time: 2.5 hours
Elevation gain: 800 feet
Maps: U.S.G.S. Northeast Missoula · Missoulian Hike Bike Run guide

Mount Jumbo sits to the north of Mount Sentinel between Rattlesnake Valley and Marshall Canyon. The North Loop Trail winds through the northern region of Mount Jumbo Recreation Area and connects with Woods Gulch in the Rattlesnake National Recreation Area. The steep hillsides are a wintering range for herds of elk and mule deer. It is closed to hikers throughout the winter until May 1. This trail (an old road) has a gentle grade and offers great views of Rattlesnake Canyon, Marshall Canyon, and across the Missoula Valley to the Bitterroot Range. Dogs are allowed.

To the trailhead

From I-90 in Missoula, take the Van Buren Street exit, and head 2.1 miles north to Lincoln Hills Drive. (En route, Van Buren Street curves into Rattlesnake Drive.) Turn right on Lincoln Hills Drive, and continue 1.5 miles to the signed trailhead. Parking is available on both sides of the road.

The hike

Head north past the trailhead map and up the grassy slope to a trail split. To the right is the Saddle Trail (Hike 11). Bear left, cross under the power lines, and continue gradually uphill into a pine forest and around Danny O'Brien Gulch. At one mile the path leaves the forest and crosses the hillside. At the northwest point, loop back to the right and head southeast. Traverse the edge of the mountain up to the ridge and a junction. The left fork follows the Ridge Trail, connecting with the Sheep Mountain Trail and Woods Gulch (Hike 10). Bear to the right, heading south on the North Loop Trail. Descend through the Douglas fir forest above Marshall Canyon for a mile to a junction with the Saddle Trail. Go right on the Saddle Trail, and cross the rolling slopes between the peaks of Mount Jumbo. Continue past the Backbone Trail on the left, which leads to the Loyola L (Hike 13). Complete the loop and return to the trailhead. ■

N
W　　E
S

Woods Gulch Road

WOODS GULCH

10 P

10

SHEEP MTN TRAIL

RIDGE TRAIL

REFERENCE MAPS
P. 16 • 44

DANNY O'BRIEN

GULCH

NORTH LOOP TRAIL

To Marshall Ski Area

RATTLESNAKE NATIONAL RECREATION AREA

MOUNT JUMBO RECREATION AREA

Mt Jumbo (north peak) 4,451'

F.S. 2122

NORTH LOOP TR

MARSHALL CANYON

12

SADDLE TRAIL

11
12 P

Drive

P

POWER LINES

pool

BACKBONE TRAIL

Lincoln Hills

11

To Rattlesnake Drive and Missoula

To L Trail (Hike 13)

12.
North Loop Trail
MOUNT JUMBO RECREATION AREA

13. L Trail
MOUNT JUMBO RECREATION AREA

Hiking distance: 1.5—7 miles round trip (optional loop)
Hiking time: 1—3 hours
Elevation gain: 500—1,400 feet
Maps: U.S.G.S. Southeast Missoula · The Missoula Bike Map

**map
page 52**

Mount Jumbo lies just north of Mount Sentinel, Hellgate Canyon, and the Clark Fork River in the Mount Jumbo Recreation Area. The north end of the recreation area is a winter range for elk and mule deer (Hike 12). It is closed to hikers through May 1. The hike to the prominent Loyola High School L in the south end of the recreation area—this hike—is open year round. The trail is less crowded than the University of Montana M Trail (Hike 22) but has equally rewarding views of Missoula, the Rattlesnake Valley, and the surrounding mountains.

To the trailhead

From I-90 in Missoula, take the Van Buren Street exit. Head one block north to Poplar Street and turn right. Continue three blocks to the trailhead on the left at the intersection of Poplar Street and Polk Street. Parking is available on both sides of the road.

The hike

Head east up the hillside to the unpaved U.S. West access road, which traverses the south side of Mount Jumbo (Hike 14). The left fork leads to another access at Cherry Street. Cross the road and pick up the footpath towards the L, which can be seen up ahead. Continue to the ridge. Follow the edge of the hillside and cross the grassy flat. Begin the final steep ascent to the painted white rocks forming the large L, the turn-around point for a 1.5-mile round trip hike.

OPTIONAL LOOP HIKE: To extend the hike, curve right and continue climbing past the L to a trail split 0.5 miles past the L. The left fork ascends to the 4,768-foot summit of Mount Jumbo, then follows the Backbone Trail along the ridge to the Saddle Trail (Hike 11). The right fork returns down the south-facing slope, forming a 3.4-mile loop back to the trailhead. ∎

14. Mount Jumbo Traverse in Hellgate Canyon

MOUNT JUMBO RECREATION AREA

Hiking distance: 3.5 miles round trip
Hiking time: 2 hours
Elevation gain: 400 feet each way
Maps: U.S.G.S. Southeast Missoula · The Missoula Bike Map

**map
page 52**

The Mount Jumbo Traverse crosses the exposed southern face of Mount Jumbo. The hike offers bird's-eye views of Hellgate Canyon, the Clark Fork River, and the forested north face of University Mountain. The trail winds through native grasses, connecting Rattlesnake Valley with East Missoula. A portion of the trail follows a U.S. West easement road high above Interstate 90.

To the trailhead

From I-90 in Missoula, take the Van Buren Street exit. Head 0.1 mile north on Van Buren Street to Cherry Street, the second street. Turn right and continue 2.5 blocks to the trailhead at the end of the road. Park alongside the curb.

The hike

Walk to the posted trailhead at the end of Cherry Street. Pass the gate and head up the slope on the narrow gravel road. Views quickly open up across the University of Montana and the Missoula Valley. A spur trail from Poplar Street merges from the right. On the left is the trail to the L (Hike 13). Continue straight ahead to a junction on a horseshoe left bend at a quarter mile. Veer right on the U.S. West access road, and traverse the south slope of Mount Jumbo in Hellgate Canyon. Slowly gain elevation on the grassy slope while overlooking the Clark Fork River and the forested north slope of Mount Sentinel. Top the slope directly across the canyon from the Hellgate Canyon Trail (Hike 28). Traverse the steep hillside at a level grade. Gradually descend and curve right on the hillside dotted with ponderosa pines above East Missoula. Weave down the hillside to the east trailhead at the end of Highton Street at 1.75 miles, just off of Highway 200. Return by retracing your steps. ■

13.
L Trail
14.
Mount Jumbo Traverse in Hellgate Canyon
MOUNT JUMBO RECREATION AREA

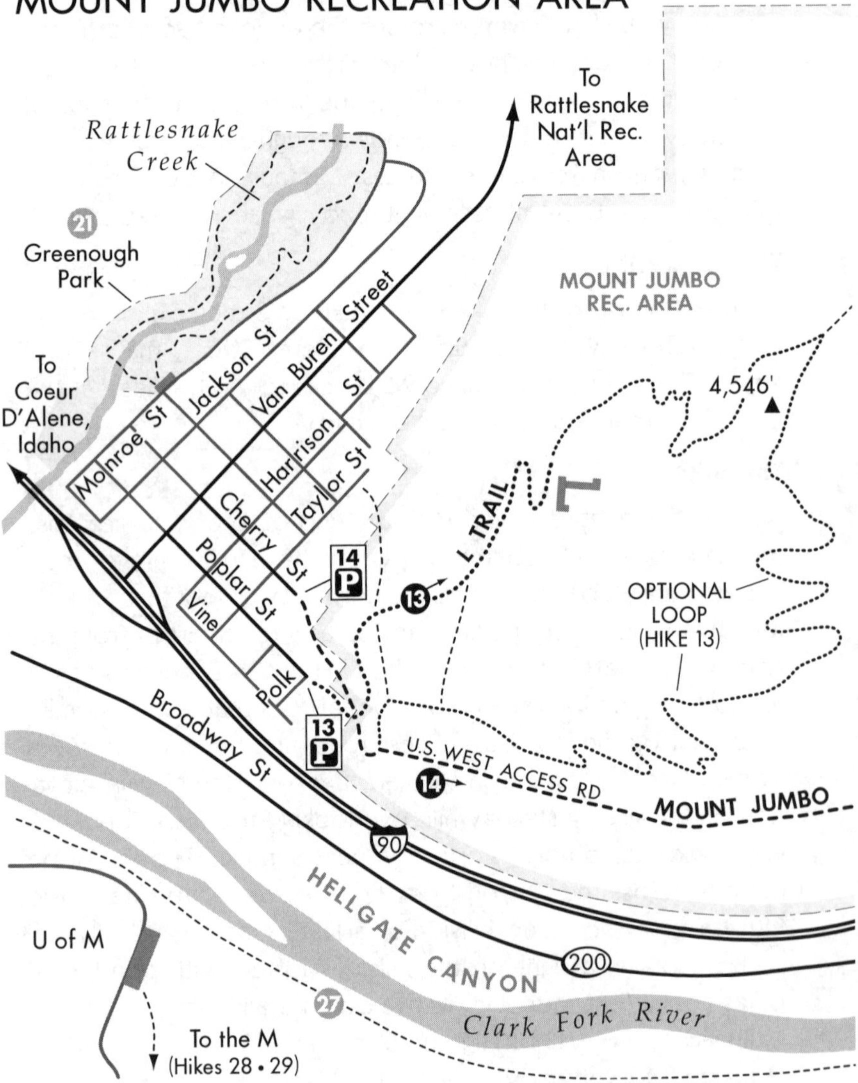

Rattlesnake Creek

21 Greenough Park

To Coeur D'Alene, Idaho

To Rattlesnake Nat'l. Rec. Area

MOUNT JUMBO REC. AREA

4,546'

Monroe St

Jackson St

Van Buren Street

Harrison St

Taylor St

Cherry St

Poplar St

Vine

Polk

14 P

13

L TRAIL

OPTIONAL LOOP (HIKE 13)

13 P

14

U.S. WEST ACCESS RD.

MOUNT JUMBO

Broadway St

90

U of M

HELLGATE CANYON

200

27

Clark Fork River

To the M (Hikes 28 • 29)

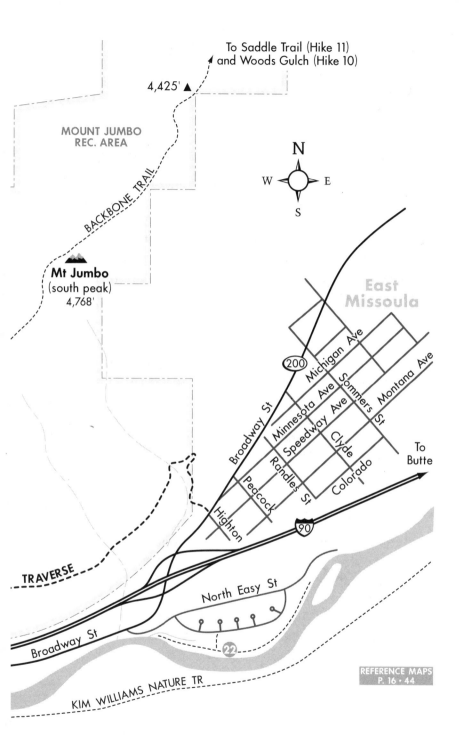

To Saddle Trail (Hike 11)
and Woods Gulch (Hike 10)

4,425' ▲

MOUNT JUMBO
REC. AREA

BACKBONE TRAIL

N
W ⬥ E
S

Mt Jumbo
(south peak)
4,768'

East
Missoula

Michigan Ave

200

Minnesota Ave

Sommers St

Montana Ave

Broadway St

Speedway Ave

Clyde

Randles St

Colorado

Peacock

To
Butte

Highton

90

TRAVERSE

North Easy St

22

Broadway St

KIM WILLIAMS NATURE TR

REFERENCE MAPS
P. 16 · 44

15. Canyon River Trail

Hiking distance: 2 miles round trip
Hiking time: 1 hour
Elevation gain: level
Maps: U.S.G.S. Northeast Missoula
   Canyon River Golf Community map
   Beartooth Publishing: Missoula, Hamilton, Lost Trail Pass

The Canyon River Trail is located in the Canyon River Golf Community in East Missoula. The public trail is one mile long and follows a big bend in the Clark Fork River. The level, dog-friendly path begins at the club house and connects with the community center. From the low bluffs, side paths lead down to the banks of the river. Throughout the hike are picturesque views of Mount Jumbo and Mount Sentinel.

To the trailhead

From I-90 and the East Missoula exit 107, head north 1.3 miles on Broadway Street/Highway 200 to Speedway Avenue. Turn right and go 0.2 miles to Deer Creek Road. Turn left and continue 0.9 miles to Bandmann Trail, signed for the Canyon River Golf Club House. Turn left and drive 0.1 miles to the club house parking lot on the left. Turn left and veer right to the far end of the parking lot, nearest to the Clark Fork River by the trailhead sign.

The hike

Pass the trailhead sign and descend to the Clark Fork River. Curve left and follow the river downstream on the wide gravel path. The trail skirts the perimeter of the golf course on a low bluff above the river. Pass scattered ponderosa pines and side paths that lead to the water's edge. At the far west end of the trail, leave the waterway and curve left along the outside boundary of the golf course. The gravel path ends and joins the golf cart road by the 7th tee. The golf cart road crosses Deer Creek Road and leads to the Canyon River Golf Community Center. Return by retracing your steps. ∎

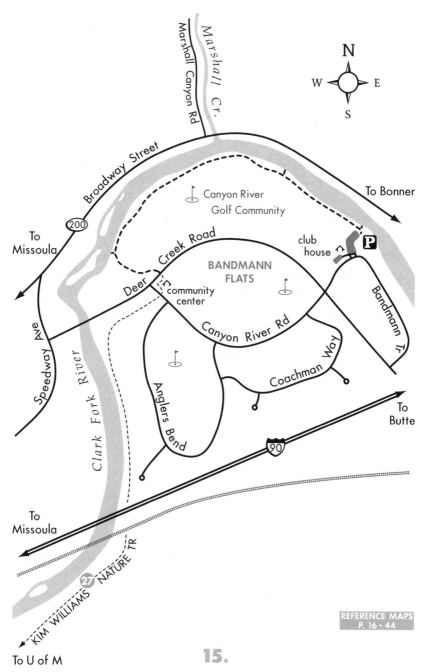

N
W   E
S

Marshall Canyon Rd

Marshall Cr.

Broadway Street

⚐ Canyon River
Golf Community

To Bonner

(200)

To
Missoula

Deer   Creek Road

BANDMANN
FLATS

club
house

P

community
center

Canyon River Rd

Bandmann Tr

Speedway Ave

Clark Fork River

Anglers Bend

Coachman Way

To
Butte

(90)

To
Missoula

KIM WILLIAMS NATURE TR

(27)

To U of M

15.

Canyon River Trail

16. Upper Rattlesnake Greenway

Hiking distance: 2.8 miles round trip
Hiking time: 1.5 hours
Elevation gain: 80 feet
Maps: U.S.G.S. Northeast Missoula · The Missoula Bike Map

The headwaters of Rattlesnake Creek form at McLeod Peak in the Rattlesnake National Recreation Area and Wilderness. The creek flows south through the heart of the wilderness and recreation area, cascading down Rattlesnake Valley before joining the Clark Fork River between the Madison Street Bridge and the Van Buren Street Bridge. This hike follows Rattlesnake Creek in the upper end of the valley on a near-level trail, meandering through ponderosa pines and riparian habitat. At its north end, the trail connects with the main Rattlesnake corridor (Hike 3), providing access to the extensive trail system in the Rattlesnake National Recreation Area.

To the trailhead

From the intersection of Broadway Street and Madison Street just east of downtown, drive 0.1 mile north on Madison Street to a T-junction. Turn right on Greenough Drive and continue 3 miles (passing under I-90) to the end of the road by the posted trailhead. Park alongside the shoulder. (Greenough Drive becomes Duncan Drive after Lolo Street.)

The hike

Walk 200 yards past the trailhead gate to Rattlesnake Creek. Cross the Rattlesnake Creek bridge, a beautiful log and metal bridge, to a T-junction. Bear right and head downstream through the ponderosa pine forest. The path ends in a quarter mile at a horseshoe bend on Timberlane.

Return 50 yards and veer left on a footpath. Follow the edge of Rattlesnake Creek, forming a loop back at the bridge. Continue north and cross a bridge over Williams Water Ditch. Enter a public access easement by a map panel, and cross an access road to the Mountain Water Company dam and reservoir. Walk between a horse pasture and barn on the right and the reservoir on the left.

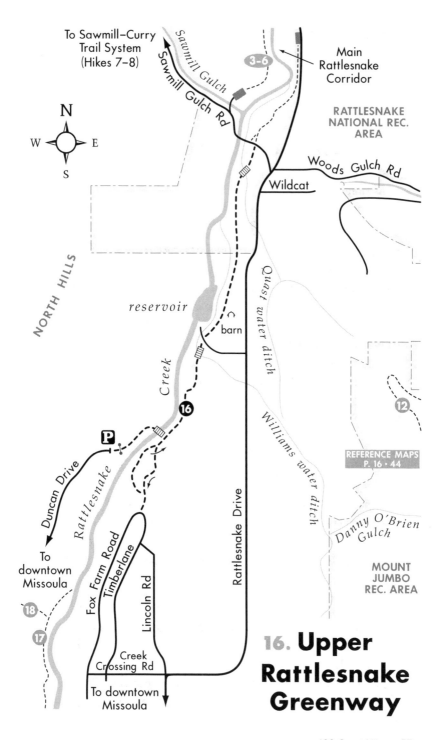

To Sawmill–Curry
Trail System
(Hikes 7–8)

Sawmill Gulch

Sawmill Gulch Rd

3-6

Main
Rattlesnake
Corridor

N
W   E
S

RATTLESNAKE
NATIONAL REC.
AREA

Woods Gulch Rd

Wildcat

NORTH HILLS

reservoir

barn

Quast water ditch

Creek

16

Williams water ditch

12

P

REFERENCE MAPS
P. 16 · 44

Rattlesnake

Duncan Drive

Rattlesnake Drive

*Danny O'Brien
Gulch*

MOUNT
JUMBO
REC. AREA

To
downtown
Missoula

Fox Farm Road

Timberlane

Lincoln Rd

18

17

Creek
Crossing Rd

To downtown
Missoula

16. Upper Rattlesnake Greenway

Meander through meadows and forest, then cross a bridge over Quast Water Ditch. A short distance ahead is Sawmill Gulch Road, the turn-around point .

To extend the hike, continue up the main Rattlesnake corridor—Hike 3. ■

17. Lower Rattlesnake Greenway

Hiking distance: 2.6 miles round trip
Hiking time: 1.5 hours
Elevation gain: 80 feet
Maps: U.S.G.S. Northeast Missoula · The Missoula Bike Map

The Rattlesnake Valley stretches northward out of Missoula, tucked between Mount Jumbo and the North Hills. Rattlesnake Creek, the centerpiece of the valley, cascades down canyon en route to the Clark Fork of the Columbia River. The drainage is part of the municipal watershed for the city of Missoula. This hike weaves along Rattlesnake Creek through city parks and natural areas with lush riparian vegetation. The trail offers views of Mount Jumbo, the North Hills, and the Rattlesnake Mountains

To the trailhead

From the intersection of Broadway Street and Madison Street just east of downtown, drive 0.1 mile north on Madison Street to a T-junction. Turn right on Greenough Drive, and continue 1.1 miles (passing under I-90) to Lolo Street. Turn right and go 0.3 miles, crossing over Rattlesnake Creek, to Wylie Avenue. (Wylie Avenue can also be reached 0.2 miles west of Rattlesnake Drive.) Turn north and drive a quarter mile to the posted trailhead at the end of the road. Park on the shoulder of the unpaved cul-de-sac.

The hike

Head north into the riparian corridor along the east side of Rattlesnake Creek. Stroll through the lush canopy, parallel to the cascading creek. Climb above the creek and enter Tom Green Park. Skirt the west edge of the park to Mountain View Drive by Old Pond Road at 0.4 miles. Bear left on the paved path, and cross a pedestrian bridge over Rattlesnake Creek. Pass Woodland

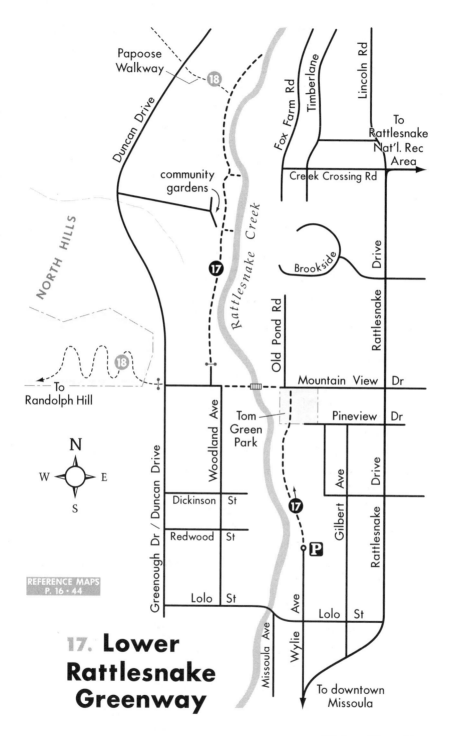

17. Lower Rattlesnake Greenway

Avenue on the left to the posted trail sign on the right. Head 130 yards north on the asphalt road to the gated trail, a gravel road. Pass the Community Gardens on the left. Stroll through the grasslands, and descend to the edge of the bluffs above Rattlesnake Creek. Walk upstream, passing a few river access paths, to a posted junction at 1.2 miles. To the left, the Papoose Walkway leads 0.15 miles up to Duncan Road across from the North Hills trails (Hike 18). Continue on the main trail straight ahead, and descend into the pine forest above the creek. The trail ends at a fenced property line 220 yards beyond the junction. Return along the same route. ■

18. North Hills: Rattlesnake Greenway Loop
NORTH HILLS OPEN SPACE

Hiking distance: 3.5-mile loop
Hiking time: 2 hours
Elevation gain: 400 feet
Maps: U.S.G.S. Northeast Missoula
Missoulian Hike Bike Run guide
Beartooth Publishing: Missoula, Hamilton, Lost Trail Pass

The North Hills rise above Missoula to the north on the west side of Rattlesnake Valley. A trail system through the open space connects Waterworks Hill in the south, the Moon–Randolph Homestead in the north, and the Rattlesnake Greenway in the west. This loop hike climbs the grassy slope to the ridge, following the ridge toward the summit of Randolph Hill. From the ridge are vistas across Missoula Valley and the surrounding mountains. A side trail leads to the Moon–Randolph Homestead, a century-old farm with an orchard and a barn. The hike returns along Rattlesnake Creek.

To the trailhead

From the intersection of Broadway Street and Madison Street just east of downtown, drive 0.1 mile north on Madison Street to a T-junction. Turn right on Greenough Drive, and continue 2.3 miles

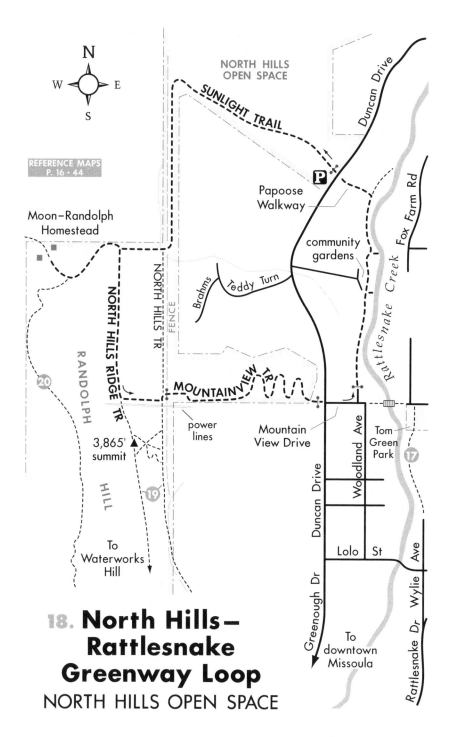

N
W · E
S

NORTH HILLS
OPEN SPACE

SUNLIGHT TRAIL

Duncan Drive

Fox Farm Rd

REFERENCE MAPS
P. 16 · 44

🅿

Papoose
Walkway

Moon–Randolph
Homestead

community
gardens

Rattlesnake Creek

NORTH HILLS TR

Brahms

Teddy Turn

FENCE

NORTH HILLS RIDGE TR

20

RANDOLPH

MOUNTAINVIEW TR

power
lines

Mountain
View Drive

Duncan Drive

Woodland Ave

Tom
Green
Park

17

3,865'
summit

HILL

19

To
Waterworks
Hill

Lolo   St

Wylie Ave

Greenough Dr

To
downtown
Missoula

Rattlesnake Dr

18. North Hills–
Rattlesnake
Greenway Loop
NORTH HILLS OPEN SPACE

(passing under I-90) to the posted trailhead parking on both sides of the road. Park on the grassy shoulder on the left/west. (Greenough Drive becomes Duncan Drive after Lolo Street.)

The hike

Walk past the entrance gate and climb a short hill on the Sunlight Trail. Ascend the grassy slope, cross a small ravine, and continue northwest amidst the rolling hills. At a half mile, cross under power lines and bear left. Descend along the fenceline, parallel to the power lines, with vistas across Missoula Valley. At the base of the hill bear right. Pass through an opening in the fence, and head west to a junction on the ridge. The right fork descends to the Moon–Randolph Homestead, open to the public on Saturdays (Hike 20).

Follow the ridge left (south) up the spine of Randolph Hill. At the power lines, about 100 yards shy of the 3,865-foot summit, veer left. Descend the slope to the fence. Bear left 40 yards and walk through a trail gate. Continue east and curve right to the fence at the top of the knoll. Bear left, following the fence east on the Mountainview Trail. Zigzag down the slope on seven switchbacks above the Rattlesnake drainage. Descend rock steps and go through a trail gate to Duncan Drive. Cross the road and walk one block on Mountain View Drive to the posted Rattlesnake Greenway. Straight ahead, the path crosses a pedestrian bridge over Rattlesnake Creek to Tom Green Park (Hike 17). Instead, go left and head 130 yards north on the asphalt road to the gated trail, a gravel road. Continue past the community gardens on the left. Stroll through the grasslands, and descend to the edge of the bluffs above Rattlesnake Creek. Walk upstream, passing a few river access paths, to a posted junction. The main trail, straight ahead, drops into the forest and ends at a fenced property line in 220 yards. Take the Papoose Walkway to the left, and climb 0.15 miles up to Duncan Road across from the trailhead. ∎

19. Waterworks Hill—Randolph Hill— Cherry Gulch Loop
NORTH HILLS OPEN SPACE

Hiking distance: 2.5-mile loop
Hiking time: 1.5 hours
Elevation gain: 550 feet
Maps: U.S.G.S. Northeast Missoula

map page 65

    The Missoula Bike Map · Missoulian Hike Bike Run guide
    Beartooth Publishing: Missoula, Hamilton, Lost Trail Pass

Waterworks Hill and Randolph Hill are the grassy slopes that lie north of Missoula on the west side of Rattlesnake Valley. The hills were the site of the well-known peace sign, a Missoula landmark that could be seen across the Missoula Valley for 25 years. Perched near the summit of Randolph Hill, the sign was dismantled, despite protests, and removed in 2001. A new peace sign has since been installed lower down the hillside. This hike climbs Waterworks Hill along the windswept, treeless ridge to the summit of Randolph Hill, passing the site of the former peace sign. The loop hike returns down Cherry Gulch, a wooded draw with shrubs and scattered cottonwoods. Atop the ridge are sweeping vistas across Missoula, the Rattlesnake Valley, Mount Jumbo, Mount Sentinel, and the Bitterroot Mountains. Dogs are allowed.

To the trailhead

From the intersection of Broadway Street and Madison Street just east of downtown, drive 0.1 mile north on Madison Street to a T-junction. Turn right on Greenough Drive and pass under I-90. Take the first left turn after I-90. Drive one block on the gravel road to the signed trailhead at the end of the road.

The hike

Walk past the trailhead gate to a posted junction. The Cherry Gulch Trail—the return route—is on the right. Begin the loop on the North Hills Ridge Trail, staying to the left on the unpaved road. Climb up the grassy, tree-dotted slope while enjoying the sweeping views across Missoula Valley to the surrounding mountains. At 200 yards is a trail fork. The left fork detours a quarter mile along the south-facing hillside to the Missoula Peace Park. The park has benches and a 60-foot peace sign built into the hillside slope. The park, established in 2007, was a gift to the community from the Jeanette Rankin Peace Center (www.jrpc.org). A path from the peace sign climbs up and rejoins the North Hills Ridge Trail. (From the ridge, the two paths to the Peace Park are 160 yards apart.) Continue up the North Hills Ridge Trail towards the distinct communication tower. Near the summit, 200 yards shy of the antenna, is a Y-fork. The left fork leads to the Moon–Randolph Homestead and the Orange Avenue Trailhead (Hike 20). Stay to the right atop the ridge to the towers. From the towers, follow the exposed ridge north toward the 3,865-foot summit of Randolph Hill. Pass the site of the old Missoula peace sign, where a hand-made rock peace symbol has been placed. Top the summit and savor the 360-degree vistas.

Slowly descend to the power lines (running perpendicular to the trail) and a junction. The main trail continues north and descends to the Moon–Randolph Homestead (Hike 20). For this hike, bear right on the footpath, and head down the slope to the fence. Curve right and follow the fence 300 yards south to a Y-fork, just before the hill and the fence head downward into Cherry Gulch. Veer right to a 5-way junction. The two right forks lead up to the ridge. The left two forks descend into Cherry Gulch. The first left fork is steep. The second left fork zigzags down at an easy grade. At the gully bottom, curve right, continuing down the draw. Pass an old tin-roof barn, completing the loop at the trailhead. ■

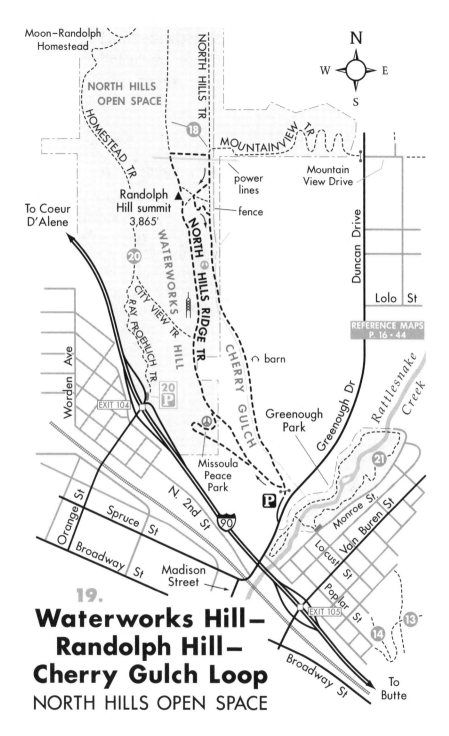

19.
Waterworks Hill –
Randolph Hill –
Cherry Gulch Loop
NORTH HILLS OPEN SPACE

20. Moon—Randolph Homestead
from the Orange Avenue Trailhead
NORTH HILLS OPEN SPACE

Hiking distance: 3 miles round trip
Hiking time: 1.5 hours
Elevation gain: 450 feet
Maps: U.S.G.S. Northeast Missoula
    Beartooth Publishing: Missoula, Hamilton, Lost Trail Pass

The Moon-Randolph Homestead is an old ranch in the northwest corner of the North Hills Open Space. The century-old farm was purchased by the city of Missoula in 1996, preserving the homestead for animals, plants, and people. The 470-acre property is adjacent to the Waterworks Trail and connects with the North Hills Trail system. The historic farm buildings and apple orchard are tucked into a draw below the highest knoll in the North Hills. The homestead site and buildings are open to the public every Saturday from May through October, 11 a.m. to 5 p.m.

There are several trail routes to access the ranch: from Waterworks Hill (Hike 19), from Duncan Drive (Hike 18), and this hike from the northern terminus of Orange Street. The hike climbs the grassy hillside overlooking Missoula to the top of the hill on an exposed ridge. From this overlook, drop down into the draw below Randolph Hill to the homestead. Dogs are allowed.

To the trailhead

The trailhead parking area is at the northern terminus of Orange Street, north of downtown Missoula. It is located just north of I-90 at Exit 104. The trailhead parking area is on the large pullout on the north side of the street.

The hike

Head north, parallel to the I-90 on-ramp, then drop down to the trailhead gate. Take the posted Ray Froehlich Trail, and skirt the base of the hill, gently gaining elevation. Curve right and weave up the open, grassy slope with great views across Missoula to the surrounding mountains. At 0.4 miles is a signed junction with the City View Trail, a two-track dirt road. The right fork leads 0.9

miles to the North Hills Ridge Trail and the Waterworks Trailhead (Hike 19). Bear left on the Homestead Trail, and take the footpath uphill, topping the flower-covered slope at one mile. Descend into the rolling North Hills terrain while overlooking the Moon–Randolph Homestead and Waterworks Hill. Cross a draw to a posted junction at 1.4 miles. The right fork leads up to the North Hills Ridge Trail. Bear left and descend 0.1 mile to the Moon–Randolph Homestead . At the site is the house, barn, an apple orchard, black locust trees, the goats, sheep, and chickens. Return by retracing your steps. ■

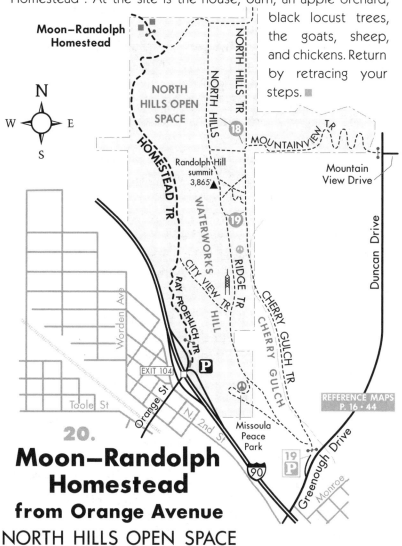

20.

Moon–Randolph Homestead
from Orange Avenue
NORTH HILLS OPEN SPACE

21. Greenough Park
Bolle Birdwatching Trail

Hiking distance: 1-mile loop
Hiking time: 30 minutes
Elevation gain: level
Maps: U.S.G.S. Northeast Missoula
Missoulian Hike Bike Run guide

Greenough Park has hiking paths that wind along Rattlesnake Creek as it flows through this 42-acre city park at the mouth of the Rattlesnake Valley. The park has mature ponderosa pines, spruce, cottonwoods, maples, and lush riparian vegetation along Rattlesnake Creek. Greenough Park, prime bird habitat, was donated to the city of Missoula in 1902 by the Greenough Family. The gift included a provision that the land would be "forever maintained in its natural state."

As many as 120 varieties of birds have been known to inhabit the area. Educational stations about birds are located along the path. The Bolle Birdwatching Trail is named for Arnold Bolle, a conservationist and Dean of Forestry at the University of Montana. The trail has paved and natural sections that loop through the park. Two footbridges cross over the creek. Benches and landscaped picnic areas are available. Dogs are welcome.

To the trailhead

From I-90 in Missoula, take the Van Buren Street exit, and drive 0.3 miles north to Locust Street on the left. Turn left, and continue 2 blocks to Monroe Street. The parking lot is on the west side of Monroe Street.

The hike

From the parking lot, head to the bridge over Rattlesnake Creek. Once over the bridge, take the path to the right, hiking clockwise around the loop. (To the left is a short loop around a grassy picnic area by the creek.) The trail along the west side of Rattlesnake Creek is paved. At 0.4 miles, cross over the creek on another bridge to a foot trail on the right. The return trail is a natural path through the shady forest on the east bank of the creek. ■

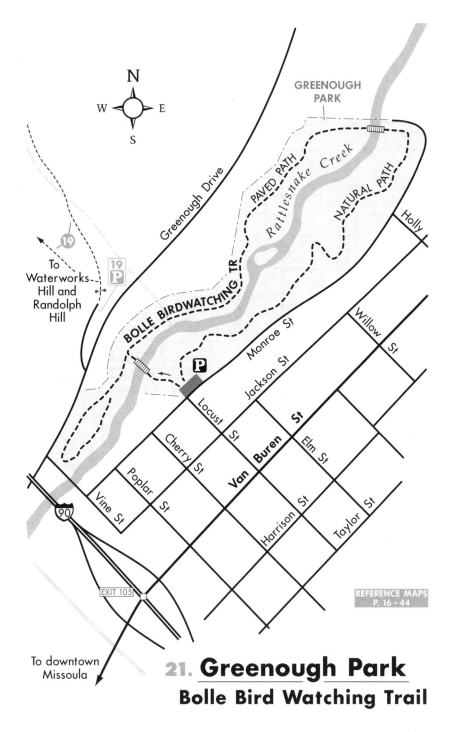

N
W · E
S

GREENOUGH PARK

Greenough Drive

PAVED PATH

Rattlesnake Creek

NATURAL PATH

Holly

BOLLE BIRDWATCHING TR

To Waterworks Hill and Randolph Hill

19
19 P

P

Monroe St

Willow St

Jackson St

Locust St

Cherry St

Van Buren St

Elm St

Poplar St

Vine St

90

Harrison St

Taylor St

EXIT 105

REFERENCE MAPS
P. 16 · 44

To downtown Missoula

21. **Greenough Park**
Bolle Bird Watching Trail

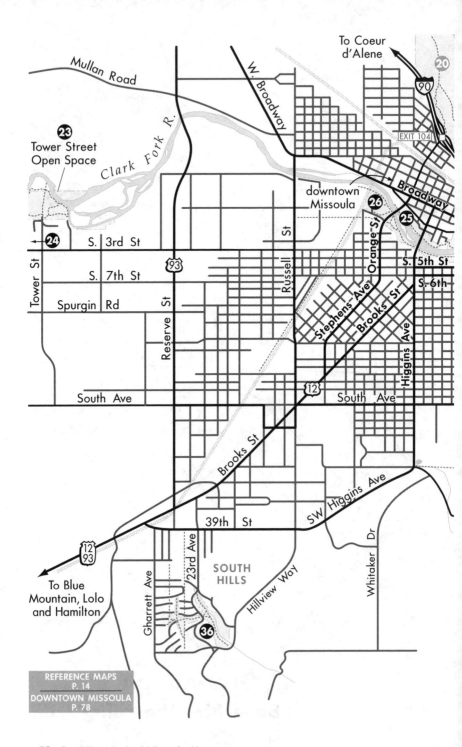

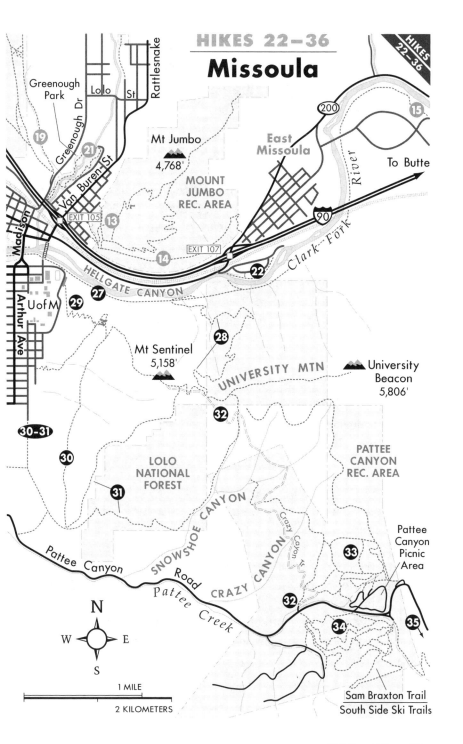

Greenough Park

Lollo St

Rattlesnake

Greenough Dr

Greenough

19

21

Mt Jumbo
4,768'

East Missoula

200

15

To Butte

MOUNT JUMBO REC. AREA

River

Van Buren St

EXIT 105

13

EXIT 107

14

22

90

Clark-Fork

Madison

HELLGATE CANYON

27

U of M

29

Arthur Ave

Mt Sentinel
5,158'

UNIVERSITY MTN

University Beacon
5,806'

28

32

PATTEE CANYON REC. AREA

30-31

30

LOLO NATIONAL FOREST

31

Pattee Canyon

SNOWSHOE CANYON

Crazy Canyon Tr

CRAZY CANYON

Pattee Canyon

Road

Pattee Creek

33

Pattee Canyon Picnic Area

32

34

35

N
W · E
S

1 MILE

2 KILOMETERS

Sam Braxton Trail
South Side Ski Trails

22. Clark Fork River Trail in Hellgate Canyon

BEN HUGHES PARK

Hiking distance: 1 mile round trip
Hiking time: 30 minutes
Elevation gain: level
Maps: U.S.G.S. Southeast Missoula

The Clark Fork of the Columbia River flows through a narrow cleft in Hellgate Canyon between Mount Sentinel and Mount Jumbo before continuing through the heart of Missoula. An unnamed footpath in Ben Hughes Park follows the north bank of the river for a half mile between University Mountain, towering more than 2,500 feet above the trail, and Mount Jumbo, stretching to 1,300 feet on the north side of the trail. This short, level route is a hidden gem with sandy beaches, cottonwoods, and low-elevation pine groves.

To the trailhead

From Broadway Street and Van Buren Street east of downtown Missoula, drive 1.5 miles east on Broadway Street to North Easy Street in Hellgate Canyon. Turn right and go one block to South Easy Street. Turn right and continue 0.1 mile to the trail access, directly across from Jason Court. Park along the curb.

The hike

Walk down the trail access on the west (river side) of 187 South Easy Street to a T-junction at the Clark Fork River. Bear right, cross a wash, and stroll through a meadow with pockets of pine and cottonwood trees. Continue downstream between the river and a water channel. The trail ends at 0.15 miles on a point of land where the water channel and river meet. Return to the T-junction and follow the river upstream. Curve left, passing an access trail from David Court. Veer right and follow the narrow path through cottonwoods and willows to the trail's end. Return along the same route.■

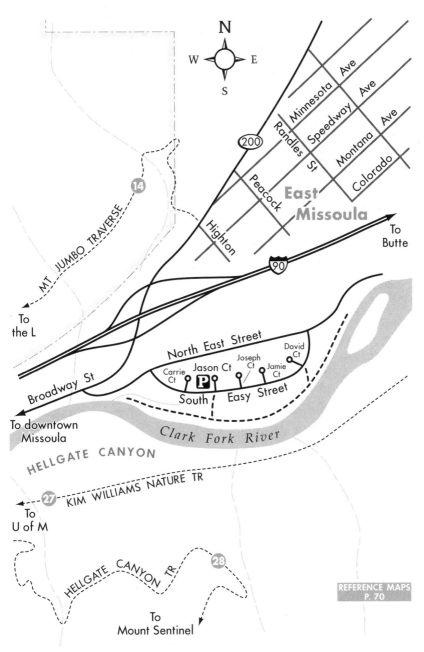

22. Clark Fork River Trail
IN HELLGATE CANYON

23. Tower Street Open Space along the Clark Fork River

Hiking distance: 1.5-mile double loop
Hiking time: 45 minutes
Elevation gain: level
Maps: U.S.G.S. Southwest Missoula · Missoulian Hike Bike Run guide

The Clark Fork of the Columbia River flows 310 miles from the Continental Divide near Butte, emptying into Lake Pend Oreille near the town of Clark Fork in the northern Idaho panhandle. The Clark Fork is the largest river (by volume) in Montana, receiving water from the Little Blackfoot River, the Blackfoot River, the Bitterroot River, the Flathead River, and the Thompson River. The Clark Fork runs through the heart of Missoula, providing swimming, fishing, and boating opportunities.

The Tower Street Open Space is a new addition to the steadily expanding trail system in the city of Missoula. The 120-acre open space sits at the north end of Tower Street and borders the Clark Fork of the Columbia River. This double loop weaves through a wildlife sanctuary in a lush riparian habitat with cottonwoods, pines, willows, chokecherry, serviceberry, aspen, and dogwood. The trail follows the river corridor, leads to a fishing access, and is a great area for birdwatching.

To the trailhead

From the intersection of Reserve Street and South 3rd Street in Missoula, drive 1.1 miles west on South 3rd Street to Tower Street. Turn right and head a quarter mile north to the end of the road and the trailhead parking lot on the right.

The hike

These trails are in a flood plain area, so the trails may alter as the level of the river rises and falls.

Walk 30 yards past the wooden trail gate to a fork. The right fork will be our second loop. For now, continue straight ahead. Stroll through the pine-covered meadows to the banks of the Clark Fork River among willows, thickets, and views of the river islands. Return a short distance and take the footpath to the west.

Follow the river downstream, curving left. Meander through the forest, completing the loop near the trailhead.

A few feet towards the trailhead to the right is the beginning of the second loop on the left. Head east through the quiet of the forest to a Y-fork. Both paths lead to the Clark Fork River, forming a small loop. The right fork leads up to a levee overlooking a fork of the river. Veer left and follow the levee to the river, where the two paths rejoin. Parallel the edge of the river to a junction with the trail extension from Tower Street. Bear left and return to the trailhead.. ∎

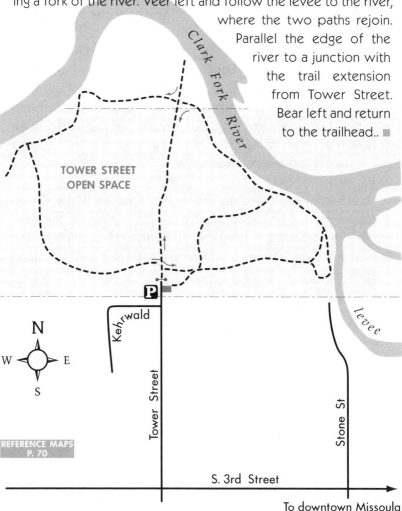

23. Tower Street Open Space
along the Clark Fork River

24. Kelly Island

Hiking distance: 1.5-mile loop
Hiking time: 1 hour
Elevation gain: level
Maps: U.S.G.S. Southwest Missoula

Kelly Island is formed at the confluence of the Bitterroot and Clark Fork Rivers on the west end of Missoula. The 650-acre undeveloped island actually encompasses one large island and eight smaller islands that are divided by springs, backwater sloughs, and channels of the Clark Fork River. The protected river corridor is a mix of cottonwood bottoms, lush meadows, and old-growth ponderosa pines. The wetland oasis has large populations of waterfowl and wildlife. Great blue herons, Canada geese, great horned owls, and red-tailed hawks commonly nest on the island. Lewis' woodpeckers, bald eagles, white-tailed deer, and beaver may also be spotted.

Kelly Island has three access points. One is off of Mullan Road, 3.5 miles west of Reserve Street; another is near the west end of Spurgin Road. This access offers the easiest hiking route due to the river crossings, which at times can be difficult and hazardous.

To the trailhead

From the intersection of Reserve Street and South 7th Street, drive 2.4 miles west on South 7th Street to Humble Road and the signed Kelly Island Access. Park in the pullouts on the side of the road.

The hike

Walk down the grassy lane along a fenced horse and sheep pasture. Pass through a grove of cottonwoods and willows to the banks of a water channel of the Clark Fork River at 0.2 miles, where the water splits into two channels. Follow the edge of the waterway downstream to a large downfall tree spanning the river. Cross the log to a meadow and a trail fork. Begin the loop to the right, and follow the opposite side of the river braid upstream to the channel split. Follow the other river fork downstream. Veer left, away from the waterway, through a dense riparian habitat, returning to the banks of the Clark Fork. The serpentine path weaves through the lush vegetation, staying close to the island perimeter. Continue along a wide branch of the river to a trail split. The right fork follows the river sixty yards and ends. Take the left fork, cutting inland, and meander through the cottonwood-dotted grassland. Complete the loop at the log crossing. Cross the log and retrace your route.■

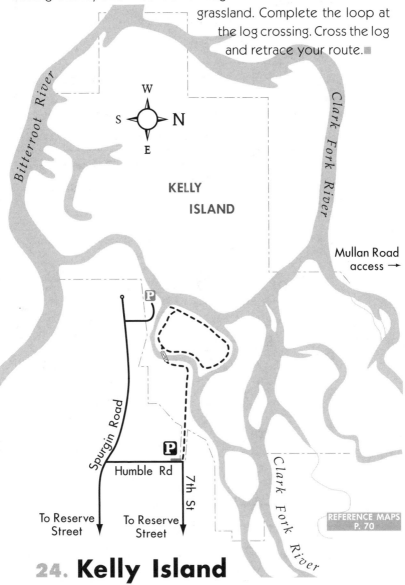

24. Kelly Island

25. Clark Fork Northside Riverfront Trail
ORANGE STREET BRIDGE to
VAN BUREN STREET PEDESTRIAN BRIDGE

Hiking distance: 2 miles round trip
Hiking time: 1 hour
Elevation gain: level
Maps: U.S.G.S. Southwest Missoula and Southeast Missoula
The Missoula Bike Map
Missoulian Hike Bike Run guide

map page 80

The Northside Riverfront Trail is in the heart of Missoula above the banks of the Clark Fork River. The bike and pedestrian path leads through the city parks of Caras Park, Bess Reed Park, and Kiwanis Park. From Caras Park to Bess Reed Park, the path is paved

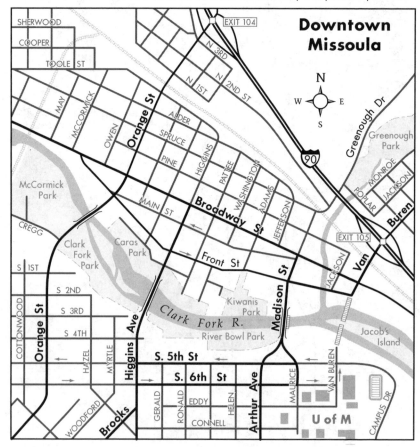

and wheelchair accessible. Various side paths lead down to the river's edge. The hike can begin from several access points. This hike begins by the hand-carved carousel in Caras Park, where the parking is most convenient.

The Riverfront Trails connect to three street bridges: Orange Street, Higgins Avenue, and Madison Street. They also connect to three footbridges: one off Van Buren Street, another under the Madison Street Bridge, and a third off of California Street just west of downtown. Watch for colonies of cliff swallows that build their adobe nests under the bridges.

To the trailhead

From downtown Missoula, drive to the entrance of the Caras Park parking lot, located one block west of Higgins Avenue off of Front Street (by the carousel).

The hike

Take the paved path west, heading downstream past the carousel. Near the west end, the path crosses under the Orange Street Bridge and ends at the hospital property line. Return to the east and go under the Higgins Street Bridge into Bess Reed Park. At the east end of the park, go to the right a half block on Lavasseur Street to the paved pathway and trail sign. Bear left on the path 60 yards. Curve right and walk through Kiwanis Park, returning to the Riverfront Trail and the Clark Fork River. Head east on the levee above the river. Cross under the Madison Street Bridge to the trail's end. The Madison Street Pedestrian Bridge crosses the river directly below the vehicle bridge, connecting with the Southside Riverfront Trail in River Bowl Park (Hike 26).

To hike farther, detour up to Front Street and bear right for two blocks to Van Buren Street. To the right is the Van Buren Street Pedestrian Bridge, crossing the river onto Jacob's Island. The path connects with the Kim Williams Trail on the left (Hike 27) and the Southside Riverfront Trail on the right (Hike 26). ■

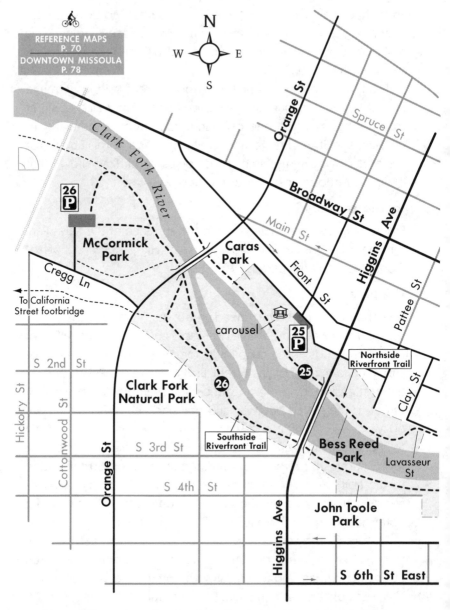

Clark Fork Riverfront Trail:

25. Northside Riverfront Trail
26. Southside Riverfront Trail

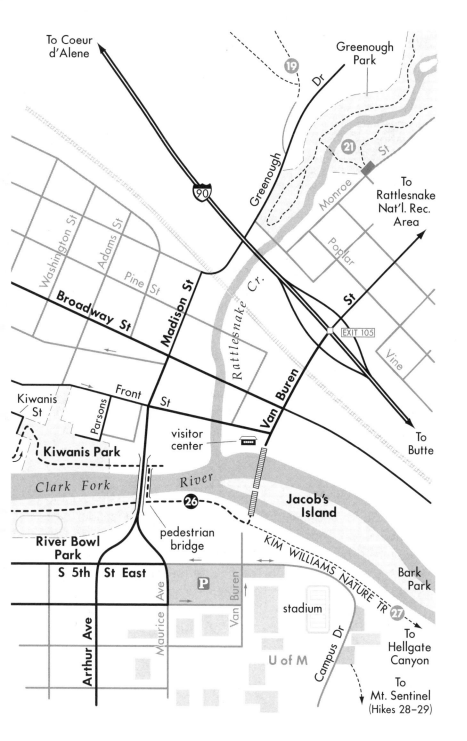

To Coeur
d'Alene

Greenough
Park

19

Dr

Greenough

21

St

Monroe

To
Rattlesnake
Nat'l. Rec.
Area

Poplar

St

I-90

Washington St

Adams St

Pine St

Broadway St

Madison St

Rattlesnake Cr.

Van Buren

EXIT 105

Vine

To
Butte

Front St

Parsons

Kiwanis St

Kiwanis Park

visitor
center

Clark Fork River

26

Jacob's
Island

River Bowl
Park

pedestrian
bridge

KIM WILLIAMS NATURE TR

Bark
Park

27

S 5th St East

P

Van Buren Ave

stadium

To
Hellgate
Canyon

Arthur Ave

Maurice Ave

U of M

Campus Dr

To
Mt. Sentinel
(Hikes 28–29)

26. Clark Fork Southside Riverfront Trail
MCCORMICK PARK to
UNIVERSITY OF MONTANA

Hiking distance: 2 miles round trip
Hiking time: 1 hour
Elevation gain: level

map
page 80

Maps: U.S.G.S. Southwest Missoula and Southeast Missoula
The Missoula Bike Map
Missoulian Hike Bike Run guide

The Southside Riverfront Trail is a wide, unpaved path that extends from McCormick Park to the University of Montana. The open space corridor was once the Old Milwaukee Railroad bed. The level path connects 26-acre McCormick Park to Clark Fork Natural Park, John Toole Park, the University of Montana River Bowl Park, and Jacob's Island Park in the Clark Fork River. (On the east end of Jacob's Island is an off-leash dog park called Bark Park.) Various side paths lead down to the river.

To the trailhead

From downtown Missoula, drive west to Orange Street. Turn left and cross the Orange Street Bridge over the Clark Fork River. Immediately after crossing, turn right and park in the McCormick Park parking lot on the right.

The hike

Head upstream to the east on the wide path. Cross under the Orange Street Bridge into Clark Fork Natural Park. Meander past a wooden footbridge, native plants, beautiful rock work, and art sculpture. Cross under the Higgins Street Bridge into John Toole Park and River Bowl Park. The Southside Trail ends at Jacob's Island Park at the north end of the University of Montana.

To continue hiking, the Van Buren Street Pedestrian Bridge is to the left, which connects to Jacob's Island and the Northside Trail—Hike 25. Straight ahead is the Kim Williams Trail to Hellgate Canyon—Hike 27. The campus road to the right (south) leads to the Mount Sentinel trailhead—Hikes 28 and 29.■

27. Kim Williams Nature Trail

Hiking distance: 5 miles round trip
Hiking time: 2.5 hours
Elevation gain: level
Maps: U.S.G.S. Southeast Missoula
The Missoula Bike Map
Missoulian Hike Bike Run guide
Beartooth Publishing: Missoula, Hamilton, Lost Trail Pass

**map
page 85**

The Kim Williams Nature Trail (named for the Missoula author and naturalist) begins at the University of Montana adjacent to Jacob's Island, where the Southside Riverfront Trail ends (Hike 26). This rails-to-trails route is a wide hiking, biking, and equestrian trail that follows the abandoned Milwaukee Railroad bed along the canyon bottom. The trail heads east into the maw of Hellgate Canyon along the base of the steep north face of Mount Sentinel. The 134-acre natural corridor borders the Clark Fork River along a diverse community of riparian plants.

To the trailhead

Park south of the Clark Fork River by the University of Montana, one block east of Maurice Avenue. During classes or school events, this parking lot may be full. If so, park north of the Clark Fork River near Van Buren Street. Cross the Van Buren Street Pedestrian Bridge over the river via Jacob's Island to the trail.

From I-90 in Missoula, take the Van Buren Street exit and head south to Broadway—turn right. Drive a short distance east to Madison Street and turn left, crossing the bridge over the Clark Fork River. After curving onto Arthur Avenue, turn left at South 6th Street into the University of Montana. Park in the lot between Maurice Avenue and Van Buren Street.

The hike

The well-defined trail heads east along the south side of the Clark Fork River. (To the west is the Southside Riverfront Trail—Hike 26.) Once past the vehicle gate, enter Hellgate Canyon along the base of Mount Sentinel. At one mile is a junction with the Hellgate Canyon Trail on the right (Hike 28). Continue straight ahead, following the Clark Fork River upstream. To the left are several narrow connecting side paths that run parallel to the Kim Williams Trail. Various fisherman trails lead down to the river's edge. The trail ends just beyond the railroad bridge spanning the river. Return along the same trail. ▪

28. Hellgate Canyon— Mount Sentinel Loop

Hiking distance: 5-mile loop
Hiking time: 3 hours
Elevation gain: 1,950 feet

**map
page 87**

Maps: U.S.G.S. Southeast Missoula
The Missoula Bike Map
Pattee Canyon Recreation Area map
Missoulian Hike Bike Run guide
Beartooth Publishing: Missoula, Hamilton, Lost Trail Pass

The Hellgate Canyon Trail climbs from the floor of Hellgate Canyon up the forested north slope of Mount Sentinel. Access is from the Kim Williams Nature Trail at the University of Montana, an abandoned railroad bed on the banks of the Clark Fork River. The strenuous trail climbs 2.5 miles up the south wall of Hellgate Canyon, gaining 1,600 feet before the final quarter-mile ascent of Mount Sentinel. The peak of Mount Sentinel towers over the city at an elevation of 5,158 feet. From the summit are sweeping vistas across Missoula Valley to the Bitterroot Mountains and Frenchtown, and across Hellgate Canyon to the Rattlesnake National Recreation Area and Wilderness. This loop hike descends the west face of the mountain on the M Trail (Hike 29). The Hellgate Canyon Trail also connects with the Crazy Canyon Trail to Pattee Canyon (Hike 32).

To the trailhead

Park south of the Clark Fork River by the University of Montana, one block east of Maurice Avenue. During classes or school events, this parking lot may be full. If so, park north of the Clark

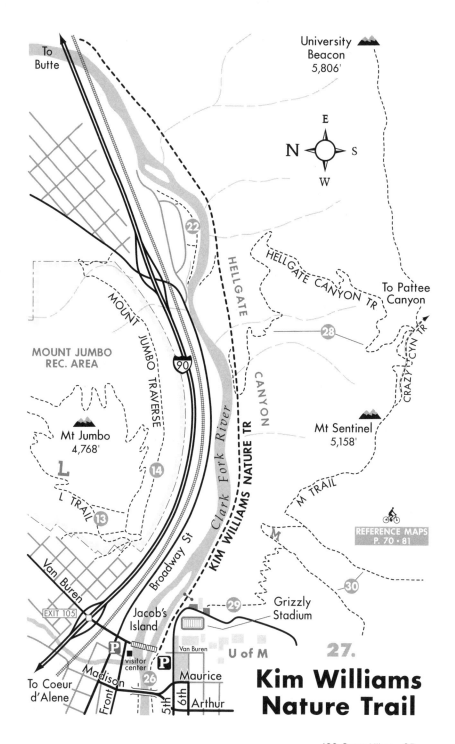

To
Butte

University
Beacon
5,806'

E

N S

W

To Pattee
Canyon

HELLGATE CANYON TR

HELLGATE CANYON

CRAZY CYN TR

22

28

MOUNT JUMBO
REC. AREA

MOUNT JUMBO TRAVERSE

I-90

Mt Jumbo
4,768'

Clark Fork River

KIM WILLIAMS NATURE TR

Mt Sentinel
5,158'

L

L TRAIL

M TRAIL

14

13

M

REFERENCE MAPS
P. 70 · 81

30

Van Buren

EXIT 105

Broadway St

Jacob's
Island

29

Grizzly
Stadium

Madison

visitor
center

P

P

Van Buren

U of M

26

Maurice

27.

**Kim Williams
Nature Trail**

To Coeur
d'Alene

Front

5th

6th

Arthur

Fork River near Van Buren Street. Cross the Van Buren Street Pedestrian Bridge over the river via Jacob's Island to the trail.

From I-90 in Missoula, take the Van Buren Street exit and head south to Broadway—turn right. Drive a short distance east to Madison Street and turn left, crossing the bridge over the Clark Fork River. After curving onto Arthur Avenue, turn left at South 6th Street into the University of Montana. Park in the lot between Maurice Avenue and Van Buren Street.

The hike

Begin along the well-defined Kim Williams Nature Trail and head east, parallel to the south side of the Clark Fork River. Once past the vehicle gate, enter Hellgate Canyon along the base of Mount Sentinel. At one mile is a junction with the Hellgate Canyon Trail on the right. Take this trail up the switchbacks. The well-groomed trail is not steep, but steadily climbs up the mountain's northern rampart. At 3.5 miles—at the top of the canyon—is a junction with the Crazy Canyon Trail (Hike 32). Take a sharp right for the final quarter mile ascent to the Mount Sentinel summit. The trail crisscrosses its way to the top. After resting, relaxing, and enjoying the 360-degree views, follow the path one mile down the west face of Mount Sentinel to the M. From here, zigzag down to the university. At the bottom, head to the right through the university, back towards the Clark Fork River and the trailhead. ■

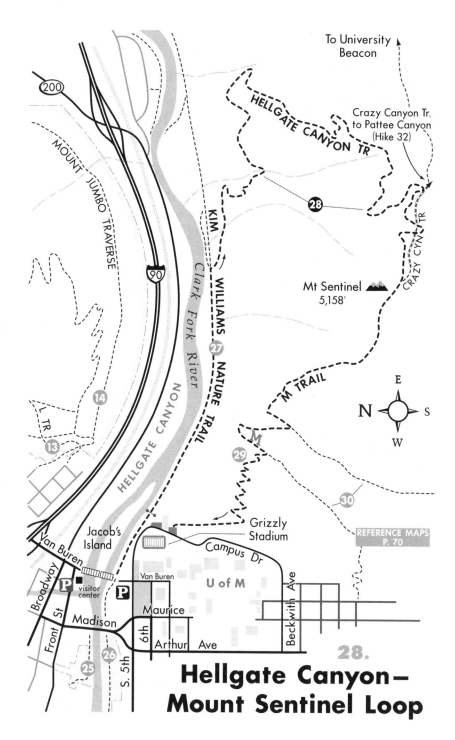

To University
Beacon

HELLGATE CANYON TR

Crazy Canyon Tr.
to Pattee Canyon
(Hike 32)

28

CRAZY CYN TR

Mt Sentinel
5,158'

M TRAIL

KIM WILLIAMS NATURE TRAIL

Clark Fork River

MOUNT JUMBO TRAVERSE

27

I-90

HELLGATE CANYON

200

14

TR

13

E
N ✦ S
W

M

29

30

REFERENCE MAPS
P. 70

Jacob's
Island

Grizzly
Stadium

Van Buren

Campus Dr

P
visitor
center

P

Van Buren

Broadway

Front St

Madison

Maurice

6th

S. 5th

Arthur Ave

26

25

U of M

Beckwith Ave

28.

Hellgate Canyon –
Mount Sentinel Loop

29. M Trail

Hiking distance: 1.5 miles round trip
Hiking time: 1 hour
Elevation gain: 620 feet
Maps: U.S.G.S. Southeast Missoula
  The Missoula Bike Map · Missoulian Hike Bike Run guide

Mount Sentinel, the western peak of University Mountain, over-looks the city of Missoula from the south side of the Clark Fork. The landmark M at the University of Montana, dating back to 1908, sits a third of the way up Mount Sentinel at 3,820 feet. It can be spotted from anywhere in the city. The M Trail begins at the eastern end of the campus near Grizzly Stadium. The steep trail zigzags up the sunny west face of the mountain to the concrete M. Throughout the hike are bird's-eye views of Missoula Valley, the Clark Fork and Bitterroot Rivers, Lolo Peak, and the Bitterroot Mountains. This popular trail has a steady stream of hikers throughout the day.

To the trailhead

From I-90 in Missoula, take the Van Buren Street exit and head south to Broadway—turn right. Drive a short distance east to Madison Street and turn left, crossing the bridge over the Clark Fork River. After curving onto Arthur Avenue, turn left at South 6th Street into the University of Montana. Follow the one-way street, curving around to the south side of Washington Grizzly Stadium. The trailhead parking lot is on the left.

The hike

Head east up the steps to the trailhead gate and kiosk. Bear right and begin steadily ascending the mountain. Zigzag 0.75 miles up thirteen switchbacks to the concrete M, savoring the great vistas across the Missoula Valley. After enjoying the views, descend along the same path.

To extend the hike, an old road continues up the west face of the mountain on a steep grade to the 5,158-foot summit of Mount Sentinel, one mile past the M. From the top are views across Hellgate Canyon to Mount Jumbo, the North Hills, and the Rattlesnake National Recreation Area and Wilderness. The Hellgate Canyon Trail loops back down to the Clark Fork canyon floor (Hike 28). The Crazy Canyon Trail heads south down to Pattee Canyon (Hike 32). ■

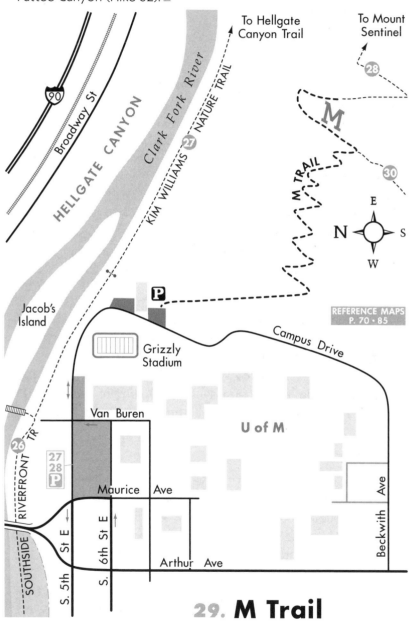

29. M Trail

30. Mount Sentinel Loop
Mount Sentinel Fire Road to the M

Hiking distance: 4.3 mile loop
Hiking time: 2 hours
Elevation gain: 800 feet
Maps: U.S.G.S. Southeast Missoula
        Beartooth Publishing: Missoula, Hamilton, Lost Trail Pass

Mount Sentinel is the landmark mountain overlooking Missoula with the large concrete M. The 5,158-foot mountain stretches from Hellgate Canyon in the north to Pattee Canyon in the south while towering over the University of Montana. This hike forms a loop on the dry western slope of Mount Sentinel, offering sweeping views across Missoula. The hike begins at the base of the mountain near the university and climbs to an overlook of Pattee Canyon. The trail—the Mount Sentinel Fire Road—traverses the exposed mountain slope through Missoula open space land, crossing the top of the M and returning along the base of the M. This hike is a great alternative to the ever-popular M Trail (Hike 29)

To the trailhead

From the intersection of Broadway and Madison Street in downtown Missoula, drive south on Madison Street, crossing the bridge over the Clark Fork River. Curve onto Arthur Avenue and continue 1.1 miles to South Avenue. Turn left and go one block to Maurice Avenue, the second right turn. Turn right and drive 0.1 mile to the posted trailhead at the end of the road. Park along the side of the road.

The hike

From the south end of Maurice Avenue, head up the unpaved fire road—the Mount Sentinel Fire Road. For the first quarter mile, the road is a public access route through private property. Traverse the base of Mount Sentinel on an upward slope, overlooking the University of Montana and the U of M Golf Course. At 0.4 miles, pass the Community Gardens Access Trail on the right, and at 0.8 miles, pass the Gravel Pit Access Trail, also on the right. (The trailhead for the connector trail from the gravel pit is located 0.7 up

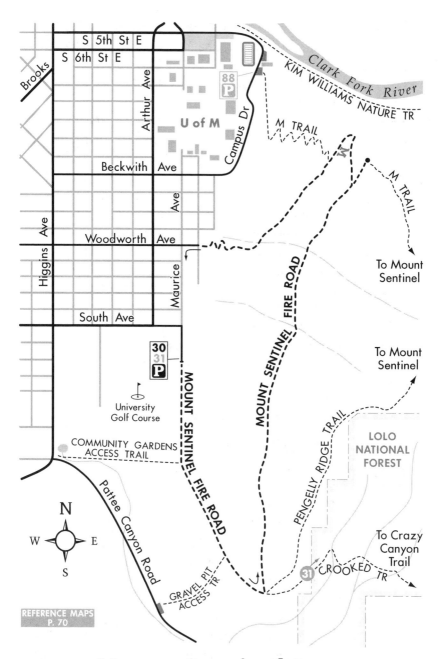

30. **Mount Sentinel Loop**
MOUNT SENTINEL FIRE ROAD

Pattee Canyon Road from Higgins Avenue.) Traverse the exposed grassy slope to a 3-way split at one mile. The right fork leads to Crooked Creek and the Crazy Canyon Trail (Hikes 31—32). The left (center) route climbs 1.75 miles on the Ridge Trail to the Mount Sentinel south summit.

For this hike, take the left switchback and head straight north towards the M. Climb higher up the mountain, with sweeping views across Missoula. When the trail is directly above the university, watch for a trail veering left. This path leads to the M. Detour straight ahead 150 yards to an overlook of Hellgate Canyon, Mount Jumbo, and the Rattlesnake.

Return to the junction and walk down to the M. Walk past the top of the M and switchback left. Return and walk along the base of the M. At the second switchback, leave the M Trail and continue straight ahead on the footpath. Traverse the lower slope, steadily losing elevation. Cross through an opening in the fence, and drop down with the aid of switchbacks to the east end of Woodworth Avenue. Walk one block down Woodworth Avenue to Maurice Avenue. Go left to the trailhead at the end of the street. ∎

31. Crooked Trail—
Pengelly Ridge Trail Loop

Hiking distance: 5 miles round trip or 6-mile loop
Hiking time: 2.5 to 3.5 hours
Elevation gain: 800—1,600 feet
Maps: U.S.G.S. Southeast Missoula
Beartooth Publishing: Missoula, Hamilton, Lost Trail Pass

The Crooked Trail connects the west face of Mount Sentinel with Crazy Canyon and the Pattee Canyon National Recreation Area. The trail begins at the southern terminus of Maurice Avenue, near the university, and traverses the western face of Mount Sentinel, where there are great views across Missoula. The Crooked Trail then curves around the slope of Mount Sentinel and brings into view Pattee Canyon. After meandering through gently sloping meadows covered in native grasses and wildflowers, the trail

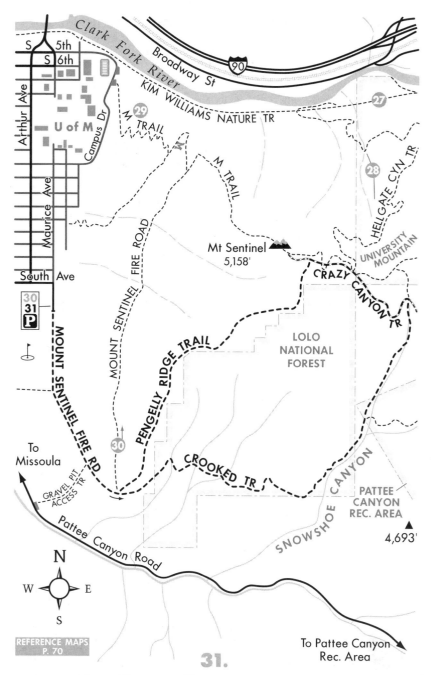

Crooked Trail–Pengelly Ridge

descends into a wooded drainage alongside Crooked Creek in Snowshoe Canyon. The creek bottom is shaded with ponderosa pine and Douglas fir. For a more strenuous loop hike, return via the Pengelly Ridge Trail, descending on the exposed west-facing slope with far-reaching vistas.

To the trailhead

From the intersection of Broadway and Madison Street in downtown Missoula, drive south on Madison Street, crossing the bridge over the Clark Fork River. Curve onto Arthur Avenue and continue 1.1 miles to South Avenue. Turn left and go one block to Maurice Avenue, the second right turn. Turn right and drive 0.1 miles to the posted trailhead at the end of the road. Park along the side of the road.

The hike

From the south end of Maurice Avenue, head up the unpaved fire road—the Mount Sentinel Fire Road. For the first quarter mile, the road is a public access route through private property. Traverse the base of Mount Sentinel on an upward slope, overlooking the University of Montana and the U of M Golf Course. At 0.4 miles, pass the Community Gardens Access Trail on the right, and at 0.8 miles, pass the Gravel Pit Access Trail, also on the right. (The trailhead for the connector trail from the gravel pit is located 0.7 up Pattee Canyon Road from Higgins Avenue.) Traverse the exposed grassy slope to a 3-way split at one mile. The left switchback continues on the Mount Sentinel Fire Road and heads north towards the M (Hike 30). The left (center) route climbs 1.75 miles on the Ridge Trail to the Mount Sentinel south summit.

For this hike, stay to the right on the Crooked Trail. Curve around the hill to great views up Pattee Canyon. Enter the Lolo National Forest and gradually descend. Curve around a seasonal drainage with wildflowers. Wind along the sloping grasslands, and drop down to the west bank of Crooked Creek in Snowshoe Canyon. Follow the creek upstream through the lush riparian vegetation. As the narrow canyon widens, the path veers away from the creek to a posted junction on the northwest corner of the Pattee

Canyon Recreation Area at 2.5 miles. This is the turn-around point for a 5-mile, out-and-back hike.

For a 5.5-mile loop hike, gaining an additional 800 feet in elevation, take the left fork straight ahead. (The right fork continues on the Crooked Trail a half mile to the Crazy Canyon Trail and the Pattee Canyon trail system.) Gently climb a half mile through the lodgepole pine forest to a T-junction with the Crazy Canyon Trail, an unpaved fire road. The right fork leads 2 miles to the Crazy Canyon trailhead (Hike 32). Bear left on the narrow road. Stroll through the open forest with sloping meadows to a posted 3-way trail split. The right fork descends 2.5 miles on the Hellgate Canyon Trail to the Kim Williams Trail alongside the Clark Fork River (Hike 28). The center and left forks are parallel paths leading to the Mount Sentinel summit. Take the left path, passing the metal gate, and steeply climb up the trail. When the path levels out, watch for footpaths on both sides of the trail. The right fork leads a short distance to an overlook of Hellgate Canyon, Mount Jumbo, East Missoula, and the Rattlesnake Wilderness. The main trail leads up to the 5,158-foot summit, overlooking Missoula with 360-degree vistas.

For this hike, bear left on the unsigned Pengelly Ridge Trail, and head into the pine forest. (If you miss this footpath and arrive at the final steep ascent of Mount Sentinel, return 200 yards to the Pengelly Ridge Trail.) Weave through the pine forest, and ascend a hill to the ridge that overlooks Pattee Canyon and south Missoula. Follow the flower-filled ridge between meadows and pockets of pines to the west-facing mountaintop. The vistas extend across the entire city. Descend the open grassy slope, losing 1,500 feet over 1.75 miles. There are great views the entire way. Complete the loop at the junction with the Crooked Trail and Mount Sentinel Fire Road. ∎

32. Crazy Canyon Trail to Mount Sentinel
PATTEE CANYON RECREATION AREA

Hiking distance: 7 miles round trip or 4.7-mile shuttle
Hiking time: 3.5 hours
Elevation gain: 1,250 feet
Maps: U.S.G.S. Southeast Missoula
Pattee Canyon Recreation Area map
Missoulian Hike Bike Run guide

The Crazy Canyon Trail crosses the southwest slope of University Mountain, connecting the Pattee Canyon Recreation Area with Hellgate Canyon and the University of Montana. This hike begins in Pattee Canyon on the east side of Missoula and follows an unpaved, vehicle-restricted road that was once used for logging. The trail leads through Crazy Canyon in the Lolo National Forest to the summit of Mount Sentinel. From the 5,158-foot peak towering above the university, the vistas span from Missoula Valley to the Bitterroot Mountains and Frenchtown, and from Hellgate Canyon to the Rattlesnake National Recreation Area and Wilderness. For a one-way, 4.7-mile hike, leave a shuttle car by the university.

To the trailhead

From downtown Missoula, drive 2 miles south on Higgins Avenue to Pattee Canyon Road and turn left. Continue 3.4 miles to the Crazy Canyon trailhead parking lot on the left.

SHUTTLE CAR: From I-90 in Missoula, take the Van Buren Street exit and head south to Broadway—turn right. Drive a short distance east to Madison Street and turn left, crossing the bridge over the Clark Fork River. After curving onto Arthur Avenue, turn left at South 6th Street into the University of Montana. Follow the one-way street, curving around to the south side of Washington Grizzly Stadium. The trailhead parking lot is on the left.

The hike

Head north, taking the right fork uphill through the forest to a vehicle restricted road. Follow the road to the left. Stay on the road rather than veering off on the various footpaths. Cross Crazy Canyon, curving to the left (west). At 2 miles, pass a posted junction on the left with the Crooked Trail (Hike 31). Continue uphill to a 3-way trail split at 2.6 miles. The right fork descends 2.5 miles on the Hellgate Canyon Trail to the Clark Fork River (Hike 28). The center and left forks are parallel paths that lead to the Mount Sentinel summit. Take either path towards Mount Sentinel and follow the ridge. Before the final ascent, the two paths merge. Climb to the 5,158-foot summit to 360-degree vistas of the Missoula Valley. After savoring the views, return by retracing your steps. For the shuttle hike, begin the 1.7-mile descent to the university, passing the M on the way down. Reference Hike 29 for hiking directions. ■

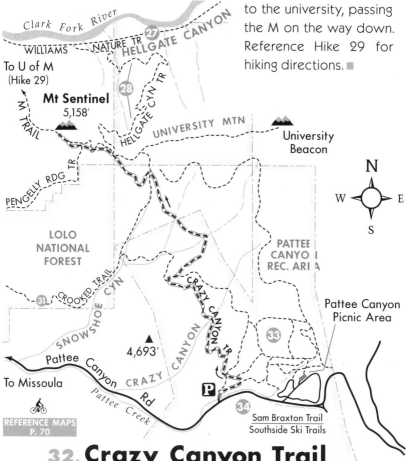

32. Crazy Canyon Trail to Mount Sentinel
PATTEE CANYON RECREATION AREA

33. Northside Trails: Meadow Loop Trail
PATTEE CANYON RECREATION AREA

Hiking distance: 2.2-mile loop
Hiking time: 1 hour
Elevation gain: 100 feet
Maps: U.S.G.S. Southeast Missoula
      The Missoula Bike Map · Missoulian Hike Bike Run guide
      Pattee Canyon Recreation Area map
      Beartooth Publishing: Missoula, Hamilton, Lost Trail Pass

Pattee Canyon sits on the south side of University Mountain in Missoula's backyard, a few miles southeast of the city. The area is named for David Pattee, an early Bitterroot Valley settler who homesteaded near the mouth of the canyon in the early 1870s. The Nez Perce and Salish traveled through this area en route to the plains for buffalo hunting. They used this route to avoid Blackfeet warrior attacks in Hellgate Canyon. From the 1920s through 1940, the meadow was the site of an old rifle range built and used by army soldiers from Fort Missoula.

The Northside Trails are a network of unsigned hiking, biking, equestrian, and cross-country ski trails north of the Pattee Canyon Picnic Area. The trails weave through open meadows and traverse the forested hills with old-growth ponderosa pine and western larch at an elevation on 4,100 feet. The Meadow Loop Trail is a pleasant loop around the meadow, where earthen-mound firing lines are still visible.

To the trailhead

From downtown Missoula, drive 2 miles south on Higgins Avenue to Pattee Canyon Road and turn left. Continue 3.9 miles to the Pattee Canyon Picnic Area on the left. Turn left and drive 0.3 miles to the group parking on the left.

The hike

From the parking area, hike north past the picnic tables into the open meadow. Several spur trails lead from the parking area to the Meadow Loop Trail. At 300 yards is an unsigned junction. Take the left route, heading west to the edge of the meadow.

Curve to the right into the ponderosa pine woodland. Head north through the trees as the trail curves to the east. Along the way are several unsigned trail forks. Most of these trails interconnect and lead back down the meadow to the picnic area and trailhead. ∎

CRAZY CANYON

PATTEE
CANYON
REC. AREA

MEADOW LOOP

NORTHSIDE
TRAILS

To Mount
Sentinel

CRAZY CANYON TR

N
W E
S

32
P

32 Pattee Creek

Pattee Canyon Rd

P

Pattee
Canyon
Picnic Area

To
Missoula

SAM BRAXTON TRAIL

34
P

34

SKI TRAILS

SOUTH SIDE

REFERENCE MAPS
P. 70

SAM BRAXTON TR

33.
Northside Trails: Meadow Loop
PATTEE CANYON RECREATION AREA

34. Sam Braxton National Recreation Trail
PATTEE CANYON RECREATION AREA

Hiking distance: 3.4-mile loop
Hiking time: 1.5 hours
Elevation gain: 350 feet
Maps: U.S.G.S. Southeast Missoula
The Missoula Bike Map · Missoulian Hike Bike Run guide
Pattee Canyon Recreation Area map
Beartooth Publishing: Missoula, Hamilton, Lost Trail Pass

The Sam Braxton Trail is located in the Pattee Canyon Recreation Area four miles southeast of Missoula. An old homestead was once located here, but the area has since been named after Braxton, a well-known local skier, biker, and outdoorsman. This national recreation trail is a winding, curving trail looping through a forest of old growth western larch, ponderosa pine, and aspen trees. The trail completely encircles the Southside Ski Trails, one of Missoula's more popular cross-country ski areas. Old logging skid trails crisscross through the area.

To the trailhead

From downtown Missoula, drive 2 miles south on Higgins Avenue to Pattee Canyon Road and turn left. Continue 4.2 miles to the posted Pattee Canyon trailhead parking lot on the right.

The hike

From the parking lot, hike south past the gate to the posted trailhead. Bear to the right 0.1 mile to a junction. Take the posted Sam Braxton Recreation Trail to the left, winding gently uphill. The trail weaves through the forest like a maze. At times the route may be confusing due to the old logging paths that cross through the area. At any of the unmarked junctions, follow the direction arrows or the national recreation trail insignia on the trees. When you least expect it, the trail completes the loop back to the trailhead. ■

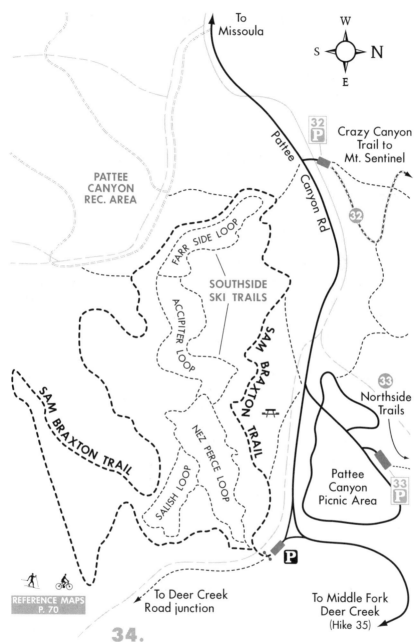

To
Missoula

W
S · N
E

PATTEE
CANYON
REC. AREA

Pattee Canyon Rd

32
P

Crazy Canyon
Trail to
Mt. Sentinel

32

FARR SIDE LOOP

SOUTHSIDE
SKI TRAILS

ACCIPITER LOOP

SAM BRAXTON TRAIL

SAM BRAXTON TRAIL

NEZ PERCE LOOP

SALISH LOOP

33
Northside
Trails

Pattee
Canyon
Picnic Area

33
P

REFERENCE MAPS
P. 70

P

To Deer Creek
Road junction

To Middle Fork
Deer Creek
(Hike 35)

34.
Sam Braxton Nat'l. Rec. Trail
PATTEE CANYON RECREATION AREA

35. Middle Fork Deer Creek Trail

Hiking distance: 2.2 miles round trip
Hiking time: 1.25 hours
Elevation gain: 600 feet
Maps: U.S.G.S. Southeast Missoula

Deer Creek, a tributary of the Clark Fork of the Columbia River, flows through the Lolo National Forest east of Mount Sentinel and Pattee Canyon. Three tributaries flow into Deer Creek at its headwaters. This hike follows the Middle Fork of Deer Creek where it merges with the West Fork. The lush trail follows a regenerated logging road and heads upstream in a pristine forested drainage that is rich with wildflowers.

To the trailhead

From downtown Missoula, drive 2 miles south on Higgins Avenue to Pattee Canyon Road and turn left. Continue 5.5 miles to Road 2127.1, a side road on a U-shaped left bend in the road. Veer right on Road 2127.1, and drive 0.25 miles to a gated road/trail on the left. Park on the left. If the gate at the bottom of Road 2127.1 is closed, park on the shoulder of the road, and walk 0.3 miles up the road to the trailhead.

The hike

Cross over the West Fork of Deer Creek, and walk past the vehicle gate. Head up the grassy road, following the east side of the creek. Pass the confluence of the Middle Fork and West Fork of Deer Creek to a Y-fork. The dirt road crosses the Middle Fork on the right and leads into the West Fork drainage high above the creek. Instead, continue straight ahead on the grassy path, heading south along the Middle Fork of Deer Creek. Miller Peak is in view to the south. The old logging road narrows to a footpath and enters the shade of the forest. Stroll through the forest, steadily climbing above the creek on the east canyon wall. At one mile, the trail returns to the creek. The path soon fades and becomes overgrown with vegetation. This is the turn-around spot. Return along the same path. ■

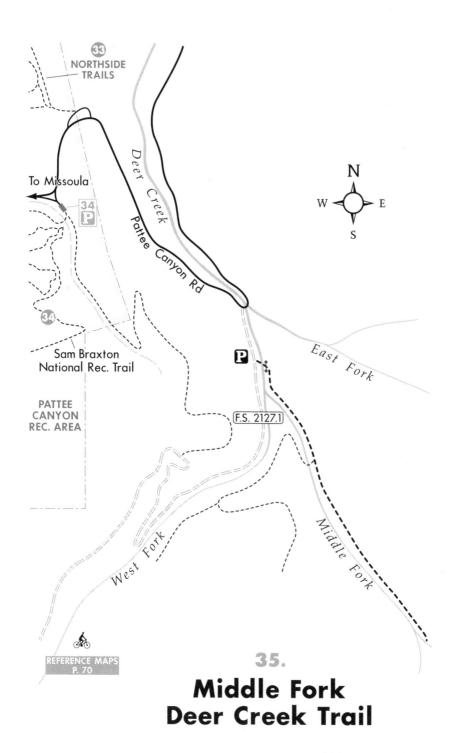

33
NORTHSIDE
TRAILS

Deer Creek

To Missoula

34
P

N
W E
S

Pattee Canyon Rd

East Fork

34

P

Sam Braxton
National Rec. Trail

F.S. 2127.1

PATTEE
CANYON
REC. AREA

Middle Fork

West Fork

REFERENCE MAPS
P. 70

35.

Middle Fork
Deer Creek Trail

36. Moose Can Gully and Peery Park
SOUTH HILLS TRAIL SYSTEM

Hiking distance: 1.3 miles round trip
Hiking time: 45 minutes
Elevation gain: 150 feet
Maps: U.S.G.S. Southwest Missoula

The South Hills Trail System was developed by South Hills landowners, local volunteers, and the Missoula Parks and Recreation Department. The trails link the South Hills neighborhoods through greenbelt corridors, pedestrian easements, and parklands. The Moose Can Gully Trail winds through parkland meadows and climbs up Moose Can Gully, a forested ravine with ponderosa pines and a natural understory of riparian vegetation. Peery Park traverses open hillside prairie with great views of Missoula.

To the trailhead

From the intersection of 39th Street and 23rd Avenue in south Missoula, drive 0.7 miles south on 23rd Avenue to Peery Park on the right. Park along the shoulder of the road.

The hike

Cross the street to the trailhead map sign. Walk across the meadow to the southwest edge of Moose Can Gully. Bear left and descend into the gully. Head down the canyon into Garland Park. The path ends at the corner of Garland Drive and 23rd Avenue. Return back up Moose Can Gully into a narrow, forested draw, leaving Garland Park. Climb up the footpath to a meadow on the southwest slope of the gully. The trail gently ascends the drainage to the head of the gully and ends at 55th Street at a bend in the road. Return to the trailhead.

To extend the hike an additional mile, cross the street into posted Peery Park. Head west through a wide greenbelt with views across Missoula. Cross the 24th Street Trail to the end of the trail at the Blackthorn Drive cul-de-sac or the Kinnikinnick Court cul-de-sac. ∎

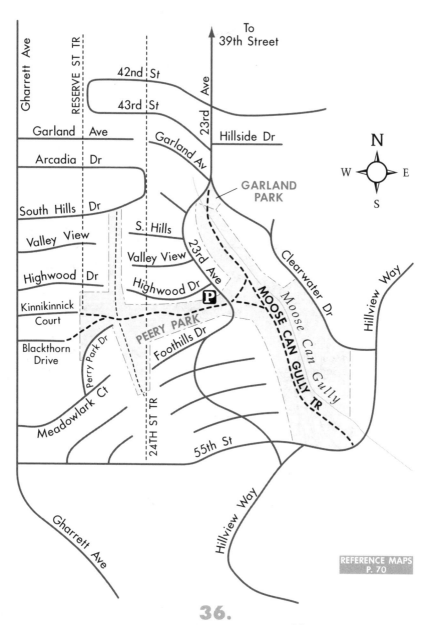

36.
Moose Can Gully
and Peery Park
SOUTH HILLS TRAIL SYSTEM

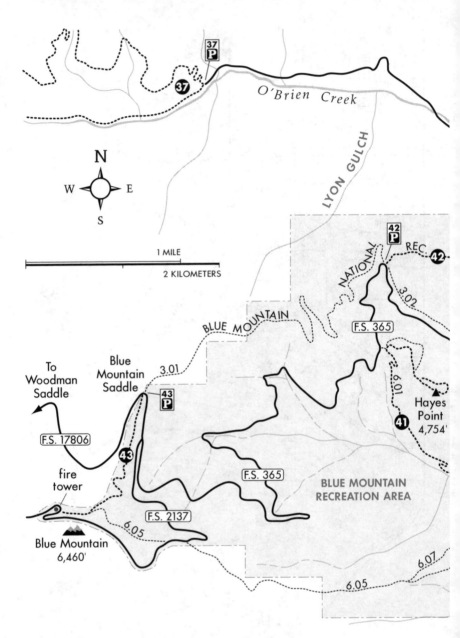

O'Brien Creek

LYON GULCH

N
W E
S

1 MILE
2 KILOMETERS

BLUE MOUNTAIN

NATIONAL

REC

F.S. 365

3.02

3.01

To
Woodman
Saddle

Blue
Mountain
Saddle

43
P

F.S. 17806

43

6.01

Hayes
Point
4,754'

41

fire
tower

F.S. 365

F.S. 2137

6.05

BLUE MOUNTAIN
RECREATION AREA

Blue Mountain
6,460'

6.05

6.07

HIKES 37–43
Blue Mountain
Recreation Area

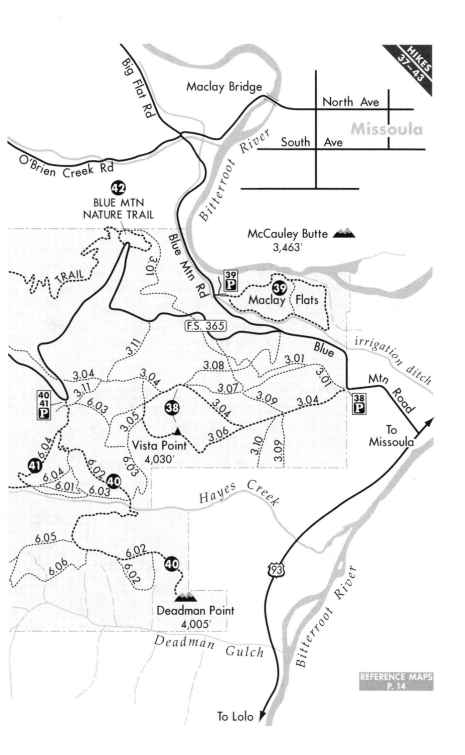

Big Flat Rd

Maclay Bridge

North Ave

South Ave

Missoula

O'Brien Creek Rd

Bitterroot River

42
BLUE MTN
NATURE TRAIL

McCauley Butte
3,463'

TRAIL

3.01

Blue Mtn Rd

39 P

39 Maclay Flats

irrigation ditch

F.S. 365

Blue

3.11

3.04   3.04   3.08   3.01

3.07

40 41 P   3.11   3.04   3.09   3.04   Mtn Road

6.03   3.05   3.04   **38 P**

38

3.06   To Missoula

6.04   Vista Point
4,030'

41   6.04   6.02   3.10   3.09

6.01   6.03   **40**

Hayes Creek

6.05

6.06   6.02   **40**

6.02

93

Deadman Point
4,005'

Bitterroot River

Deadman Gulch

REFERENCE MAPS
P. 14

To Lolo

37. South O'Brien Creek Loop

Hiking distance: 7.5-mile loop
Hiking time: 4 hours
Elevation gain: 1,000 feet
Maps: U.S.G.S. Blue Mountain · O' Brien Creek Area trailhead map

map
page 110

O'Brien Creek forms on the east slope of the Grave Creek Range west of Missoula and north of the Blue Mountain Recreation Area. The creek, a tributary of the Bitterroot River, flows 10 miles to its confluence with the river just north of Maclay Flats. En route, the waterway skirts the northern base of Blue Mountain. The South O'Brien Creek Loop is a little known gem that follows the waterway and loops back on the north canyon wall. Along the way, the path weaves through canyons, open meadows, and lush, forested waterways. Overlooks from the trail offer views across Missoula to Mount Jumbo and Mount Sentinel. The trail is closed from December 1 through May 15 to protect wintering elk and deer populations.

To the trailhead

From Highway 93 in Missoula, drive 2 miles south of Reserve Street to Blue Mountain Road and turn right. Continue 2.9 miles to O'Brien Creek Road. Turn left and continue 3.1 miles to the posted trailhead at the end of the road. Park in the spaces on the right. SECOND DRIVING ROUTE: From the intersection of South Avenue

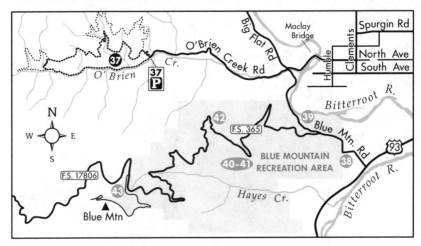

and Reserve Street in Missoula, drive 2.5 miles west on South Avenue to Humble Road. With humility, turn right and go 0.2 miles to North Avenue. Turn left and continue one mile, crossing the Maclay Bridge over the Bitterroot River, to the Blue Mountain Road—Big Flat Road junction. (North Avenue becomes River Pines Road after the Maclay Bridge.) Drive through the intersection onto O'Brien Creek Road, and go 3.1 miles to the posted trailhead at the end of the road. Park in the spaces on the right.

The hike

Follow the dirt road past the gate, and parallel the north side of O'Brien Creek through the forest. Pass a home on the left, and continue through private land on an easement for a half mile. Steadily head up canyon, passing flower-filled meadows along the meandering creek. Pass through a second vehicle gate, staying on the north side of the creek. At 2.5 miles, by a meadow on the right, is a posted junction. Leave the road and veer right, gently ascending the hillside into a side canyon. Head up the minor canyon, then weave up the east wall to a posted junction on a narrow dirt road. Take the road to the right—the South O'Brien Creek Loop—following the contours of the mountain on a level grade. Traverse the slope among flower-clad meadows. The views span across O'Brien Canyon to Blue Mountain and across the city to Mount Sentinel. At 5 miles is another signed junction. The North O'Brien Creek Loop continues straight ahead, adding an additional 2.7 miles to the hike.

For this hike, curve right, staying on the South O'Brien Creek Loop. Drop down into the forested drainage, and cross a tributary stream. Follow the waterway downstream through lush riparian vegetation. Curve left, cross the stream, and go to the right. Traverse the hillside to a signed junction on a dirt road at 5.5 miles. Bear right and slowly loose elevation, weaving in and out of small drainages and around knolls, which offer views of the L on Mount Jumbo and the M on Mount Sentinel. Make a long, sweeping bend around a knoll to a posted fork with the North O'Brien Creek Loop on the left at 7 miles. Go to the right and wind a half mile down the forested hillside to the trailhead. ■

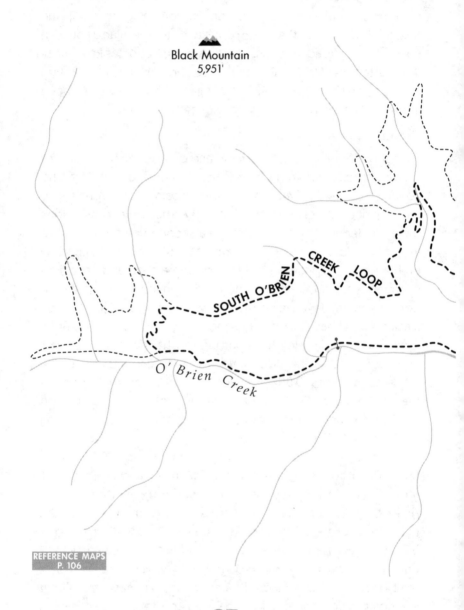

Black Mountain
5,951'

CREEK LOOP

SOUTH O'BRIEN

O'Brien Creek

REFERENCE MAPS
P. 106

37.
South O'Brien Creek Loop

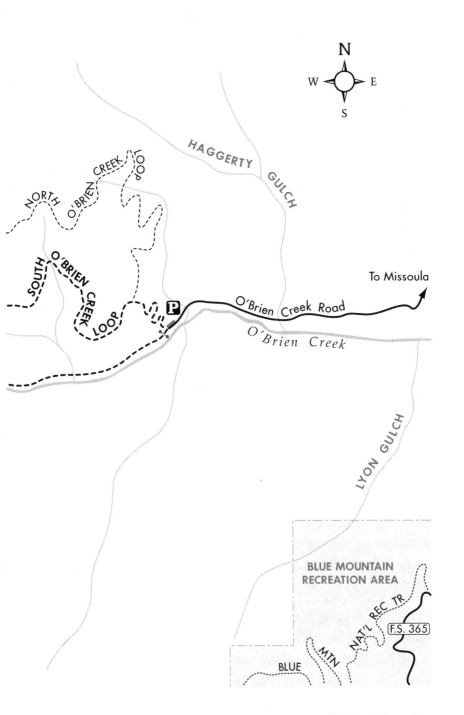

N

W   E

S

HAGGERTY GULCH

NORTH O'BRIEN CREEK LOOP

SOUTH O'BRIEN CREEK LOOP

P

O'Brien Creek Road

To Missoula

O'Brien Creek

LYON GULCH

BLUE MOUNTAIN RECREATION AREA

NAT'L REC TR

F.S. 365

BLUE MTN

38. Vista Point Loop
BLUE MOUNTAIN RECREATION AREA

Hiking distance: 3.2-mile loop
Hiking time: 1.5 hours
Elevation gain: 800 feet
Maps: U.S.G.S. Southwest Missoula
Blue Mountain Recreation Area map · The Missoula Bike Map
Beartooth Publishing: Missoula, Hamilton, Lost Trail Pass

Blue Mountain Recreation Area is a popular 5,500-acre outdoor destination only two miles from Missoula. An army military reservation was once located here. In 1986 the land was designated as a recreation area, and a network of multi-use trails was established. The picturesque landscape, part of the Lolo National Forest, includes a grassy valley bottom adjacent to several mountain peaks. Vista Point is a 4,030-foot rounded hilltop that offers unobstructed panoramas in every direction. The dog-friendly trail to the point crosses meadows and loops through a ponderosa pine and Douglas fir forest.

To the trailhead

From Highway 93 in Missoula, drive two miles south of Reserve Street to Blue Mountain Road and turn right. Continue 0.5 miles to the trailhead parking lot on the left.

The hike

Cross the grassy slope, heading west toward the mountains on Trail 3.04. Pass two intersecting trails while heading to the west end of the meadow and a signed trail split. Bear left and enter the pine forest, beginning the loop on Trail 3.06. Head steeply up the hillside to a saddle overlooking the Blue Mountain backcountry. Curve right along the ridge to the Vista Point overlook at 4,030 feet. After enjoying the 365-degree views, descend to the west to a signed junction. Take the right fork on Trail 3.05 a short distance to another signed junction. Go to the right again on Trail 3.03. Continue downhill and bear right a third time on Trail 3.04. The forested path passes Trails 3.07 and 3.08 on the left, completing the loop at the west end of the meadow. Cross the meadow, returning to the trailhead. ■

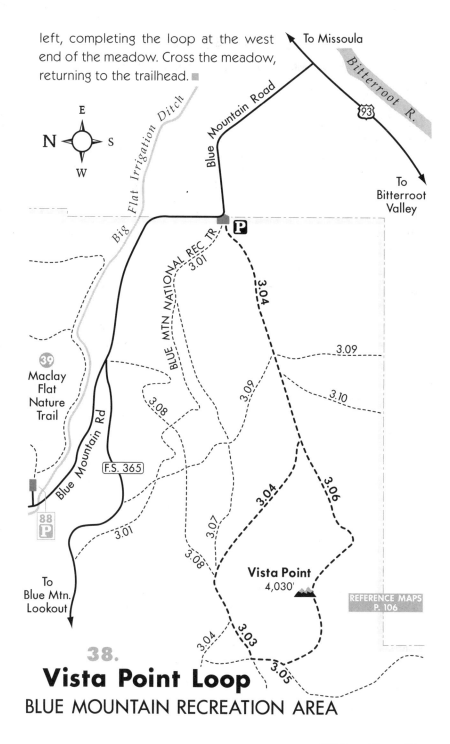

38.
Vista Point Loop
BLUE MOUNTAIN RECREATION AREA

39. Maclay Flat Nature Trail
BLUE MOUNTAIN RECREATION AREA

Hiking distance: 1.25-mile or 1.8-mile loop
Hiking time: 1 hour
Elevation gain: level
Maps: U.S.G.S. Southwest Missoula
      Blue Mountain Recreation Area map
      Missoulian Hike Bike Run guide
      Beartooth Publishing: Missoula, Hamilton, Lost Trail Pass

The Maclay Flat Trail is a wide, level interpretive trail that lies at the base of Blue Mountain between the Bitterroot River and the Big Flat Irrigation Ditch. The area was a camping site for the Salish Indians while they gathered roots of the bitterroot flower. The trail meanders through open grasslands and a rich riparian forest with aspen, cottonwood, ponderosa pine, dogwood, and willow. The wetlands, forest, and river make it a year-round haven for watching wildlife. The irrigation ditch is used by farms and ranches through Big Flat before emptying into the Clark Fork River. Sixteen information stations along the trail describe the geology; river system; vegetation; and wildlife in the area, including bald eagles, osprey, and tree swallows. Benches, picnic tables, and a boat ramp are available along this wheelchair accessible trail. Leashed dogs are allowed.

To the trailhead

From Highway 93 in Missoula, drive two miles south of Reserve Street to Blue Mountain Road and turn right. Continue 1.7 miles to the Maclay Flat parking lot on the right.

The hike

From the parking lot, the well-defined trail heads east. Begin hiking clockwise on the left fork. At 0.3 miles the trail parallels the banks of the Bitterroot River and passes a grassy riverfront picnic area. At 0.6 miles is a junction with a cut-across trail. The right fork shortens the hike to a 1.25-mile loop. Continue straight ahead for a 1.8-mile loop. Curve south and return back to the trailhead along the north edge of the Big Flat Irrigation Ditch. ■

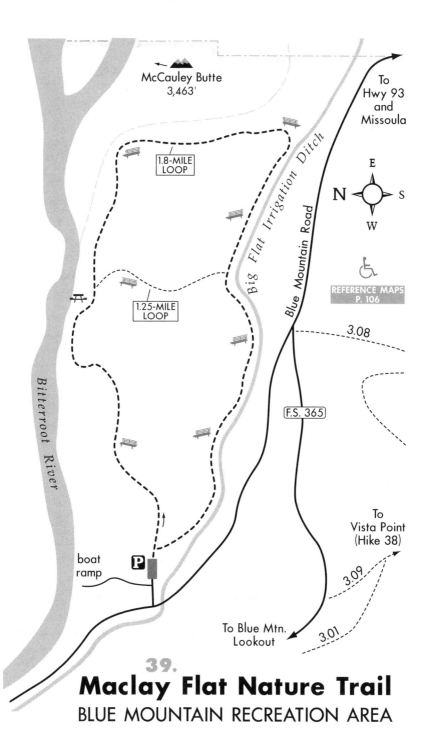

McCauley Butte
3,463'

To
Hwy 93
and
Missoula

1.8-MILE
LOOP

Big Flat Irrigation Ditch

Blue Mountain Road

E
N ⊕ S
W

REFERENCE MAPS
P. 106

3.08

1.25-MILE
LOOP

F.S. 365

Bitterroot River

To
Vista Point
(Hike 38)

boat
ramp

P

3.09

To Blue Mtn.
Lookout

3.01

39.
Maclay Flat Nature Trail
BLUE MOUNTAIN RECREATION AREA

40. Deadman Point
BLUE MOUNTAIN RECREATION AREA

Hiking distance: 5.6 miles round trip
Hiking time: 2.5 hours
Elevation gain: 600 feet
Maps: U.S.G.S. Blue Mountain and Southwest Missoula
   Blue Mountain Recreation Area map
   The Missoula Bike Map
   Beartooth Publishing: Missoula, Hamilton, Lost Trail Pass

Deadman Point is a rounded grassy knoll at the south edge of the Blue Mountain Recreation Area. The trail heads south in a lodgepole pine forest, crosses Hayes Creek on a footbridge, and climbs to the 4,005-foot knoll. From the summit are panoramic 360-degree views of the Missoula Valley, the Bitterroot River, and the Sapphire and Bitterroot Mountains.

To the trailhead

From Highway 93 in Missoula, drive two miles south of Reserve Street to Blue Mountain Road and turn right. Continue 1.3 miles to a road fork, and bear left on unpaved Forest Road #365. Drive 3 miles to the signed motorcycle trailhead on the left.

The hike

From the back of the parking lot, walk through the fence opening. Take the well-defined middle trail through the pine forest. At 0.1 mile is a signed junction. The right fork—Trail 6.04—leads to Hayes Point (Hike 41). Take the left fork on Trail 6.01, descending down four switchbacks to another signed junction. Bear left on Trail 6.02. Descend to Hayes Creek at a four-way junction by a log rail fence. Cross the wooden bridge over Hayes Creek, staying on Trail 6.02. Climb up the hillside to the ridge at a junction with Trail 6.05 on the right. Follow the ridge straight ahead, staying to the left past three consecutive intersecting trails. The path curves south for the final ascent to the rounded summit of Deadman Point. Return on the same trail. ∎

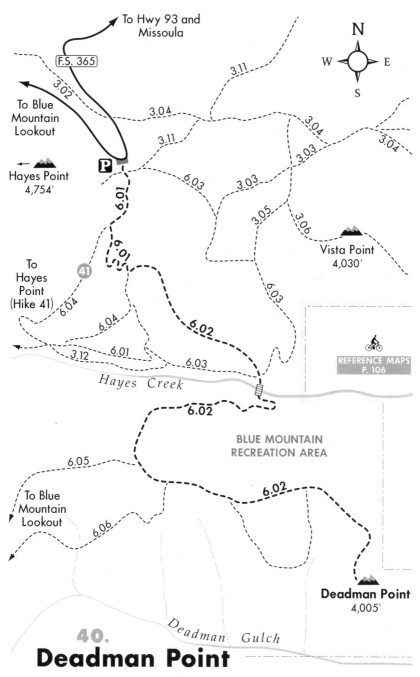

To Hwy 93 and
Missoula

F.S. 365

3.02

To Blue
Mountain
Lookout

N

W   E

S

3.11

3.04

3.11

Hayes Point
4,754'

P

3.04

3.04

3.04

3.03

6.03

6.01

3.03

3.05

3.06

Vista Point
4,030'

To
Hayes
Point
(Hike 41)

41

6.01

6.04

6.04

6.03

6.03

3.12

6.01

6.03

6.02

REFERENCE MAPS
P. 106

Hayes   Creek

6.02

**BLUE MOUNTAIN
RECREATION AREA**

6.05

To Blue
Mountain
Lookout

6.06

6.02

Deadman Point
4,005'

Deadman Gulch

40.
Deadman Point
BLUE MOUNTAIN RECREATION AREA

41. Hayes Point

BLUE MOUNTAIN RECREATION AREA

Hiking distance: 5.4 miles round trip
Hiking time: 3 hours
Elevation gain: 1,200 feet
Maps: U.S.G.S. Blue Mountain and Southwest Missoula
      Blue Mountain Recreation Area map · The Missoula Bike Map
      Beartooth Publishing: Missoula, Hamilton, Lost Trail Pass

Hayes Point is a rocky, tree-covered overlook in the center of Blue Mountain Recreation Area. The trail loops through the forest, skirting a segment of Hayes Creek en route to the overlook. From the 4,754-foot summit are sweeping vistas of the Missoula Valley, the Bitterroot River, and the surrounding mountains.

To the trailhead

From Highway 93 in Missoula, drive two miles south of Reserve Street to Blue Mountain Road and turn right. Continue 1.3 miles to a road fork, and bear left on unpaved Forest Road #365. Drive 3 miles to the signed motorcycle trailhead on the left.

The hike

From the back of the parking lot, walk through the fence opening. Take the well-defined middle trail through the pine forest. At 0.1 mile is a signed junction. The left fork—Trail 6.01—leads to Deadman Point (Hike 40). Take the right fork on Trail 6.04, and continue through the forest. Traverse the edge of the hillside, curving right high above Hayes Creek. Descend to the creek and a four-way junction at one mile. Take the right fork—Trail 6.01—heading upstream. Leave the stream and begin the ascent. The trail is never steep, but it is steady and requires a few rest stops. At the top, the trail meets the road on the left at a trail junction. Bear right and head east to a trail split. Both trails lead to Hayes Point, creating a loop. The more direct route to the overlook is to the right. After enjoying the views, continue around the loop and return on the same trail. For a shorter return, at the junction by the road, take Forest Road #365 back to the parking lot. ■

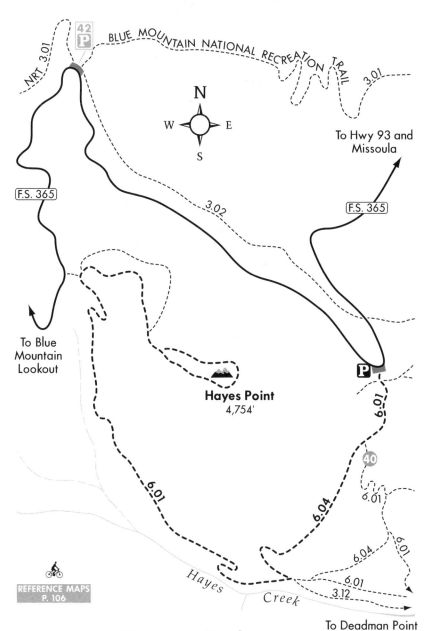

NRT 3.01

42 P

BLUE MOUNTAIN NATIONAL RECREATION TRAIL

3.01

N
W · E
S

To Hwy 93 and
Missoula

F.S. 365

F.S. 365

3.02

To Blue
Mountain
Lookout

Hayes Point
4,754'

P

6.01

40

6.01

6.04

6.01

6.04

6.01

REFERENCE MAPS
P. 106

Hayes

Creek

6.01

3.12

To Deadman Point

41. Hayes Point

BLUE MOUNTAIN RECREATION AREA

42. Blue Mountain National Recreation Trail

Blue Mountain Nature Trail

BLUE MOUNTAIN RECREATION AREA

Hiking distance: 4.2 miles round trip
Hiking time: 2 hours
Elevation gain: 700 feet
Maps: U.S.G.S. Blue Mountain and Southwest Missoula
Blue Mountain Recreation Area map
Missoulian Hike Bike Run guide
Beartooth Publishing: Missoula, Hamilton, Lost Trail Pass

The Blue Mountain National Recreation Trail is an 8-mile trail that traverses the entire length of the park, from the trailhead at the eastern boundary to the Blue Mountain Lookout at the western boundary. The trail is open to hikers and equestrians only. This hike follows a two-mile section of the trail along a beautiful forested path through ponderosa pine and Douglas fir. The Blue Mountain Nature Trail is a quarter-mile wheelchair-accessible loop at the east end of this hike. The trail leads to an overlook with a panoramic photograph identifying the surrounding peaks and canyons. (Brochures are available at the trailhead.) The road passes the signed Blue Mountain Nature Trail en route to the trailhead if you prefer to hike only the quarter-mile loop.

To the trailhead

From Highway 93 in Missoula, drive two miles south of Reserve Street to Blue Mountain Road and turn right. Continue 1.3 miles to a road fork, and bear left on unpaved Forest Road #365. Drive 4.2 miles to the gate on the right at a sharp left bend in the road. Park in the pullout on the right.

The hike

Walk through the opening in the fence on the right side of the metal gate. Head east through the forest on the well-defined footpath. At 0.5 miles, views open up across the Missoula Valley. Descend through the forest on a winding course with switchbacks, reaching the Blue Mountain Nature Trail at two miles. Circle the quarter-mile nature loop on the level path, over-looking Missoula Valley, the Bitterroot River, and the surrounding peaks. Return along the same route. ■

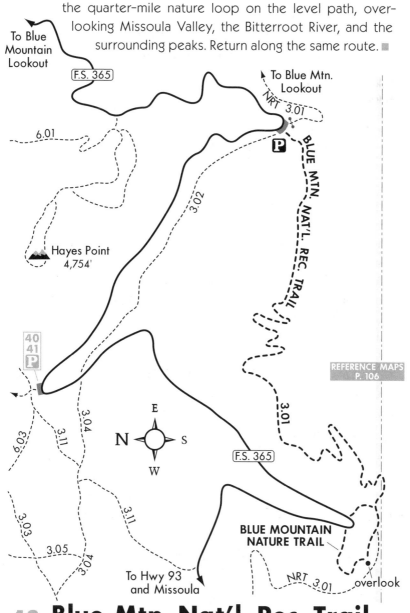

To Blue Mountain Lookout

F.S. 365

6.01

To Blue Mtn. Lookout

NRT 3.01

P

BLUE MTN. NAT'L. REC. TRAIL

3.02

Hayes Point
4,754'

40
41
P

REFERENCE MAPS
P. 106

3.01

3.04

3.11

N
E ⊕ S
W

F.S. 365

6.03

3.03

3.11

BLUE MOUNTAIN
NATURE TRAIL

3.05

3.04

To Hwy 93
and Missoula

NRT 3.01

overlook

42. **Blue Mtn. Nat'l. Rec. Trail**
Blue Mtn. Nature Trail
BLUE MOUNTAIN RECREATION AREA

43. Blue Mountain Lookout from Blue Mountain Saddle

BLUE MOUNTAIN RECREATION AREA

Hiking distance: 2.2 miles round trip
Hiking time: 1.5 hours
Elevation gain: 660 feet
Maps: U.S.G.S. Blue Mountain and Southwest Missoula
      Blue Mountain Recreation Area map
      Missoulian Hike Bike Run guide
      Beartooth Publishing: Missoula, Hamilton, Lost Trail Pass

The hike from Blue Mountain Saddle up to the fire lookout follows the last mile of the 8-mile Blue Mountain National Recreation Trail (Hike 42). The lookout tower, at the top of Blue Mountain, is a working Forest Service fire lookout. From the summit are incredible panoramic views of the Garnet, Swan, Rattlesnake, Mission Mountain, and Cabinet Ranges; the Scapegoat, Bob Marshall, and Selway-Bitterroot wilderness areas; the Missoula Valley; and Lolo Peak. During fire season, the lookout is open to the public. Visitors are welcome to climb the steps up to the 50-foot tower and take a tour. Forest Service Road #2137 also winds up to the fire lookout (in season). The scenic drive to the summit is highly recommended if you prefer not to hike.

To the trailhead

From Highway 93 in Missoula, drive two miles south of Reserve Street to Blue Mountain Road and turn right. Continue 1.3 miles to a road fork, and bear left on unpaved Forest Road #365. Drive 10.3 miles to a signed junction with F.S. 2137. The left fork leads to the Blue Mountain Lookout. Take the right fork straight ahead for 0.3 miles to the signed Blue Mountain Saddle at a horseshoe bend in the road. Park in the pullouts on the right by the post and rail fence.

The hike

Cross the road and pass through the fence to the grassy knoll. Follow the ridge southwest toward the lookout, which can be seen above the trees at the top of Blue Mountain. The path straddles the ridge, overlooking the Grave Creek Range to the west and the Missoula Valley to the east. The wide trail enters the shady forest while steeply climbing the mountain. At 0.7 miles, follow the switchbacks moderately uphill to the top of Blue Mountain. Bear right on Trail 6.05 (which is un-marked), and walk a short distance to the fire lookout. After enjoying the views, retrace your steps. ■

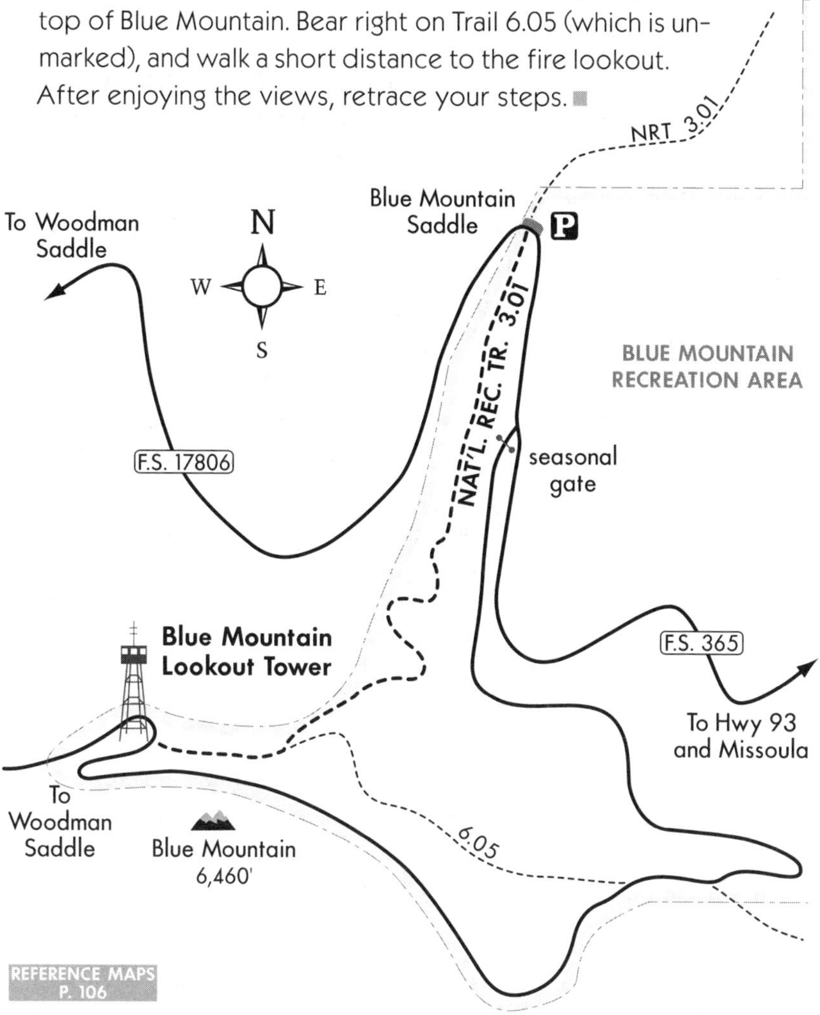

NRT 3.01

To Woodman
Saddle

N

W ← → E

S

Blue Mountain
Saddle

P

BLUE MOUNTAIN
RECREATION AREA

NAT'L. REC. TR. 3.01

F.S. 17806

seasonal
gate

Blue Mountain
Lookout Tower

F.S. 365

To Hwy 93
and Missoula

To
Woodman
Saddle

Blue Mountain
6,460'

6.05

REFERENCE MAPS
P. 106

33.
Blue Mountain Lookout
from Blue Mountain Saddle
BLUE MOUNTAIN RECREATION AREA

44. Council Grove State Park

Hiking distance: 1 mile round trip
Hiking time: 40 minutes
Elevation gain: level
Maps: U.S.G.S. Primrose

Council Grove State Park marks the location of the July 16, 1855 council between Isaac Stevens (Governor of Indian Affairs) and the Salish (Flathead), Kootenai, and the Pend d' Orielle (Kalispel) Indians. The council resulted in the signing of the Hellgate Treaty, which created the Flathead Reservation in the Jocko and Mission Valleys. The reluctant tribes relinquished their 12 million acres of ancestral lands—almost all of their land in Western Montana—for the 1.25-million acre Flathead Reservation. The Salish were removed from the Bitterroot Valley.

The 187-acre Council Grove State Park sits along the banks of the Clark Fork River (known as the Hellgate River in the 1800s) at the far west end of Missoula. The primitive park contains open meadows, old-growth ponderosa pine, cottonwoods, and an aspen grove fed by a vernal pool (a natural depression that holds water seasonally). A path with interpretive panels wanders along a slough to the Clark Fork River. It is a great park for picnicking, bird watching, dog walking, and fishing.

To the trailhead

From the intersection of Reserve Street and Mullan Road in Missoula, drive 6.4 miles west on Mullan Road to the posted Council Grove State Park turnoff. Turn left and continue a half mile on the dirt road to the trailhead parking lot.

The hike

Two paths leave from the trailhead. Take the right trail past the Treaty Memorial display. Head through open grasslands with ponderosa pines and cottonwoods to the banks of Warm Slough, a channel of the Clark Fork River. An informal trail follows the edge of the river channel 200 yards downstream to the park boundary, adjacent to privately owned land.

Return upstream and head east to a junction with the other

trailhead path, our return route. Continue straight ahead, following the river. Stroll atop the 8-foot bluff through grasslands and riparian vegetation. Pass fishing access spots, rock and sand beach pockets, and an aspen grove fed by the vernal pool. The trail ends at fenced pastureland. Return to the junction and cross the meadow back to the trailhead. ■

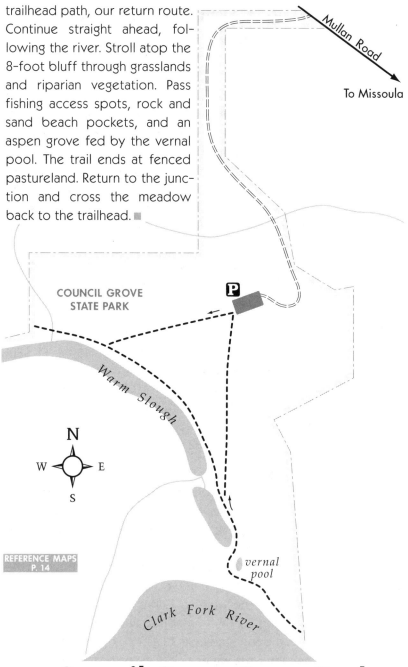

44. Council Grove State Park

45. Erskine Fishing Access Trail

Hiking distance: 3 miles round trip
Hiking time: 1.5 hours
Elevation gain: level
Maps: U.S.G.S. Huson

The Erskine Fishing Access is located in Frenchtown on the west end of the Missoula Valley. The 700-acre public site is bordered by the Clark Fork of the Columbia River to the south and pasture-land to the north. The floodplain contains islands and an adjoining U-shaped oxbow bend in the river. The 1.5-mile fishing access trail follows the waterway as the river curves along the base of the mountains. The dog-friendly path leads through the lush riverside wetland with a rich complex of cottonwoods, ponderosa pines, aspen groves, willow bottoms, cattails, hawthorn thickets, and beaver ponds. The area is a haven for birds.

To the trailhead

From Missoula, drive 14 miles west on I-90 to Frenchtown/Exit 89. Turn south 0.2 miles to a T-junction. Turn left and a quick right onto Ducharme Street. Drive 0.1 mile south to Mullan Road and turn right. Continue 2.2 miles west to the posted Erskine Fishing Access turnoff. Turn left and go 0.7 miles to the trailhead parking area at the end of the road.

The hike

Begin on the trail to the east (left). Walk east along the southern edge of the dry grassland, skirting the lush riparian vegetation on the right. Follow a slow-moving branch of the Clark Fork River. Curve right through a grove of cottonwoods into a riverfront meadow along the oxbow at a half mile.

After checking out the gorgeous habitat, return a half mile to the trailhead. Head west, passing a few ponderosa pines while skirting the north edge of the wetland. Curve left into the wetlands, thick with aspens and willows. Cross through a massive grassland, directly towards the forested mountains, to a branch of the Clark Fork River. Stroll along the waterway through the meadow to the main branch of the wide river. Meander downstream along the river bank through pockets of ponderosa pine. The trail officially ends at the fenced Montana Fish and Game boundary at one mile. A path continues along the river, but it is on private land. Return through the grassland, forming a loop, or return on the same path parallel to the waterway. ■

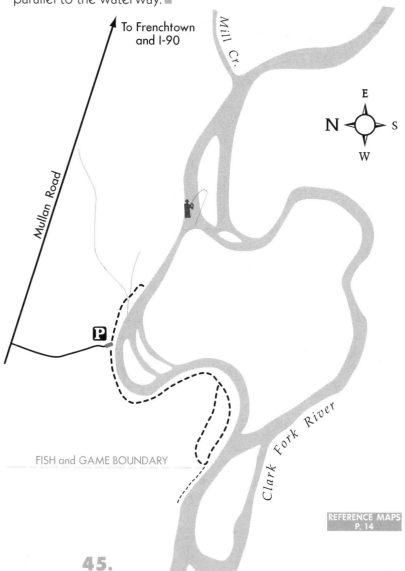

45.
Erskine Fishing Access Trail

46. Grand Menard Discovery Trail

Hiking distance: 1.3-mile loop
Hiking time: 1 hour
Elevation gain: 150 feet
Maps: U.S.G.S. Alberton
Lolo National Forest Grand Menard Discovery Trail map
Beartooth Publishing: Missoula, Hamilton, Lost Trail Pass

The Ninemile Valley is a wide, alpine valley in the Lolo National Forest 21 miles northwest of Missoula. The historic Ninemile Ranger Station and Remount Depot is located four miles from the valley's confluence with the Clark Fork River. The Grand Menard Discovery Trail, less than a mile north of the ranger station, is a self-guided interpretive trail. A brochure at the ranger station and trailhead describes the history of the Ninemile Valley, logging in the area, irrigation, the life cycle of trees, pine nuts, knapweed, wildlife, and the effects of fire. The rambling nature trail has two loops that wind through a ponderosa pine and Douglas fir forest. The inner loop is a 0.6-mile graveled, wheelchair-accessible trail. From the trail are views of Stark Mountain and the fire lookout.

To the trailhead

From Missoula, drive 21 miles west on I—90 to Ninemile Road/Exit 82. Turn right (north) and drive 1.4 miles to Remount Road. Turn right and drive 2.7 miles to the Ninemile Ranger Station. Continue 0.8 miles to the Grand Menard turnoff. Turn left and drive 0.2 miles to the parking lot on the left.

The hike

Head south from the end of the parking lot, passing the interpretive trail sign. At the first trail junction, take the fork to the right and hike counter-clockwise. A short distance ahead is a bridge over a stream. Continue to the next fork, and again take the trail to the right. The trail crosses another bridge to the west side of the loop. Head south, overlooking a large meadow and pasture to the west. Loop back toward the trailhead, crossing two additional bridges before completing the loop. Take the trail to the right, and return to the parking lot. ∎

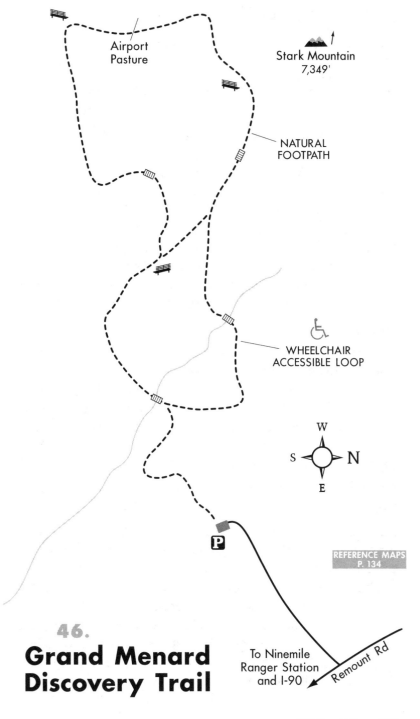

Airport
Pasture

Stark Mountain
7,349'

NATURAL
FOOTPATH

WHEELCHAIR
ACCESSIBLE LOOP

W
S ✦ N
E

P

REFERENCE MAPS
P. 134

46.
Grand Menard
Discovery Trail

To Ninemile
Ranger Station
and I-90

Remount Rd

47. Kreis Pond Trail

Hiking distance: 2.5-mile loop or 3.4 miles round trip
Hiking time: 2.5 hours
Elevation gain: 300 feet
Maps: U.S.G.S. Alberton · Kreis Pond Mountain Bike Trails map
   Beartooth Publishing: Missoula, Hamilton, Lost Trail Pass

Kreis Pond is an eight-acre pond that sits at 3,677 feet in the Lolo National Forest, a couple miles north of the Ninemile Ranger Station. The pond was developed in the 1940s as an irrigation reservoir for 200 acres of local hayfields. Water diverted from the creek was dammed to form the pond. The reservoir is no longer used for irrigation. At a depth of 24 feet, it instead offers fishing for trout and largemouth bass from the shoreline or from small watercraft. Picnic areas and campsites surround the pond. The Kreis Pond Trail weaves through the forest to the pond on an easy, uncrowded hiking, mountain biking, and equestrian trail.

To the trailhead

From Missoula, drive 21 miles west on I—90 to Ninemile Road/Exit 82. Turn right (north) and go 1.4 miles to Remount Road. Turn right and drive 2.7 miles to the historic Ninemile Ranger Station. Continue 1.5 miles to a Y-fork. Veer left on Forest Service Road 456, and go 2.2 miles to a posted road split. Bear left on F.S. Road 2176. Drive 0.8 miles to a dirt road on the left, located 0.4 miles before the campground entrance. Park in the pullout on the left shoulder of the road.

The hike

Head south into the ponderosa pine and Douglas fir forest on the two-track road. Curve right and steadily descend to a posted junction at 0.7 miles. The left fork loops back up 2.5 miles to the Civilian Conservation Corp (CCC) Camp, built for the Forest Service during the Great Depression of the 1930s. (The Civilian Conservation Corp also built many of the roads and trails in the Ninemile area.) Continue straight and make a horseshoe right bend. Descend to a trail on the right by a trail sign and bear right. A short distance ahead, make a wide, sweeping left curve and head southwest. Weave down two more wide curves and emerge at the northeast corner of Kreis Pond by Campsite 8. ■

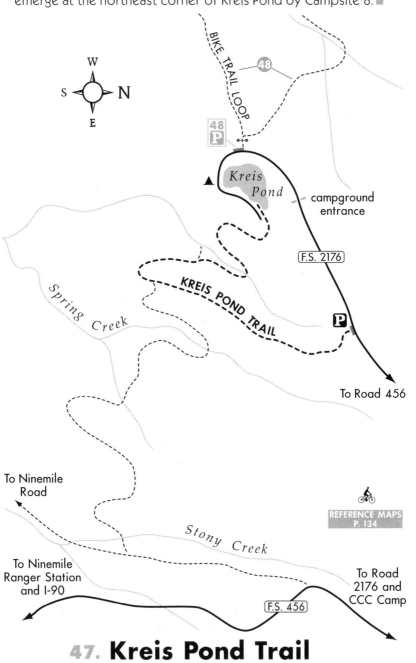

47. **Kreis Pond Trail**

48. Bike Trail Loop at Kreis Pond

Hiking distance: 2.6-mile loop
Hiking time: 1.5 hours
Elevation gain: 250 feet
Maps: U.S.G.S. Alberton
Kreis Pond Mountain Bike Trails map

The Kreis Pond area, two miles north of the historic Ninemile Ranger Station, is a great spot for hiking, mountain biking, horseback riding, fishing, and picnicking. More than 25 miles of multiuse trails in the Lolo National Forest can be accessed near the pond. This uncrowded trail includes views of the surrounding mountains as it loops through flower-filled meadows, an evergreen forest, valley grasslands, and small wetlands.

To the trailhead

From Missoula, drive 21 miles west on I—90 to Ninemile Road/Exit 82. Turn right (north) and go 1.4 miles to Remount Road. Turn right and drive 2.7 miles to the historic Ninemile Ranger Station. Continue 1.5 miles to a Y-fork. Veer left on Forest Service Road 456, and go 2.2 miles to a posted road split. Bear left on F.S. Road 2176. Drive 1.5 miles to the parking area on the right by a restroom and information board. The parking area is a quarter mile from the campground entrance.

The hike

Walk past the restrooms and trail gate, heading west through an open pine and fir forest. Gradually descend 200 yards to a Y-fork. Begin the loop on the right fork, following the trail signs. Descend north into a meadow with vistas of the surrounding mountains. Cross through the meadow and re-enter a forest with Douglas firs, steadily losing elevation. The path levels out and curves left, meandering through the valley bottom grasslands with pockets of trees. Pass a small wetland on the left, and cross a small bridge over a tributary of Ninemile Creek to a Y-fork. Stay to the left, following the trail signs. Steadily gain elevation through the quiet of the forest and complete the loop. Return 200 yards to the right. ■

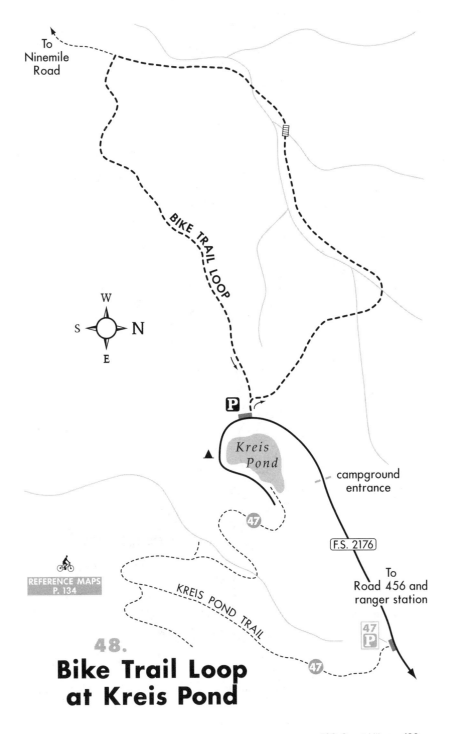

To
Ninemile
Road

BIKE TRAIL LOOP

W
S — N
E

P

Kreis Pond

▲

campground
entrance

47

F.S. 2176

To
Road 456 and
ranger station

47
P

KREIS POND TRAIL

REFERENCE MAPS
P. 134

47

48.
Bike Trail Loop
at Kreis Pond

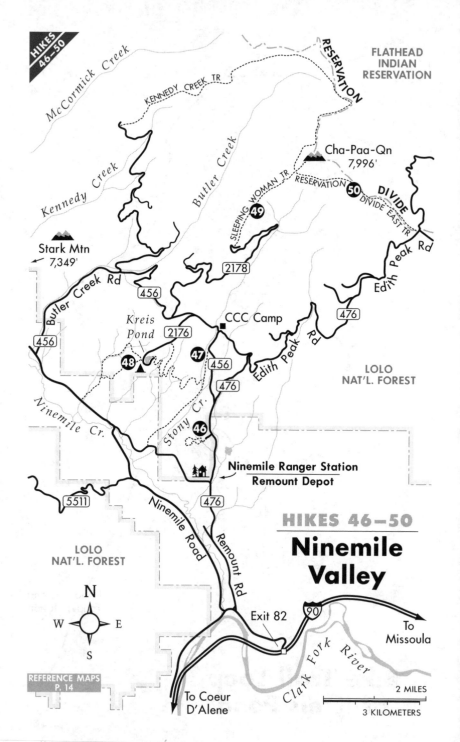

McCormick Creek

FLATHEAD
INDIAN
RESERVATION

RESERVATION

KENNEDY CREEK TR

Butler Creek

Cha-Paa-Qn
7,996'

SLEEPING WOMAN TR

RESERVATION

50

DIVIDE

DIVIDE EAST TR

Kennedy Creek

49

2178

Stark Mtn
7,349'

Butler Creek Rd

456

Edith Peak Rd

Kreis
Pond

2176

CCC Camp

476

456

48

47

456

Edith Peak Rd

476

LOLO
NAT'L. FOREST

Ninemile Cr.

Stony Cr.

46

Ninemile Ranger Station
Remount Depot

5511

Ninemile Road

476

Remount Rd

HIKES 46-50
Ninemile Valley

LOLO
NAT'L. FOREST

N
W E
S

Exit 82

90

To
Missoula

Clark Fork River

REFERENCE MAPS
P. 14

To Coeur
D'Alene

2 MILES

3 KILOMETERS

49. Sleeping Woman Trail to Cha-paa-qn

Hiking distance: 5.6 miles round trip
Hiking time: 3 hours
Elevation gain: 2,200 feet
Maps: U.S.G.S. McCormick Peak and Hewolf Mountain
Missoulian Hike Bike Run guide

map
page 138

Cha-paa-qn is Salish for treeless peak or shining peak. It is the prominent pyramid-shaped mountain on Missoula's western horizon in the Lolo National Forest. Three trails climb to Reservation Divide and ascend the talus rock summit of Cha-paa-qn: the Sleeping Woman Trail, the Reservation Divide East Trail (Hike 50), and the Kennedy Creek Trail. The Sleeping Woman Trail—this trail—is the shortest but steepest route to the 7,996-foot peak. The trail climbs through a pine and fir forest above Stony Creek Canyon to Reservation Divide. The last half mile to the summit is a slow-moving scramble over scree. From the summit above the timberline are far-reaching, 360-degree vistas of the Bitterroot Mountains; the Mission, Swan, Sapphire, Cabinet, and Bison Ranges; and the Rattlesnake and Great Burn Wilderness Areas.

To the trailhead

From Missoula, drive 21 miles west on I—90 to Ninemile Road/ Exit 82. Turn right (north) and go 1.4 miles to Remount Road. Turn right and drive 2.7 miles to the historic Ninemile Ranger Station. Continue 1.5 miles to a Y-fork. Veer left on Forest Service Road 456, and go 2.7 miles to F.S. Road 2178. Turn right and wind 6.4 miles up the narrow mountain road to the trailhead, located at the end of the accessible road on a round, flat area with horse hitching posts.

The hike

Head north up the hillside on the well-defined Sleeping Woman Trail in a forest of whitebark pines and firs. Climb high up the northwest slope of Stony Creek Canyon. Steadily gain elevation while views of the surrounding mountains emerge through the trees. Climb a switchback to the left and slowly curve right, heading toward the summit of Cha-paa-qn.

At 2.2 miles is a posted junction by a three-foot rock cairn. The left fork leads 7 miles to the Kennedy Creek Trailhead. To the right, the Reservation Divide East Trail leads 3.5 miles to the Edith Peak Road trailhead (Hike 50). To ascend the summit of Cha-paa-qn, continue straight ahead. Climb the rock and root-embedded path as the bald, rocky peak comes into view. Ascend the path to the base of the peak by a four-foot rock cairn with 180-degree vistas. Turn around here, or extend the hike up the rock-strewn mountain, scrambling your way to the summit. Return by retracing your route. ■

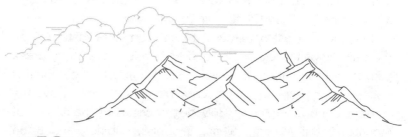

50. Reservation Divide East Trail to Cha-paa-qn

Hiking distance: 8.2 miles round trip
Hiking time: 4 hours
Elevation gain: 1,800 feet
Maps: U.S.G.S. Hewolf Mountain
        Missoulian Hike Bike Run guide

**map
page 139**

The Reservation Divide encompasses 16,000 backcountry acres west of Missoula along the ridge between the Lolo National Forest and the Flathead Indian Reservation. The Reservation Divide East Trail is a primary route to pyramid-shaped Cha-paa-qn. The trail follows the 7,000-foot divide through a quiet forest with small streams and bridges. The final ascent is a slow scramble up talus rock and boulders to the 7,996-foot pinnacle, the highest point in the Ninemile Ranger District. From the peak are panoramic views of the Mission Mountains, the Flathead Indian Reservation, the Missoula and Bitterroot Valleys, and the Rattlesnake Wilderness.

To the trailhead

From Missoula, drive 21 miles west on I—90 to Ninemile Road/ Exit 82. Turn right (north) and go 1.4 miles to Remount Road. Turn right and drive 2.7 miles to the historic Ninemile Ranger Station. Continue 1.5 miles to a Y-fork. Veer right, staying on Edith Peak Road/Forest Service Road 476, and drive 1.3 miles to a T-junction. Go to the right, again staying on Edith Peak Road/F.S. Road 476, and continue 7.1 miles to the posted trail. It is located just before the Flathead Reservation and Edith Peak Road split. Park in the large pullout on the left.

The hike

Take the posted trail northwest into the lush pine and fir forest. Begin a steady but moderate ascent, crossing over the Reservation Divide. Pass through a level, pastoral forest. Begin a steep section of the trail up to a 7,000-foot plateau, gaining 450 feet in 0.4 miles. Cross the flat plateau and Reservation Divide, walking over trickling streams on three small bridges. Slowly curve left to the west side of the divide on the south slope of Cha-paa-qn. Cross two scree fields and traverse the slope across the head of Stony Creek Canyon.

At 3.5 miles is a posted junction by a three-foot rock cairn. To the left, the Sleeping Woman Trail leads 2.2 miles to the trailhead on F.S. 2178 (Hike 49). Straight ahead the trail leads 7 miles to the Kennedy Creek Trailhead. To ascend the summit of Cha-paa-qn, take the right fork. Climb the rock and root-embedded path as the bald, rocky peak comes into view. Ascend the path to the base of the peak by a four-foot rock cairn with 180-degree vistas. Turn around here, or extend the hike up the rock-strewn mountain, scrambling your way to the summit. Return on the same trail. ▪

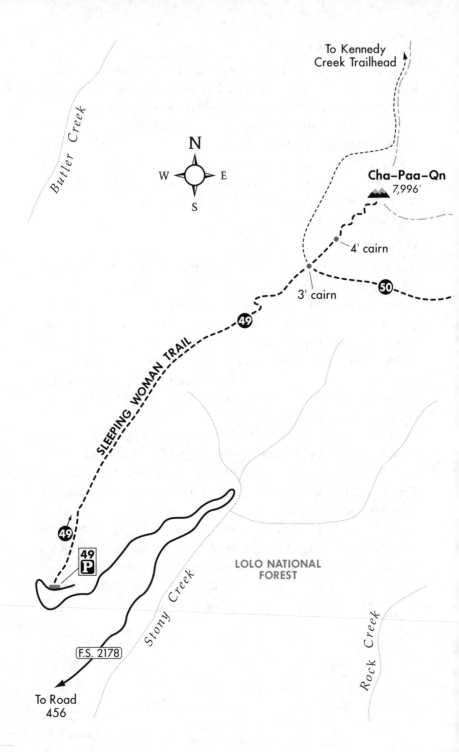

To Kennedy
Creek Trailhead

N
W E
S

Cha-Paa-Qn
7,996'

4' cairn

3' cairn

50

49

Butler Creek

SLEEPING WOMAN TRAIL

49

49
P

Stony Creek

LOLO NATIONAL
FOREST

Rock Creek

F.S. 2178

To Road
456

HIKE 49
Sleeping Woman Trail to Cha-paa-qn

HIKE 50
Reservation Divide East Trail to Cha-paa-qn

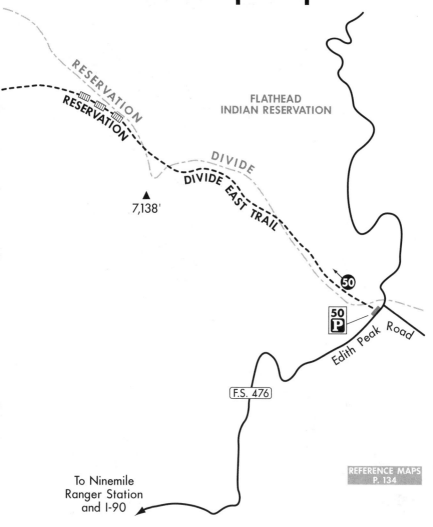

RESERVATION

RESERVATION

FLATHEAD
INDIAN RESERVATION

DIVIDE

DIVIDE EAST TRAIL

▲
7,138'

50

50
P

Edith Peak Road

F.S. 476

To Ninemile
Ranger Station
and I-90

REFERENCE MAPS
P. 134

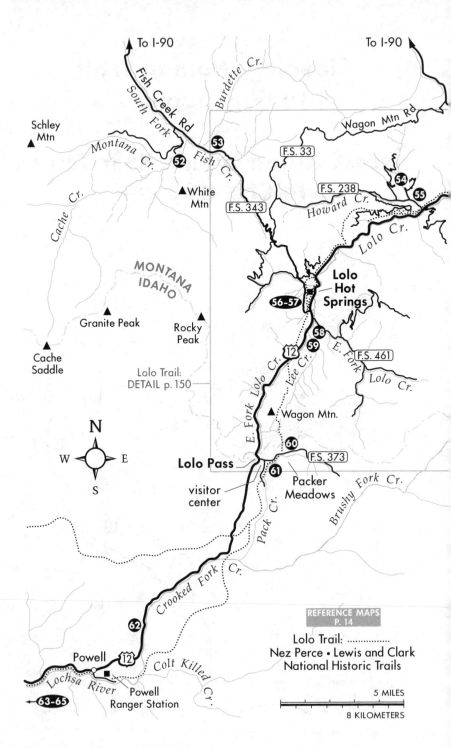

To I-90

To I-90

Burdette Cr.

Wagon Mtn Rd

Fish Creek Rd

South Fork

Schley Mtn

Montana Cr.

Cache Cr.

Fish Cr.

53

52

White Mtn

F.S. 343

F.S. 33

F.S. 238

54

55

Howard Cr.

Lolo Cr.

MONTANA
IDAHO

Granite Peak

Rocky Peak

Cache Saddle

Lolo Trail:
DETAIL p. 150

Lolo Hot Springs

56-57

58

59

12

Lee Cr.

E. Fork

F.S. 461

E. Fork Lolo Cr.

Lolo Cr.

E. Fork Lolo Cr.

Wagon Mtn.

N

W E

S

Lolo Pass

60

F.S. 373

61

Packer Meadows

visitor center

Brushy Fork Cr.

Pack Cr.

Crooked Fork Cr.

REFERENCE MAPS
P. 14

62

Lolo Trail: ....
Nez Perce • Lewis and Clark
National Historic Trails

Powell

12

Colt Killed Cr.

Lochsa River

Powell Ranger Station

63-65

5 MILES

8 KILOMETERS

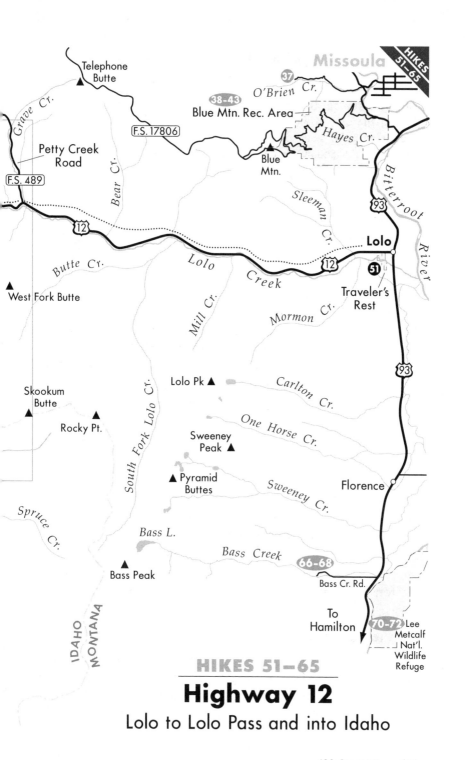

Telephone Butte

Grave Cr.

Missoula

O'Brien Cr. 37

38-43
Blue Mtn. Rec. Area

Hayes Cr.

F.S. 17806

Petty Creek Road

Bear Cr.

Blue Mtn.

Sleeman Cr.

Bitterroot River

F.S. 489

93

12

Lolo

Butte Cr.

Lolo Creek

12

West Fork Butte

Mill Cr.

Mormon Cr.

51

Traveler's Rest

93

Skookum Butte

South Fork Lolo Cr.

Lolo Pk ▲

Carlton Cr.

Rocky Pt.

One Horse Cr.

Sweeney Peak ▲

▲ Pyramid Buttes

Sweeney Cr.

Florence

Spruce Cr.

Bass L.

Bass Creek

Bass Peak

66-68

Bass Cr. Rd.

To Hamilton

70-72 Lee Metcalf Nat'l. Wildlife Refuge

IDAHO
MONTANA

HIKES 51-65

Highway 12
Lolo to Lolo Pass and into Idaho

51. Travelers' Rest Interpretive Trail
TRAVELER'S REST STATE PARK

Hiking distance: 0.6-mile loop
Hiking time: 30 minutes
Elevation gain: level
Maps: U.S.G.S. Southwest Missoula and Florence

Travelers' Rest State Park is located on the banks of Lolo Creek near its confluence with the Bitterroot River just west of the town of Lolo. The 41-acre site marks the location of a centuries-old trading and camp site for Native Americans, including the Salish, Kootenai, Nez Perce, Pend d'Oreilles, and Lemhi-Shoshone tribes. For thousands of years, the timeworn site was the hub of four trading routes—European goods came from the north, horses from the south, buffalo from the east, and salmon from the west. The crossroad was also located along the ancient route from the northern Rocky Mountains to the eastern buffalo country.

Travelers' Rest is primarily known for the Lewis and Clark Expedition, who set up camp at this site September, 1805, before their difficult journey over the Rockies. They stayed here again in June, 1806, on the return of their epic 28-month journey. The location is among the few sites containing physical proof of their visit. Excavations have led to the discovery of their central cook fire with fire-cracked rock, charcoal, and puddles of lead used for ammo, which were carbon dated to their era. The latrine was found with traces of mercury, residue from medicine that was used to purge contaminants from the body.

A self-guided interpretive trail explores this age-old camp, looping through the open meadows lined with towering black cottonwoods along Lolo Creek. A bookshop and visitor center is on site.

To the trailhead

From Missoula, drive 8 miles south on Highway 93 to Lolo. Turn right on Highway 12, and head 0.35 miles west to the posted state park entrance. Turn left and continue 0.3 miles to the parking lot.

The hike

Walk past the bookstore and visitor center on the interpretive trail. Cross over a stream to the large metal bridge spanning Lolo Creek. Cross the bridge to the open meadow. Bear right and begin the loop through the meadow. Views of the Bitterroot Mountains and Lolo Peak stretch to the southwest. At the south end of the loop is a fork. The right branch climbs a short distance to an overlook. Return to the junction and continue circling the historic camping area, returning to Lolo Creek. Follow the creek upstream to complete the loop. ∎

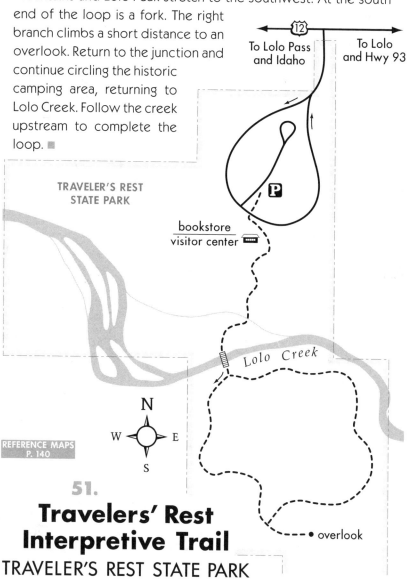

51.
Travelers' Rest
Interpretive Trail
TRAVELER'S REST STATE PARK

52. Cache Creek Trail
FISH CREEK DRAINAGE

Hiking distance: 6–10 miles round trip
Hiking time: 3–6 hours
Elevation gain: 200–800 feet through the creek drainage
3,400 feet to Cache Saddle
Maps: U.S.G.S. White Mountain, Schley Mountain, Rhodes Peak

**map
page 146**

Cache Creek is a tributary of the South Fork of Fish Creek, located in the Fish Creek drainage in Lolo National Forest. The Cache Creek Trail parallels Cache Creek through a portion of the famous 1910 Great Burn. The wildfire spread from Washington to

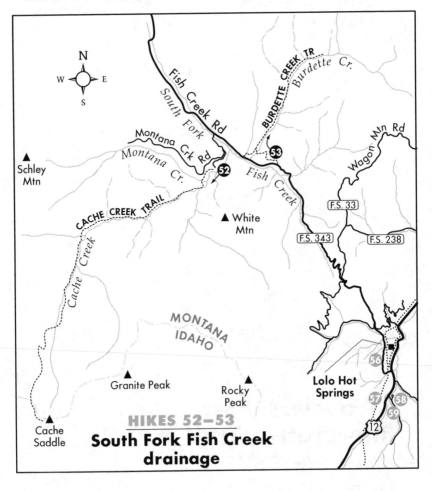

HIKES 52–53
South Fork Fish Creek drainage

Montana. Evidence of the burn is still apparent. The area is a winter range for wildlife and a fall hunting ground. This trail skirts the northwest base of White Mountain along remote Cache Creek, gently gaining elevation through the drainage. The trail continues along the creek for nine miles before ascending another mile and an additional 2,000 feet to Cache Saddle, sitting at 7,200 feet on the Montana—Idaho border.

To the trailhead

From Missoula, drive 8 miles south on Highway 93 to Lolo. Take Highway 12 west for 25.8 miles to Fish Creek Road on the right. The turnoff is located a half mile past Lolo Hot Springs, just past mile marker 7. Turn right on Fish Creek Road, and drive 11.2 miles to Montana Creek Road. (Stay on Road 343, the middle road, at a 3-way junction.) Turn left and continue 0.6 miles to a road fork, crossing the South Fork of Fish Creek. Take the left fork 0.7 miles to the trailhead parking at road's end.

From I-90, drive 38 miles west of Missoula to the Fish Creek exit. Drive 20 miles south to Montana Creek Road on the right. Turn right and continue 0.6 miles to a road fork, crossing the South Fork of Fish Creek. Take the left fork 0.7 miles to the trailhead parking at road's end.

The hike

From the parking area, head west past the Forest Service information board. The trail begins high above Cache Creek. The wide drainage offers frequent views of White Mountain. At 0.3 miles is a shallow but wide crossing of Montana Creek. To keep dry, there is a log crossing 20 yards downstream. (A narrow path leads to the crossing.) After crossing, take the main trail towards the left. The trail approaches the bank of Cache Creek, then meanders along the hillside to a second stream crossing at 1.2 miles. The trail continues 9 miles into the canyon before reaching the strenuous climb to Cache Saddle. Choose your own turn-around spot. ■

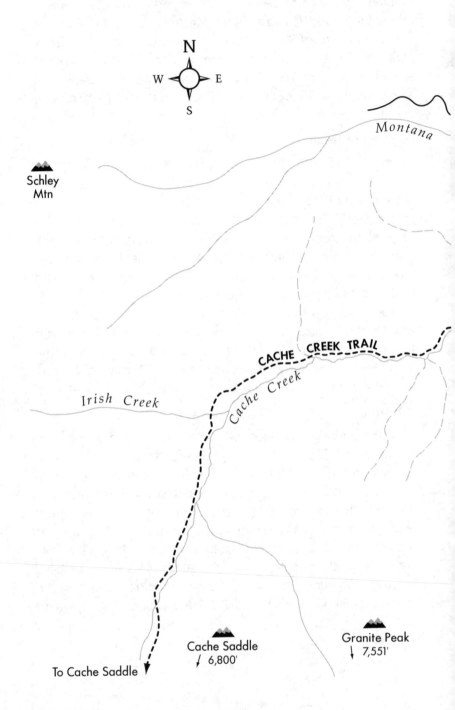

N
W   E
S

Montana

Schley
Mtn

CACHE CREEK TRAIL

Irish Creek

Cache Creek

To Cache Saddle

Cache Saddle
↓ 6,800'

Granite Peak
↓ 7,551'

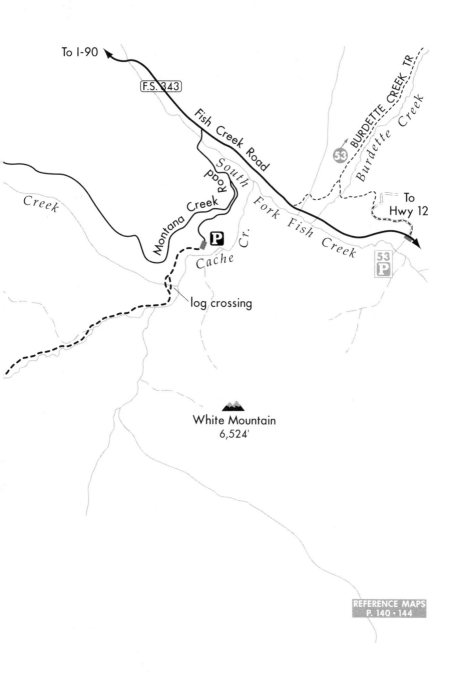

To I-90

F.S. 343

Fish Creek Road

South Fork Road

Montana Creek

Creek

South Fork Fish Creek

Cache Cr.

BURDETTE CREEK TR

Burdette Creek

53

To Hwy 12

53 P

P

Cache

log crossing

White Mountain
6,524'

REFERENCE MAPS
P. 140 • 144

52.
Cache Creek Trail

53. Burdette Creek Trail
FISH CREEK DRAINAGE

Hiking distance: 6—9 miles round trip
Hiking time: 3—5 hours
Elevation gain: 300—400 feet
Maps: U.S.G.S. Lupine Creek

Burdette Creek is a tributary of the South Fork of Fish Creek, located in the Fish Creek drainage in Lolo National Forest. The Burdette Creek Trail provides access into the remote stream-fed drainage, following the creek through an old-growth ponderosa pine forest. The gentle trail gains only 400 feet as it leads to a campsite at 4.5 miles, lying below the Petty Creek–Fish Creek divide. The route passes beaver ponds and crosses the creek three times. Known as an excellent wildlife winter range, the drainage is primarily used in the fall during hunting season.

To the trailhead

From Missoula, drive 8 miles south on Highway 93 to Lolo. Take Highway 12 west for 25.8 miles to Fish Creek Road on the right. The turnoff is located a half mile past Lolo Hot Springs, just past mile marker 7. Turn right on Fish Creek Road, and drive 9 miles to the Burdette Creek trailhead on the right. (Stay on Road 343, the middle road, at a 3-way junction.) Parking pullouts are on the left.

From I-90, drive 38 miles west of Missoula to the Fish Creek exit. Drive 22 miles south to the Burdette Creek trailhead on the left.

The hike

The trail begins one mile southeast of Burdette Creek. Hike up the forested draw and over the ridge on an old road heading north. At the top of the hill, the road fades. Watch for the footpath veering off to the left. Take this footpath and descend 300 feet towards the Burdette Creek valley. As the trail descends, there are great views of the drainage and creek below. At one mile, cross Burdette Creek, then head northeast up the wide drainage. At 2.5 miles, as the canyon narrows, is a second creek crossing.

At 3 miles, the trail crosses back again to the west side of the creek. For a 6-mile hike, this is a good turn-around spot. For a 10-mile hike, continue as the canyon narrows and curves east. The trail crosses talus fields and passes beaver ponds to the trail's end. Return along the same path. ■

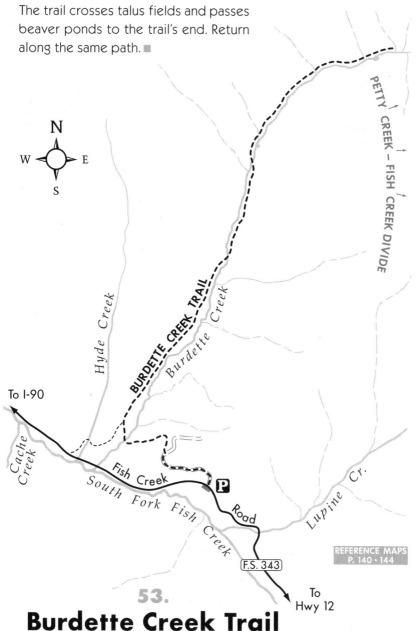

53.
Burdette Creek Trail

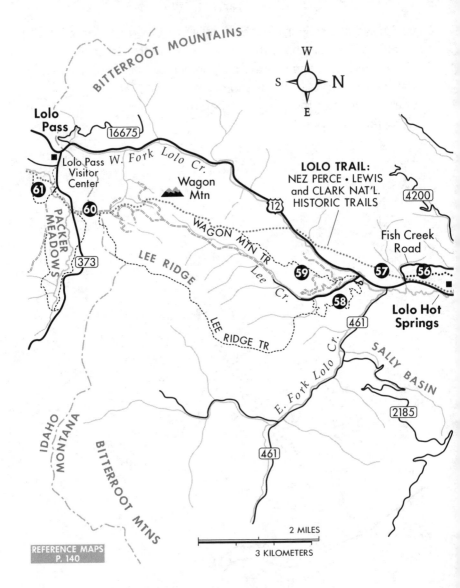

HIKES 54–61
Lolo Trail
and connecting hikes

NEZ PERCE • LEWIS and CLARK
NATIONAL HISTORIC TRAILS

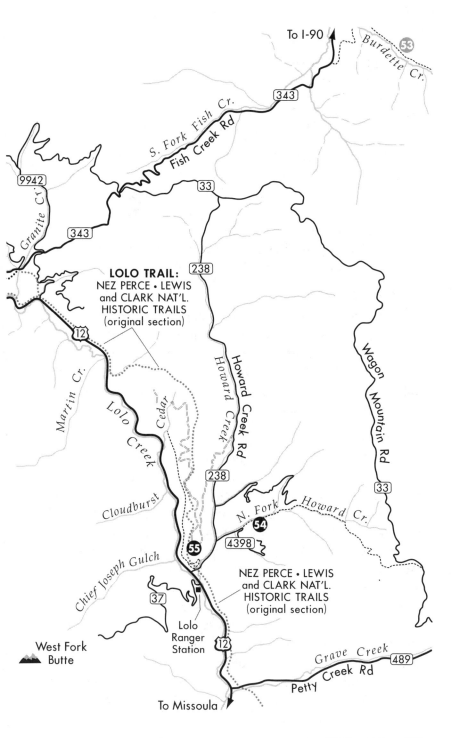

To I-90

Burdette Cr.

53

343

S. Fork Fish Cr.

Fish Creek Rd

9942

33

Granite Cr.

343

238

LOLO TRAIL:
NEZ PERCE • LEWIS
and CLARK NAT'L.
HISTORIC TRAILS
(original section)

12

Martin Cr.

Lolo Creek

Cedar

Howard Creek

Howard Creek Rd

Wagon Mountain Rd

33

238

Cloudburst

N. Fork *Howard Cr.*

54

4398

55

NEZ PERCE • LEWIS
and CLARK NAT'L.
HISTORIC TRAILS
(original section)

Chief Joseph Gulch

37

Lolo
Ranger
Station

12

**West Fork
Butte**

Grave Creek

489

Petty Creek Rd

To Missoula

54. North Fork Howard Creek

Hiking distance: 4 miles round trip
Hiking time: 2 hours
Elevation gain: 400 feet
Maps: U.S.G.S. Garden Point · U.S.F.S. Lolo National Forest
       Beartooth Publishing: Missoula, Hamilton, Lost Trail Pass

The North Fork of Howard Creek drains through a narrow, forested canyon and merges with Howard Creek shortly before its confluence with Lolo Creek. The headwaters of the remote creek begin just south of Wagon Mountain Road at 5,100 feet. This hike heads north up the canyon, following the course of the creek through a lush riparian habitat. The trail is infrequently used, offering quiet solitude in a beautiful canyon.

To the trailhead

From Missoula, drive 8 miles south on Highway 93 to Lolo. Turn right on Highway 12 and head 18.5 miles west to the signed Howard Creek turnoff on the right at mile marker 14. Turn right and go 0.7 miles to Road 4398 on the right. Turn right and drive 0.5 miles to the posted trailhead on the left on a horseshoe left bend in the road. Park on the left shoulder.

The hike

Walk up the old dirt road on the east side of the North Fork of Howard Creek. The creek can be heard, but the lush forest hides the creek from view. Follow the east wall of the canyon for a half mile to the end of the road. Continue straight on the footpath, and descend through dense riparian vegetation. Stroll through the narrow canyon as the trail traverses over small dips and rises. At 0.7 miles, cross a bridge over the North Fork. Continue up canyon on the west side of the creek. Pass through an old burned area rich with wildflowers, where canyon views emerge. Near the head of the main drainage, the canyon divides. Wade across the creek and climb the hillside, leaving the creek behind. This is a good turn-around spot. Return by retracing your steps.

To hike farther, the trail continues another 1.5 miles and an additional 500 feet in elevation to Wagon Mountain Road. ■

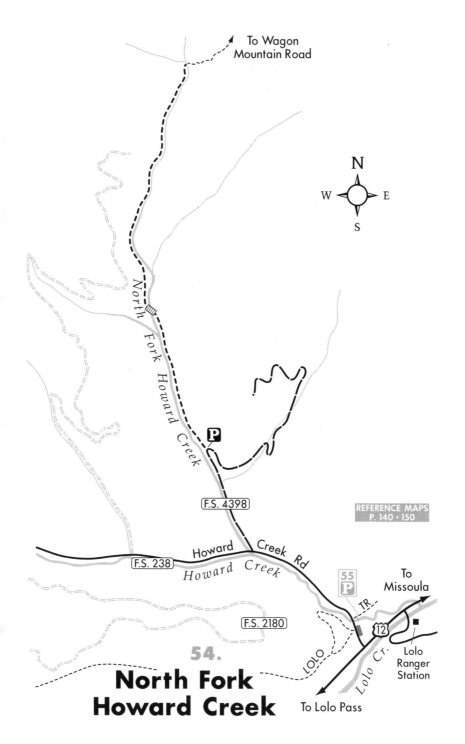

To Wagon
Mountain Road

N
W   E
S

North Fork Howard Creek

P

F.S. 4398

REFERENCE MAPS
P. 140 · 150

Howard Creek Rd
F.S. 238
Howard Creek

55 P

To
Missoula

F.S. 2180

TR

LOLO

12

Lolo Cr.

Lolo
Ranger
Station

54.
North Fork
Howard Creek

To Lolo Pass

55. Lolo Trail from Howard Creek

LEWIS AND CLARK NATIONAL HISTORIC TRAIL
NEZ PERCE (NEE-ME-POO) NATIONAL HISTORIC TRAIL

Hiking distance: 2—14 miles or more round trip
Hiking time: 1—7 hours
Elevation gain: 600 feet
Maps: U.S.G.S. Garden Point
U.S.F.S. Lolo National Forest
Beartooth Publishing: Missoula, Hamilton, Lost Trail Pass

Lawrence "Lolo" Rence was an early 19th century fur trapper who lived in a cabin on Grave Creek, a tributary of Lolo Creek. Lolo shot and wounded a grizzly bear, who charged and mauled him. Lolo died a short time later in his cabin and was buried on a grassy bench above Grave Creek. His grave was recently re-discovered and a large white cross marks the location. Since his death, a Montana town, a historic trail, a hot springs, a 5,235-foot pass, and a national forest have all been named after him.

The Lolo Trail is a portion of the Nez Perce and Lewis and Clark National Historic Trails. A 14-mile section of trail along Lolo Creek between Grave Creek and Lolo Pass is the most primitive and least altered sections of the entire 4,000-mile Lewis and Clark Trail. The trail was not built; it was created by centuries of foot travel. This hike follows an original section of the Lolo Trail beginning at Howard Creek, two miles west of Grave Creek. This trail traverses the south-facing slopes above Lolo Creek.

To the trailhead

From Missoula, drive 8 miles south on Highway 93 to Lolo. Turn right on Highway 12, and head 18.5 miles west to the signed Howard Creek turnoff on the right by mile marker 14. Turn right and park 0.1 mile ahead at the trailhead and picnic parking area on the right.

The hike

Cross Howard Creek Road to the signed trailhead. Head northwest up the hillside into a dense lodgepole forest, parallel to Howard Creek. A short distance ahead, a switchback leads southeast,

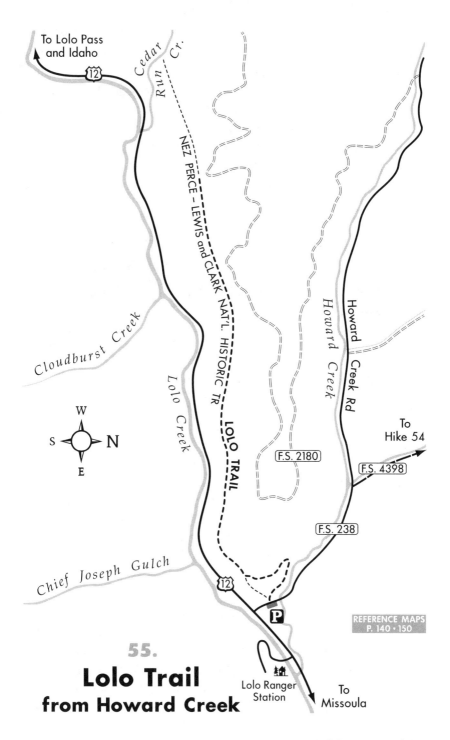

To Lolo Pass
and Idaho

12

Cedar Run Cr.

NEZ PERCE - LEWIS and CLARK NAT'L. HISTORIC TR

LOLO TRAIL

Cloudburst Creek

Lolo Creek

Howard Creek

Howard Creek Rd

F.S. 2180

To
Hike 54

F.S. 4398

F.S. 238

Chief Joseph Gulch

12

P

REFERENCE MAPS
P. 140 • 150

Lolo Ranger
Station

To
Missoula

W
N
S
E

55.
Lolo Trail
from Howard Creek

gaining more elevation to a signed junction at 0.3 miles. The left fork descends steeply, returning to the picnic and parking area. Take the right fork on the original Lolo Trail. Traverse the hillside on the narrow, rocky trail high above Lolo Creek and Highway 12. There are frequent dips and rises with a few short steep sections. Cross a logged, sloping meadow through a burned area. At one mile are beautiful rock outcroppings. The trail continues another six miles to Lolo Hot Springs (Hike 56). Choose your own turn-around spot, returning on the same path. ■

56. Lolo Trail: Fish Creek Road to Granite Creek

LEWIS AND CLARK NATIONAL HISTORIC TRAIL
NEZ PERCE (NEE-ME-POO) NATIONAL HISTORIC TRAIL

Hiking distance: 3 miles round trip
Hiking time: 1.5 hours
Elevation gain: 350 feet
Maps: U.S.G.S. Lolo Hot Springs
       Beartooth Publishing: Missoula, Hamilton, Lost Trail Pass

**map
page 158**

The Lolo Trail includes a small but perilous section of the historic Lewis and Clark Trail along Lolo Creek. For thousands of years, the Nez Perce (the Nee-Me-Poo) used the Lolo Trail to cross the Continental Divide into the Bitterroot Valley to hunt buffalo with the Salish people. Conversely, the Salish, living east of the Bitterroots, used this route to reach the salmon-rich Lochsa and Clearwater Rivers in Idaho and trade with the Nez Perce. Lewis and Clark also used this historic route during 1805 and 1806. (The Lewis and Clark Trail stretches 4,000 miles, from the Mississippi River above Saint Louis to the Pacific Ocean near Astoria, Washington.)

This portion of the trail passes Lolo Hot Springs a few miles east of Lolo Pass. It was here that the Lewis and Clark party headed west up the Lolo Creek drainage, passing through Lolo Hot Springs. They returned nine months later on June 29, 1806, where they camped, rested, and soaked in the hot mineralized spring water. This hike follows a 1.5-mile length of the trail, traversing the hills above Lolo Hot Springs to Granite Creek. The trail continues north to Howard Creek (Hike 55) and south to the canyon overlook (Hike 57).

To the trailhead

From Missoula, drive 8 miles south on Highway 93 to Lolo. Turn right on Highway 12, and head 25.7 miles west to posted Fish Creek Road on the right. The turnoff is located a half mile past Lolo Hot Springs, just past mile marker 7. Turn right on Fish Creek Road, and go 0.1 mile to the signed trailhead parking areas on both sides of the road.

The hike

From the north side of Fish Creek Road, head north past the trailhead gate. Traverse the forested hillside on a gentle, rolling grade, above and parallel to Highway 12. Cross a gravel road, and continue straight to a T-junction with a dirt road. The left fork climbs to an overlook of the Granite Creek drainage and drops down to Fish Creek Road. Bear right and climb to another overlook of the surrounding area, then weave through a pine forest to a Y-fork. Veer left and descend on the footpath to Fish Creek Road, the gravel road 50 yards west (left) of Granite Creek and 30 yards east (right) of Forest Service Road 4200. To the east of Granite Creek is a large meadow, the turn-around spot. ∎

57. Lolo Trail:
Fish Creek Road to Canyon Overlook
LEWIS AND CLARK NATIONAL HISTORIC TRAIL
NEZ PERCE (NEE-ME-POO) NATIONAL HISTORIC TRAIL

Hiking distance: 3 miles round trip
Hiking time: 1.5 hours
Elevation gain: 300 feet
Maps: U.S.G.S. Lolo Hot Springs
        Beartooth Publishing: Missoula, Hamilton, Lost Trail Pass

map
page 158

The Lolo Trail is an ancient travel corridor once used by Native Americans for 6,000—8,000 years. The trail is comprised of a network of ancient routes that formed a travel corridor across

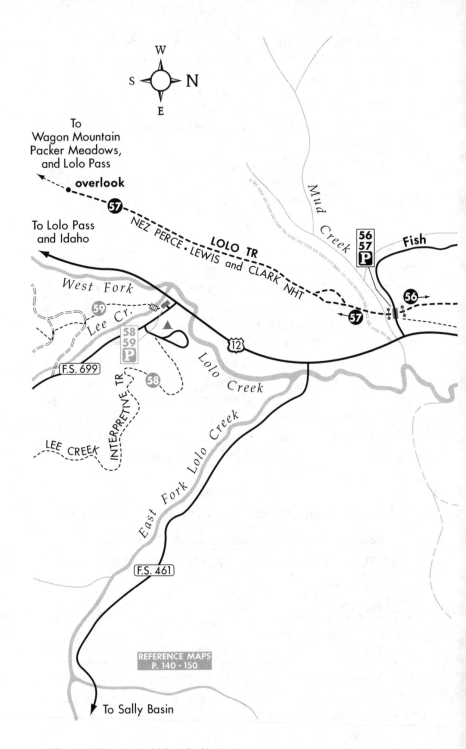

W · N · E · S

To
Wagon Mountain
Packer Meadows,
and Lolo Pass

overlook

57

NEZ PERCE · LEWIS and CLARK NHT

LOLO TR

To Lolo Pass
and Idaho

Mud Creek

Fish

56
57
P

56

57

West Fork

Lee Cr.

59

58
59
P

F.S. 699

58

INTERPRETIVE TR

LEE CREEK

Lolo Creek

12

East Fork Lolo Creek

F.S. 461

REFERENCE MAPS
P. 140 · 150

To Sally Basin

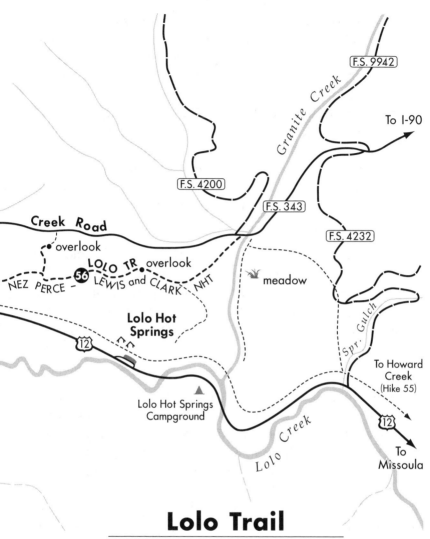

Lolo Trail

NEZ PERCE • LEWIS and CLARK
NATIONAL HISTORIC TRAILS

HIKE 56

Fish Creek Road to Granite Creek

HIKE 57

Fish Creek Road to Canyon Overlook

the northern Rocky Mountains from present day Lolo, Montana, to Weippe, Idaho, west of Lolo Pass. The trail along Highway 12, once a Native American trading and hunting route, closely follows the highway across the Bitterroot Mountains to the Clearwater River. It was the westbound route of the Lewis and Clark expedition in search of the Northwest Passage and the eastbound route of the Nez Perce traveling to hunt buffalo on the eastern plains. Lewis and Clark National Historic Trail markers face westbound hikers; Nez Perce National Historic Trail markers face eastbound hikers. This hike follows a 1.5-mile segment of the ancient trail to an overlook of the upper Lolo Creek drainage.

To the trailhead

From Missoula, drive 8 miles south on Highway 93 to Lolo. Turn right on Highway 12, and head 25.7 miles west to posted Fish Creek Road on the right. The turnoff is located a half mile past Lolo Hot Springs, just past mile marker 7. Turn right on Fish Creek Road, and go 0.1 mile to the signed trailhead parking areas on both sides of the road.

The hike

From the south side of Fish Creek Road, pass the signed trailhead and gate. Enter a grassy pine forest, crossing Mud Creek and an old dirt road. Head uphill to a fork with a trail sign on a tree. Both forks rejoin a short distance ahead, with the right fork being an easier climb. Climb to the low ridge, and stroll through the quiet forest across the long and narrow plateau. At 1.5 miles, the path reaches a partial clearing with views of Wagon Mountain. Watch for trail markers on the trees as the path fades in and out. Gradually descend to the south end of the ridge and a view of upper Lolo Creek Canyon, the turn-around point for this hike.

To extend the hike, the trail descends to Highway 12 and continues to Wagon Mountain, Packer Meadow, and Lolo Pass by the visitor center. (See Hikes 59 and 60.) ■

58. Lee Creek Interpretive Trail

Hiking distance: 2.5-mile loop
Hiking time: 1.5 hours
Elevation gain: 200 feet
Maps: U.S.G.S. Lolo Hot Springs
U.S.F.S. Lolo National Forest
Lee Creek Interpretive Trail map
Beartooth Publishing: Missoula, Hamilton, Lost Trail Pass

**map
page 162**

The Lee Creek Interpretive Trail begins from the Lee Creek Campground and loops through the forested hillside above Lee Creek. Don't let the words "interpretive trail" deter you from this hike. It is a fascinating and informative trail. Twenty descriptive panels identify ponderosa pine, lodgepole pine, and Douglas fir trees. The panels explain, with examples, the effects of logging, lightening, fire, birds, decay, and deterioration upon the trees. An interpretive brochure is available at the trailhead and at the Forest Service visitor centers.

To the trailhead

From Missoula, drive 8 miles south on Highway 93 to Lolo. Turn right on Highway 12, and head 26.5 miles west to the Lee Creek Campground on the left. The campground is located 1.3 miles west of Lolo Hot Springs and west of mile marker 6. Turn left, then take a quick right into the parking lot.

The hike

From the parking lot, walk up the main road 0.1 mile to the road fork veering left into the campground. Go left on the signed footpath along the hillside into a lodgepole pine forest. Continue uphill through the forest, passing 20 information sites. At 1.3 miles, after signpost 16, the trail levels out to a posted junction. The Lee Ridge Trail heads left and leads 8 miles to Lolo Pass. Stay to the right on the interpretive trail, and meander through the quiet forest. At signpost 17, begin a descent. Wind 0.3 miles downhill, crossing a bridge over a stream to the gravel road. Bear right and walk 0.9 miles down the forested road, completing the loop and returning to the parking lot. ■

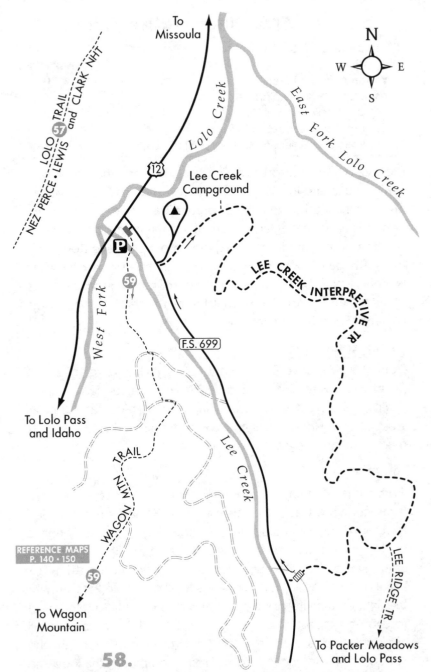

To Missoula

Lolo Creek

East Fork Lolo Creek

N
W · E
S

LOLO TRAIL
NEZ PERCE · LEWIS and CLARK NHT
57

12

Lee Creek Campground

LEE CREEK INTERPRETIVE TR

59

F.S. 699

West Fork

To Lolo Pass and Idaho

Lee Creek

WAGON MTN TRAIL

REFERENCE MAPS
P. 140 · 150

59

To Wagon Mountain

LEE RIDGE TR

To Packer Meadows and Lolo Pass

58.
Lee Creek Interpretive Trail

59. Wagon Mountain Trail from Lee Creek

LEWIS AND CLARK NATIONAL HISTORIC TRAIL
NEZ PERCE (NEE-ME-POO) NATIONAL HISTORIC TRAIL

Hiking distance: 6 miles round trip
Hiking time: 3 hours
Elevation gain: 1,200 feet
Maps: U.S.G.S. Lolo Hot Springs
U.S.F.S. Selway Bitterroot Wilderness
Beartooth Publishing: Missoula, Hamilton, Lost Trail Pass

**map
page 166**

The Nez Perce (Nee-Me-Poo) Trail extends 1,170 miles, from Wallowa Lake, Oregon, to Bear Paw Battlefield near Chinook, Montana, just shy of the Canadian border. The long, circuitous route was used only once by the Nez Perce. They reluctantly left their homeland in order to seek refuge from hostilities, conflicts, and mistreatment. Their tragic flight from the U.S. Army in 1877 led through four states. This route is now the designated Nez Perce National Historic Trail. Sections of the trail, however, were used for thousands of years prior to 1877. Many of these abandoned segments, originally formed from repeated use, have become impassable due to overgrown vegetation; downfall; and altera-tion by floods, powerlines, and manmade structures. The Wagon Mountain Trail follows a portion of the Nez Perce Trail that has been restored and maintained. It connects Lee Creek to Packer Meadows at Lolo Pass. The hike can be combined with Hike 60 for a one-way, five-mile shuttle hike.

To the trailhead

From Missoula, drive 8 miles south on Highway 93 to Lolo. Turn right on Highway 12, and head 26.5 miles west to the Lee Creek Campground on the left. The campground is located 1.3 miles west of Lolo Hot Springs and west of mile marker 6. Turn left, then a quick right into the parking lot.

The hike

Walk down and rock hop over Lee Creek. Head sharply up the hill-side on the well-defined path. At the ridge, bear left on the log-ging road for 20 yards and bear right on the unsigned footpath. Follow the ridge to another logging road. Bear left on the road for 100 yards, and again take the footpath to the right. Continue uphill through the forest to an old jeep road. The left fork leads into the Lee Creek drainage. Take the old road to the right, fol-lowing the ridge separating Lee Creek Canyon from Lolo Canyon. The trail levels out on a saddle, then enters the forest. Begin the gentle ascent of Wagon Mountain. The trail levels out again a half mile north of the Wagon Mountain summit—the destination for this hike and the next hike. The hikes can be combined for a one-way, five-mile shuttle hike. ■

60. Wagon Mountain Trail from Packer Meadows

LEWIS AND CLARK NATIONAL HISTORIC TRAIL

NEZ PERCE (NEE-ME-POO) NATIONAL HISTORIC TRAIL

Hiking distance: 4 miles round trip
Hiking time: 2 hours
Elevation gain: 400 feet
Maps: U.S.G.S. Lolo Hot Springs
      U.S.F.S. Selway Bitterroot Wilderness
      Beartooth Publishing: Missoula, Hamilton, Lost Trail Pass

**map
page 166**

For thousands of years, before the Europeans arrived, the Nez Perce crossed the rugged Bitterroot Mountains from their Idaho homeland to hunt buffalo on the eastern plains of Montana. They called the trail *K'Useyneisskt,* meaning "Trail to the Buffalo Country." This route was also used when the Nez Perce were fleeing General Howard's army in the Nez Perce War of 1877. To the Nez Perce, these trails are part of their sacred land and were once sustained through continual use. The Wagon Mountain Trail connects Lee Creek to Packer Meadows, following a segment of the Nez Perce and Lewis and Clark National Historic Trails. This hike begins in Packer Meadows, located one mile east of the Lolo Pass Visitor Center near the Montana–Idaho border. The high-elevation meadow was a Nez Perce gathering site for camas root, a prime food staple.

This hike can be combined with Hike 59 for a one-way, five-mile shuttle hike.

To the trailhead

From Missoula, drive 8 miles south on Highway 93 to Lolo. Turn right on Highway 12, and head 32.4 miles west to the Lolo Pass Visitor Center on the left at the Montana–Idaho border. Turn left on Forest Service Road 373 alongside the visitor center, and continue 1.1 mile to signed F.S. Road 5950 on the left, across the road from Packer Meadows. Park in the pullouts on the right.

The hike

Follow the forested dirt road north. At a half mile, cross into Montana to a signed junction with the Lee Ridge Trail on the right. Stay to the left, crossing an unpaved logging road. Follow the blue diamond ski trail markers up the knoll. At one mile, leave the road, bearing left at a trail sign. Descend on the footpath into the deep forest. Cross a stream and head up the hillside to a logging road. Follow the road 100 yards to the right, and pick up the trail again on the left. Follow the winding path up Wagon Mountain. Near the summit, cross another logging road and skirt the eastern edge of the ridge. At two miles the trail begins the descent towards Lee Creek Campground. Turn around here, or continue with Hike 59 for the one-way shuttle hike. ▪

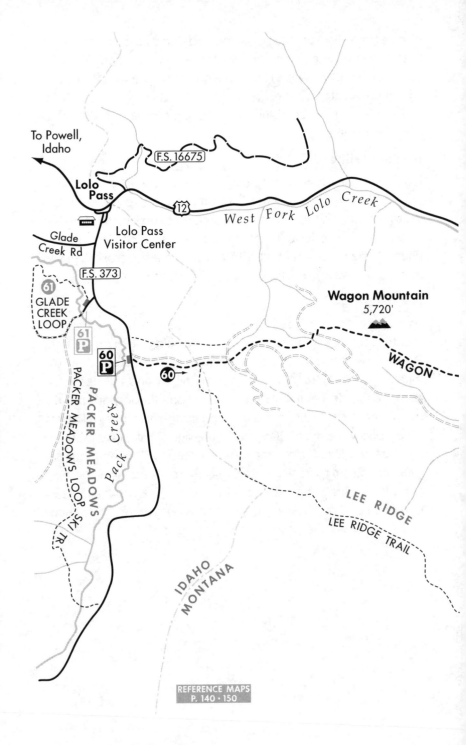

To Powell,
Idaho

F.S. 16675

Lolo
Pass

12

West Fork Lolo Creek

Glade
Creek Rd

Lolo Pass
Visitor Center

F.S. 373

Wagon Mountain
5,720'

61
GLADE
CREEK
LOOP

61
P

60
P

60

WAGON

PACKER MEADOWS LOOP SKI TR.

PACKER MEADOWS

Pack Creek

LEE RIDGE

LEE RIDGE TRAIL

IDAHO
MONTANA

REFERENCE MAPS
P. 140 · 150

166 - Day Hikes Around Missoula, Montana

Wagon Mountain Trail

NEZ PERCE • LEWIS and CLARK NATIONAL HISTORIC TRAILS

HIKE 59
Lee Creek to Wagon Mountain
HIKE 60
Packer Meadows to Wagon Mountain

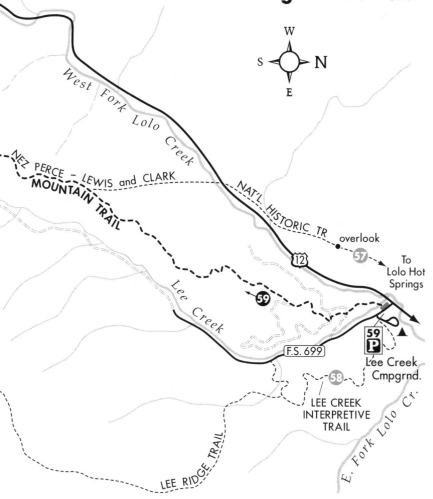

61. Glade Creek Loop

Hiking distance: 1.5-mile loop
Hiking time: 1 hour
Elevation gain: 50 feet
Maps: U.S.G.S. Lolo Hot Springs
U.S.F.S. Selway Bitterroot Wilderness

The Bitterroot Mountains form a jagged ridge along the Montana-Idaho border. Lolo Pass straddles the ridge along the state line at 5,235 feet. The pass was an ancient Native American travel corridor with intersecting east, west, north, and south routes. Packer Meadows is a pristine meadow rimmed with Engelmann spruce and sub-alpine fir that sits atop the pass. Glade (Pack) Creek meanders through the lush meadow. Thirty-five members of the Lewis and Clark expedition camped here in September, 1805. On their return journey in June, 1806, they passed through the meadow again en route to Lolo Hot Springs. The meadow has remained virtually unaltered over the last 200 years. This hike forms a loop through the lower west end of the meadow. The historic area is also a popular winter recreation site for nordic skiers, snowshoers, and snowmobilers.

Lewis and Clark named Glade Creek in their journal. The U.S.F.S. renamed it Pack Creek. It is currently referred to as Pack Creek in the spring/summer and Glade Creek during the winter.

To the trailhead

From Missoula, drive 8 miles south on Highway 93 to Lolo. Turn right on Highway 12, and head 32.4 miles west to the Lolo Pass Visitor Center on the left at the Montana-Idaho border. Turn left on Forest Service Road 373 alongside the visitor center, and continue 0.65 miles to F.S. Road 373A. Turn right and go 0.1 mile to the trailhead gate. Park on the side of the road.

The hike

Walk over Pack Creek, and pass the trailhead gate at the end of the access road. Slowly gain elevation through the forest to a Y-fork at 300 yards. The left fork follows the southern slope above Packer Meadows. Take the Glade Creek Trail to the right on

Road 5955. Climb through the tree-covered meadows marbled with streams. Curve right and head west, traversing the lower slope above Glade Creek Meadow. At a Y-fork, stay to the right on the lower path. Make a horseshoe right bend, then curve left, returning to the meadow. The road fades away, giving way to the meadow. Stroll through the meadow and an opening in the trees. Use the blue diamond ski markers as a guide. Pass through a wetland with small streams, where the path fades in and out. Cross a bridge over Pack Creek, following the orange stakes and blue diamond markers. Complete the loop on F.S. Road 373A. ■

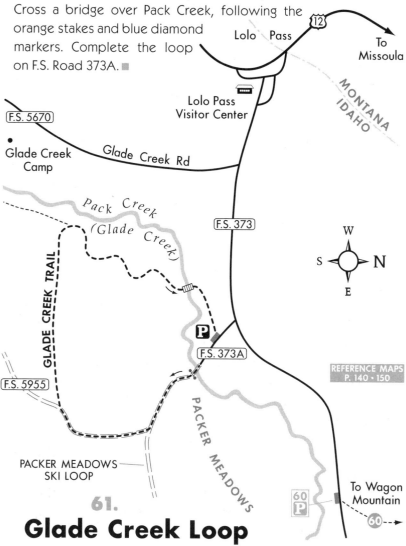

61.
Glade Creek Loop

62. DeVoto Memorial Cedar Grove

Hiking distance: 1 mile round trip
Hiking time: 30 minutes
Elevation gain: 50 feet
Maps: U.S.G.S. Rocky Point
U.S.F.S. Selway Bitterroot Wilderness

The DeVoto Memorial Cedar Grove was named for Bernard DeVoto, a conservationist and historian. The two short trails loop through a beautiful western red cedar grove where DeVoto edited the Lewis and Clark journals. These massive red cedars are the largest trees in the state of Idaho and can live up to 3,000 years. On the east side of the road is the Trail of Discovery. The wheelchair-accessible interpretive trail loops past Crooked Fork Creek, a tributary of the Lochsa River.

To the trailhead

From Missoula, drive 8 miles south on Highway 93 to Lolo. Turn right on Highway 12, and head 32.4 miles west to the Lolo Pass Visitor Center on the left at the Montana–Idaho border. Continue on Highway 12 into Idaho for another 9.3 miles to the paved DeVoto Memorial Cedar Grove parking lots on both sides of the road.

The hike

A loop trail is located on each side of Highway 12. On the west side, take the rock steps down to a trail junction. Begin the loop to the right through a grove of huge red cedars. The well-defined path meanders through the forest and zigzags up the lush, sloping hillside. Cross a wooden bridge over a trickling stream, and descend back to the trailhead. Several benches are placed alongside the trail.

Across the highway on the east is the Trail of Discovery. Walk down the ramp to a trail junction and map. Begin the loop to the right. The level trail curves left, passing interpretive signs to Crooked Fork Creek. Parallel the creek upstream and cross a wooden bridge over a small tributary stream. Complete the loop at the trailhead. ■

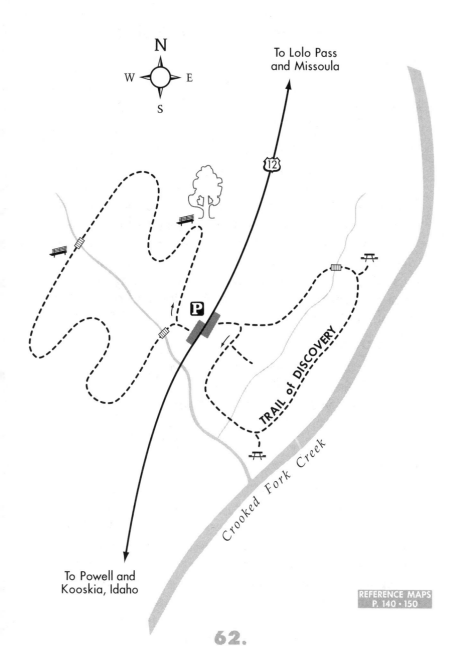

To Lolo Pass
and Missoula

N
W · E
S

12

P

TRAIL of DISCOVERY

Crooked Fork Creek

To Powell and
Kooskia, Idaho

REFERENCE MAPS
P. 140 · 150

62.
DeVoto Memorial
Cedar Grove

63. Jerry Johnson Hot Springs

Hiking distance: 2 miles round trip
Hiking time: 1 hour
Elevation gain: 200 feet
Maps: U.S.G.S. Bear Mountain and Tom Beal Peak
U.S.F.S. Selway Bitterroot Wilderness

**map
page 174**

Jerry Johnson Hot Springs is a popular destination 23 miles southwest of Lolo Pass in the Clearwater National Forest in Idaho. The area has a series of primitive pools along the east bank of Warm Springs Creek near its confluence with the Lochsa River. The trail crosses a suspension bridge over the Lochsa and follows Warm Springs Creek to the pools. Several of the rock-lined hot pools sit beneath thermal waterfalls in a beautiful forest setting. A 10-foot-wide pool sits on a hillside away from the creek overlooking a cedar grove. The clothing-optional pools are restricted to day-use only.

To the trailhead

From Missoula, drive 8 miles south on Highway 93 to Lolo. Turn right on Highway 12, and head 32.4 miles west to the Lolo Pass Visitor Center on the left at the Montana-Idaho border. Continue on Highway 12 into Idaho for another 22.8 miles to the Jerry Johnson Hot Springs parking lot on the right.

The hike

Cross the Warm Springs pack bridge (the wooden suspension bridge) over the Lochsa River to a signed junction. The left fork follows the Lochsa River to Hot Springs Point (Hike 64). Take the right fork through the forest, following the river downstream. The path soon curves away from the Lochsa and heads southeast up the drainage, parallel to Warm Springs Creek. Ascend the west-facing hillside overlooking the creek to an unsigned junction with a footpath to the right. The right fork heads steeply downhill to a series of hot waterfalls and a half dozen soaking pools at the creek. The main trail continues upstream past more pools. Another side path on the right circles a flat cedar grove meadow along the banks of the creek, looping back to the main trail. Climb up a forested knoll to the last and largest pool on the left side of the trail.

To hike farther, the trail parallels Warm Springs Creek, reaching Cooperation Creek at two miles and the Selway-Bitterroot Wilderness at 3.5 miles. The trail climbs steeply into the mountains to Bear Mountain Overlook and several connecting trails. ■

64. Hot Springs Lookout Trail along the Lochsa River

Hiking distance: 2.6 miles round trip
Hiking time: 1 hour
Elevation gain: level
Maps: U.S.G.S. Bear Mountain and Tom Beal Peak
U.S.F.S. Selway Bitterroot Wilderness

**map
page 174**

The Hot Springs Lookout Trail follows the free-flowing Lochsa River for a mile before curving away from the river and steeply climbing 2,300 feet to Hot Springs Point. This hike follows the level, lower end of the trail along the river. The trail begins on the Warm Springs Trail—the path to Jerry Johnson Hot Springs (Hike 63). The Hot Springs Lookout Trail, however, receives little use as almost everyone is headed to Jerry Johnson Hot Springs.

To the trailhead

From Missoula, drive 8 miles south on Highway 93 to Lolo. Turn right on Highway 12, and head 32.4 miles west to the Lolo Pass Visitor Center on the left at the Montana-Idaho border. Continue on Highway 12 into Idaho for another 22.8 miles to the Jerry Johnson Hot Springs parking lot on the right.

The hike

Cross Highway 12 to the Warm Springs pack bridge. Take the wooden suspension bridge over the Lochsa River to a signed junction. The right fork leads to Jerry Johnson Hot Springs (Hike 63). Take the left fork, following the Lochsa River upstream. Climb a small hill to a signed junction with the stock bypass route to Warm Springs Creek and the hot springs. Stay left and traverse the edge of the mountain above the river. Cross a moss-covered

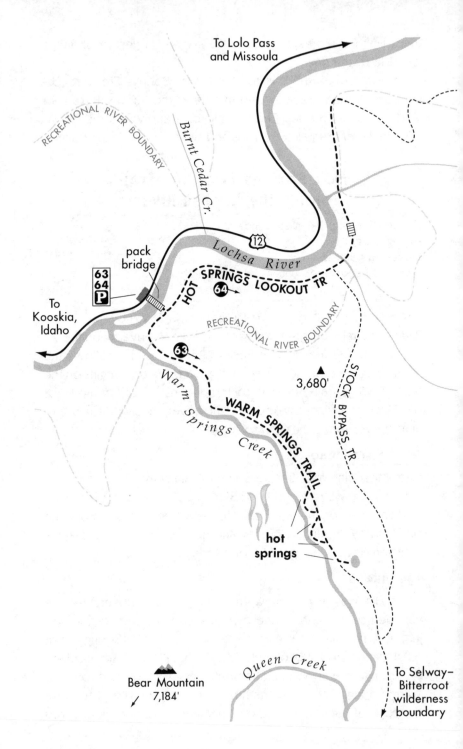

To Lolo Pass
and Missoula

RECREATIONAL RIVER BOUNDARY

Burnt Cedar Cr.

Lochsa River

12

pack
bridge

63
64
P

To
Kooskia,
Idaho

HOT SPRINGS LOOKOUT TR

64

RECREATIONAL RIVER BOUNDARY

63

3,680'

STOCK BYPASS TR

Warm Springs Creek

WARM SPRINGS TRAIL

hot
springs

Queen Creek

Bear Mountain
7,184'

To Selway-
Bitterroot
wilderness
boundary

footbridge that appears old enough to have been used by Lewis and Clark. Continue through a lush, tropical looking fern grove, and rock hop across a small stream. As the river bends sharply to the left, the trail bends 90 degrees to the right. This is the turn-around spot.

To hike farther, the trail begins an intense uphill climb for another 2.3 miles southeast, gaining 2,200 feet to Hot Springs Point at an elevation of 5,535 feet. ▪

HOT SPRINGS TRAIL

Hot Springs Point
5,535'

N
W — E
S

To Selway–Bitterroot wilderness boundary

REFERENCE MAPS
P. 14

REFERENCE MAPS
P. 14

HIKE 63
Jerry Johnson Hot Springs
HIKE 64
Hot Springs Lookout Trail
along the LOCHSA RIVER

65. Colgate Licks Nature Trail

Hiking distance: 1-mile loop
Hiking time: 30 minutes
Elevation gain: 200 feet
Maps: U.S.G.S. Bear Mountain

The Lochsa River, meaning *rough water* in the Nez Perce language, is an undammed, free-flowing river. The wild river forms in the Clearwater National Forest and joins with the Selway and Clearwater Rivers in north-central Idaho. The scenic river parallels the Lolo Highway (Highway 12) near the same route that Lewis and Clark followed in search of the Northwest Passage.

Colgate Licks is an open glade with natural, sulphur-smelling mineral deposits containing calcium, sodium, and potassium that attract wildlife. This one-mile nature trail is an easy, picturesque loop along the Lochsa River. The trail meanders through the lush forest of lodgepole pine, Douglas fir, grand fir, and western red cedar. The trail crosses open meadows with overlooks of the Lochsa River and Bear Mountain. Interpretive stations describe the effects of fire on the trees and surrounding forest.

To the trailhead

From Missoula, drive 8 miles south on Highway 93 to Lolo. Turn right on Highway 12, and head 32.4 miles west to the Lolo Pass Visitor Center on the left at the Montana-Idaho border. Continue on Highway 12 into Idaho for another 26.2 miles to the paved Colgate Licks parking lot on the right.

The hike

Walk up the wooden steps to a platform with a trail map and benches. Take the well-defined path to the right, traversing the hillside past large western red cedars. Continue uphill to a bench and overlook of the Lochsa River, which lies on the other side of the highway. Curve left and head up the shady drainage. The trail levels out and winds through the open forest and grassy meadows. To the south, Bear Mountain towers above the meadow. Rock hop across a stream and gradually descend along the hillside above Highway 12, returning to the trailhead. ■

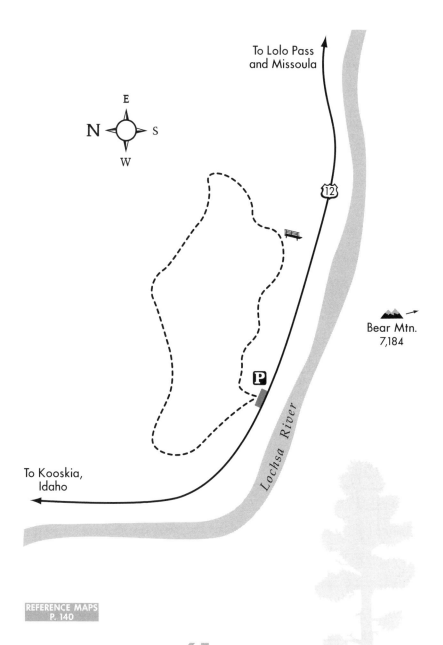

To Lolo Pass
and Missoula

N E S W

12

Bear Mtn.
7,184

Lochsa River

P

To Kooskia,
Idaho

REFERENCE MAPS
P. 140

65.
Colgate Licks
Nature Trail

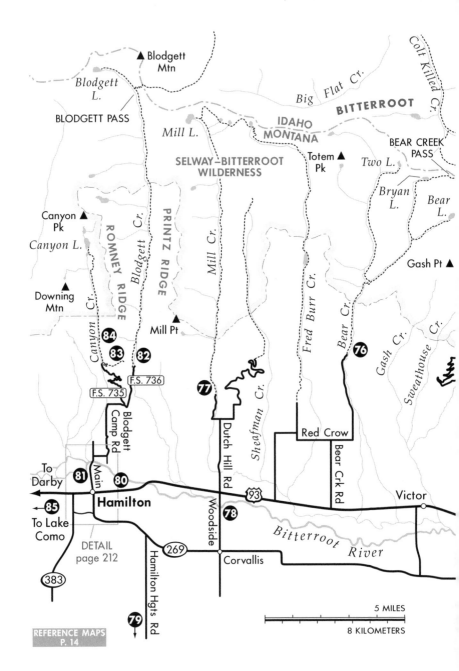

▲ Blodgett Mtn

Blodgett L.

BLODGETT PASS

Big *Flat Cr.*

Colt Killed Cr.

BITTERROOT

Mill L.

IDAHO
MONTANA

SELWAY–BITTERROOT
WILDERNESS

Totem ▲
Pk

BEAR CREEK
PASS

Two L.

Bryan L.

Bear L.

Canyon ▲
Pk

Canyon L.

ROMNEY RIDGE

PRINTZ RIDGE

Blodgett Cr.

Mill Cr.

Fred Burr Cr.

Bear Cr.

Gash Pt ▲

▲
Downing
Mtn

Canyon Cr.

Mill Pt ▲

Gash Cr.

Sweathouse Cr.

84

83

82

F.S. 736

F.S. 735

76

77

Blodgett Camp Rd

Sheafman Cr.

Red Crow

Bear Crk Rd

Dutch Hill Rd

To
Darby

81

Main

80

Hamilton

93

Woodside

78

Victor

85

To Lake
Como

DETAIL
page 212

269

Corvallis

Bitterroot River

383

Hamilton Hgts Rd

79

5 MILES

8 KILOMETERS

REFERENCE MAPS
P. 14

HIKES 66–85

Bitterroot Valley

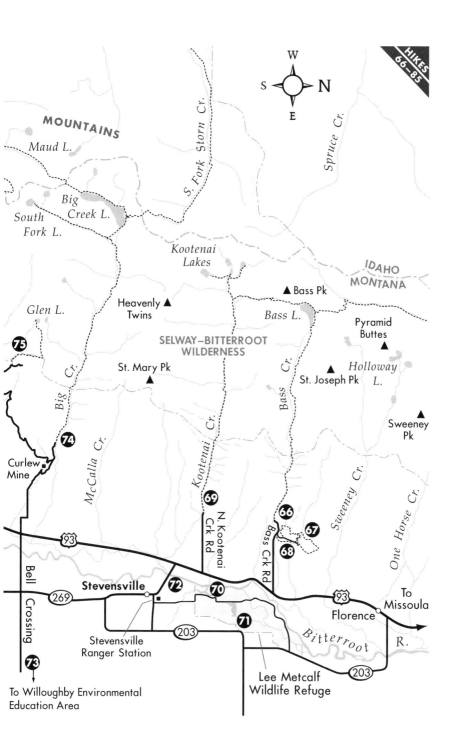

66. Bass Creek Trail

Hiking distance: 3 miles round trip
Hiking time: 1.5 hours
Elevation gain: 500 feet

map
page 182

Maps: U.S.G.S. Saint Mary Peak and Saint Joseph Peak
U.S.F.S. Selway Bitterroot Wilderness
Bass Creek Recreation Area map
Beartooth Publishing: Missoula, Hamilton, Lost Trail Pass

Bass Lake is nestled in the upper forested slopes of Bass Peak. Bass Creek cascades down the canyon from the lake, dropping more than 3,000 feet over seven miles. The 93-acre lake and creek are named for D.C. Bass, a settler along the creek in the 1860s. He built Montana's first irrigation ditch and operated one of the original sawmills in Montana. The Bass Creek Trail follows the watercourse from the Charles Waters Campground near the valley floor up to Bass Lake at 6,765 feet. The trail is along an abandoned road used to build the dam at Bass Lake in the 1890s. The first section of the Bass Creek Trail is an easy hike that gains elevation gradually, paralleling Bass Creek along a continuous series of whitewater cascades, small waterfalls, and pools. This hike heads 1.5 miles into the canyon to an old log dam. Behind the dam is a large, clear pond. For a longer hike, the trail continues west along Bass Creek into the Selway-Bitterroot Wilderness. The trail climbs the canyon's north wall for an additional 5.5 miles to Bass Lake, en route gaining 3,000 feet.

To the trailhead

From Missoula, drive 20 miles south on Highway 93 to Bass Creek Road and turn right (west). Continue 2.5 miles to the trailhead parking area at road's end.

From Hamilton, drive 23 miles north on Highway 93 to Bass Creek Road and turn left. Continue 2.5 miles to the trailhead parking area at road's end.

The hike

From the far west end of the campground, the signed Bass Creek Trail immediately enters the forested canyon on an old vehicle-restricted road. About 100 yards up the road, the trail forks left and stays close to the creek. For the first half mile, large boulders covered with moss and lichen border the trail while Bass Creek cascades down canyon on your left. The trail then climbs high above the creek along the hillside. As you near the log dam, the trail approaches the creek again. Narrow side paths to the left lead down to the dam. The valley widens beyond this area, with great views of the surrounding mountains. Return on the same trail.

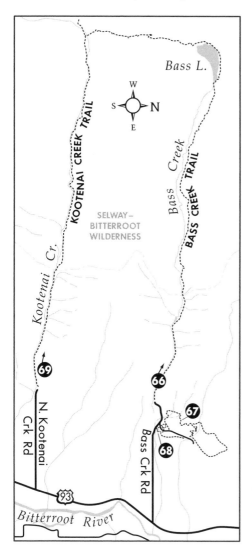

The Bass Creek Trail continues another 5.5 miles along the north side of the creek to Bass Lake. Connecting trails lead north and south along the Bitterroot Range. Head north up the saddle to the South Fork of Lolo Creek and south around Bass Lake to the Kootenai Creek Trail (Hike 69). ■

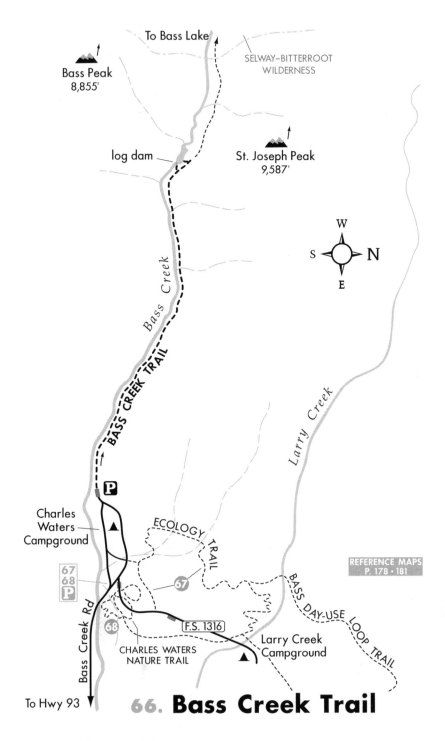

To Bass Lake

SELWAY–BITTERROOT
WILDERNESS

Bass Peak
8,855'

log dam

St. Joseph Peak
9,587'

W

S ✦ N

E

Bass Creek

BASS CREEK TRAIL

Larry Creek

REFERENCE MAPS
P. 178 • 181

P

Charles
Waters
Campground

ECOLOGY TRAIL

67

BASS DAY-USE LOOP TRAIL

67
68
P

Bass Creek Rd

68

F.S. 1316

Larry Creek
Campground

CHARLES WATERS
NATURE TRAIL

To Hwy 93

66. **Bass Creek Trail**

67. Larry Creek Fire Ecology Trail

Hiking distance: 2.5-mile loop
Hiking time: 1.5 hours
Elevation gain: 400 feet
Maps: U.S.G.S. Saint Mary Peak · U.S.F.S. Selway Bitterroot Wilderness
      Bass Creek Recreation Area map
      Beartooth Publishing: Missoula, Hamilton, Lost Trail Pass

**map
page 184**

The Larry Creek Fire Ecology Trail loops through aspen and willow stands and a ponderosa pine and fir forest in the foothills of the Bitterroot Mountains. The interpretive trail studies the effects of fire, and the lack of fire, on the forest ecology and wildlife. A trail brochure accompanies the hike, available at the Forest Service office in Stevensville or from the campground host at Charles Waters Campground.

To the trailhead

From Missoula, drive 20 miles south on Highway 93 to Bass Creek Road and turn right (west). Continue 2 miles to the trailhead parking area on the right. Turn right and park in the lot by the information kiosk.

From Hamilton, drive 23 miles north on Highway 93 to Bass Creek Road and turn left. Continue 2 miles to the trailhead parking area on the right. Turn right and park in the lot by the information kiosk.

The hike

Walk up Bass Creek Road 200 yards to the signed trail on the right, directly across from the entrance to the Charles Waters Campground. Head north up the footpath. At the top of the rise, the connector trail joins the Ecology Trail. Bear left, curving up the rolling hillside. At just over one mile—by signpost 10—is a trail split. The Bass Day-Use Loop Trail bears left (a 4.5-mile loop to the north). Take the Ecology Trail to the right, descending into the canyon. Switchbacks lead halfway down to Larry Creek through a dense forest. Continue downhill to another junction with the Loop Trail at signpost 15. Take the right fork a short distance to unpaved Forest Service Road 1316. Pick up the trail across the road a few yards south on the left. Follow the path past the horse trailer parking area. Continue through the nature trail loop (Hike 68), returning to the parking area by Bass Creek Road. ■

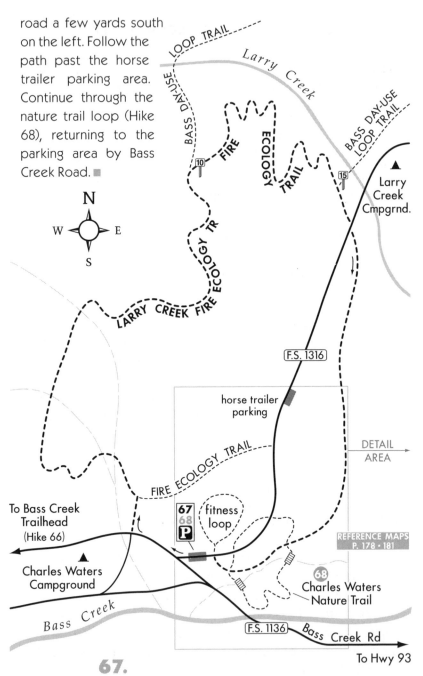

Larry Creek Fire Ecology Trail

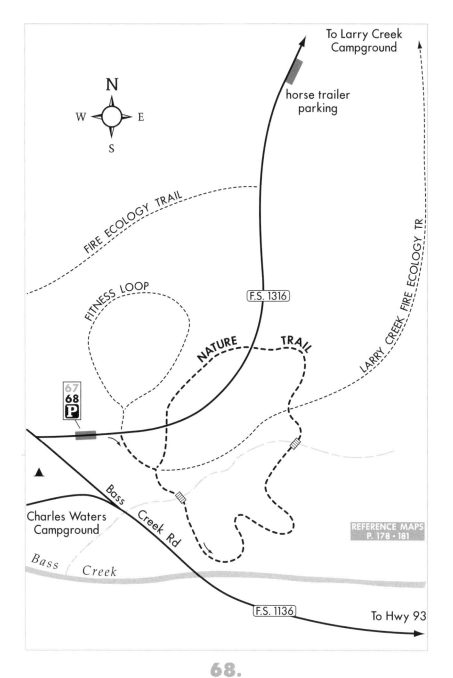

Charles Waters Nature Trail

68. Charles Waters Nature Trail

Hiking distance: 1-mile loop
Hiking time: 30 minutes
Elevation gain: level

map
page 185

Maps: U.S.G.S. Saint Mary Peak · U.S.F.S. Selway Bitterroot Wilderness
Bass Creek Recreation Area map
Beartooth Publishing: Missoula, Hamilton, Lost Trail Pass

Charles Waters Nature Trail lies at the base of the Bitterroot Mountains adjacent to the Charles Waters Campground. The trail loops through two different habitats. The hike begins in a dry ponderosa pine forest, then winds through a lush and cool old-growth forest. The trail parallels a short section of Bass Creek and includes two footbridges over a small stream. Across the road from the nature trail is a quarter-mile fitness loop with 14 exercise stations.

To the trailhead

From Missoula, drive 20 miles south on Highway 93 to Bass Creek Road and turn right (west). Continue 2 miles to the trailhead parking area on the right. Turn right and park in the lot by the information kiosk.

From Hamilton, drive 23 miles north on Highway 93 to Bass Creek Road and turn left. Continue 2 miles to the trailhead parking area on the right. Turn right and park in the lot by the information kiosk.

The hike

Walk 50 yards down Forest Service Road #1316, following the signs to the nature trail on the right. Take the footpath under the forest canopy of ponderosa pine and Douglas fir. Cross a wooden footbridge over a tributary stream. The trail leads to Bass Creek a short distance ahead, then winds back through the forest. Cross the stream again to a four-way junction. The right fork crosses the prairie alongside an irrigation ditch—the return for Hike 67. The left fork returns directly to the trailhead. Take the middle fork straight ahead. The path curves through the grassland, completing the loop near the parking area. ■

69. Kootenai Creek Trail

Hiking distance: 6 miles round trip
Hiking time: 3 hours
Elevation gain: 600 feet
Maps: U.S.G.S. Saint Mary Peak and Saint Joseph Peak
U.S.F.S. Selway Bitterroot Wilderness
Beartooth Publishing: Missoula, Hamilton, Lost Trail Pass

**map
page 188**

Kootenai Creek features a dynamic display of raging whitewater, cascades, and small waterfalls. The Kootenai Creek Trail along the creek is a popular, heavily used hiking trail. The path stays close to the picturesque creek, winding through a narrow, steep-walled canyon. The trail continues along the north side of the creek for nine miles to the four Kootenai Lakes, gaining 2,600 feet in elevation. This hike follows the easier first three miles of the trail into the Selway-Bitterroot Wilderness.

To the trailhead

From Missoula, drive 23 miles south on Highway 93 to the North Kootenai Creek Road on the right (west). The road is located one mile north of the Stevensville junction. Turn right and continue 2 miles to the trailhead parking area at the road's end.

From Hamilton, drive 20 miles north on Highway 93 to North Kootenai Creek Road on the left. Continue with the directions above.

The hike

Hike west past the trailhead information board. The trail follows the north edge of the canyon, always in view of the tumbling Kootenai Creek. There are continuous dips and rises as the trail heads west into the canyon. Enter the Selway-Bitterroot Wilderness at 2.6 miles. At 3 miles the gradient steepens. The well-defined trail parallels Kootenai Creek to the lakes for the entire distance. Choose your own turn-around point.

Shortly before reaching the lakes, a connecting trail leads north to Bass Lake (Hike 66). ▦

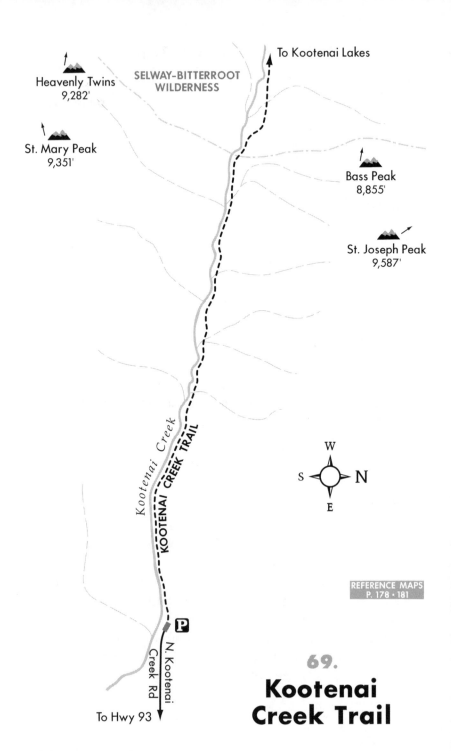

To Kootenai Lakes

Heavenly Twins
9,282'

SELWAY-BITTERROOT
WILDERNESS

St. Mary Peak
9,351'

Bass Peak
8,855'

St. Joseph Peak
9,587'

Kootenai Creek

KOOTENAI CREEK TRAIL

W
S — N
E

REFERENCE MAPS
P. 178 · 181

P

N. Kootenai
Creek Rd

To Hwy 93

69.
Kootenai
Creek Trail

70. Bitterroot River Recreation Area
LEE METCALF NATIONAL WILDLIFE REFUGE

Hiking distance: 1.8 miles round trip
Hiking time: 1 hour
Elevation gain: level
Maps: U.S.G.S. Stevensville
Lee Metcalf National Wildlife Refuge map

**map
page 191**

The 2,800-acre Lee Metcalf National Wildlife Refuge lies in the Bitterroot Valley north of Stevensville. The refuge borders the banks of the Bitterroot River and is surrounded by fertile ranch and farmland. It is a premier bird watching habitat with migrating and resident waterfowl. The refuge includes a chain of ponds, wildlife viewing areas, a meadow, river bottom woodlands, riparian and wetland habitats, and a visitor center. The 140-acre

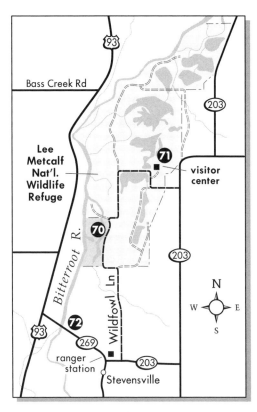

Bitterroot River Recreation Area within the refuge has two short loop trails beginning at the same trailhead. The trails meander along the Bitterroot River and Francois Slough through woodlands, meadows, and riparian habitat.

Driving directions

From Missoula, drive 24 miles south on Highway 93 to the Stevensville turnoff (Highway 269) and turn left (east). Continue 1.3 miles to the Eastside Highway (Highway 203). Turn left and go 0.2 miles to Wildfowl Lane and turn left again. Drive 2.1 miles to the trailhead parking area on the right.

From Hamilton, the Stevensville (Highway 269) turnoff is 19 miles north on Highway 93.

The hike

Cross Wildfowl Lane and take the paved path over Francois Slough to the trailhead kiosk and map. Take the right fork on the unpaved Ponderosa Loop. Walk through the meadow and forest to the Bitterroot River. At the river is a bridge leading to a sandy beach on the right. The main trail completes the loop back at the map.

The second loop is a paved, wheelchair-accessible trail. Head south on Riparian Way, following the banks of Francois Slough past a sheltered fishing deck on the right. A short distance ahead is a junction with Owl Hollow on the right, an unpaved trail reconnecting with Riparian Way. Riparian Way ends at a loop around a picnic area and covered pavilion at the Bitterroot River. ■

71. Kenai Nature Trail
LEE METCALF NATIONAL WILDLIFE REFUGE

Hiking distance: 2.5 miles round trip
Hiking time: 1.5 hours
Elevation gain: level
Maps: U.S.G.S. Stevensville
   Lee Metcalf National Wildlife Refuge map

**map
page 193**

The Lee Metcalf National Wildlife Refuge was established in 1963 to provide nesting, feeding, and cover habitat for migratory birds. A series of dikes and impoundments were constructed to hold and manage the water for wildlife. The diverse habitats within the refuge are a haven to 235 different species of migratory birds and a variety of wildlife, including 37 species of mammals and 17 species of reptiles. The Kenai Nature Trail begins at the visitor center and heads north on a gravel trail through riparian vegetation. The trail parallels wetlands and a chain of ponds with benches, viewing platforms, photo blinds, and a spotting

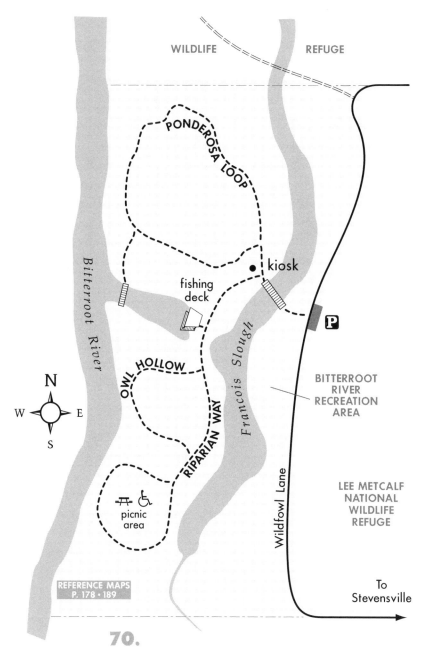

WILDLIFE   REFUGE

PONDEROSA LOOP

Bitterroot River

fishing deck

• kiosk

Francois Slough

OWL HOLLOW

RIPARIAN WAY

P

BITTERROOT
RIVER
RECREATION
AREA

N
W ⊕ E
S

picnic
area

Wildfowl Lane

LEE METCALF
NATIONAL
WILDLIFE
REFUGE

To
Stevensville

REFERENCE MAPS
P. 178 • 189

70.
Bitterroot River Rec. Area
LEE METCALF NAT'L. WILDLIFE REFUGE

scope. The ponds are home to muskrats, turtles, osprey, great blue herons, and bald eagles. Throughout the hike are sweeping panoramas of the majestic Bitterroot Mountains and the beautiful, but less dramatic, rolling Sapphire Mountains. The visitor center offers binoculars for use during the hike.

To the trailhead

From Missoula, drive 24 miles south on Highway 93 to the Stevensville turnoff (Highway 269) and turn left (east). Continue 1.3 miles to the Eastside Highway (Highway 203). Turn left and go 0.2 miles to Wildfowl Lane and turn left again. Drive 4 miles to the prominent headquarters and visitor center sign. Turn left and proceed 0.2 miles to the visitor center parking lot.

From Hamilton, the Stevensville (Highway 269) turnoff is 19 miles north on Highway 93.

The hike

Walk around the back (west) side of the visitor center to the trailhead. Cross the bridge over a pond to a T-junction. Both directions on this small loop lead to the Kenai Nature Trail. For this hike, begin to the left. Pass a large pond on the left to the massive reed-filled wetlands and sloughs. At the northeast corner of the loop, veer left and head northeast on the raised grasslands above the wetlands. Cross a wood bridge to an observation blind. A side path on the left leads fifty yards down to the blind on the edge of the pond. Continue on the main trail past a couple of cottonwood tree pockets to a bench overlooking Pond 8. Fifty yards ahead, cross a third bridge over a wetland drainage. Pass the north end of Pond 8 to a dirt maintenance road. At this road crossing is the only view of Potato Cellar Pond, located on the east side of the road. Cross the road to an overlook of Pond 8 and Pond 10. Zigzag down to the edge of the wetlands. Cross a 24-foot-long boardwalk over the wet, fragile terrain to a roofed observation shelter with a spotting scope. Beyond the observation deck, the trail forms a small loop and returns to the boardwalk. Retrace your steps back to the visitor center. ■

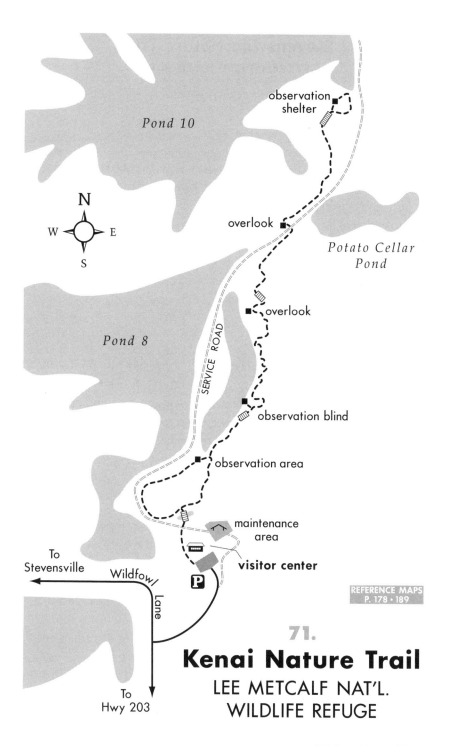

Pond 10

observation
shelter

overlook

Potato Cellar
Pond

N
W   E
S

overlook

Pond 8

SERVICE ROAD

observation blind

observation area

maintenance
area

visitor center

To
Stevensville

Wildfowl
Lane

P

REFERENCE MAPS
P. 178 · 189

To
Hwy 203

71.

Kenai Nature Trail
LEE METCALF NAT'L.
WILDLIFE REFUGE

72. Stevensville Nature Trail
STEVENSVILLE RIVER PARK

Hiking distance: 1-mile loop
Hiking time: 30 minutes
Elevation gain: level
Maps: U.S.G.S. Stevensville

Stevensville River Park resides just west of Stevensville between the banks of the Bitterroot River and fertile ranch and farmland. The park sits on a floodplain forest with cottonwood, chokecherry, and cattail wetlands. It is a popular spot for fishing, picnicking, and wildlife observation. The Stevensville Nature Trail is a river and floodplain loop through the park. It follows the freely flowing Bitterroot River and returns through the wetlands. A paved bike path connects the park with downtown Stevensville.

To the trailhead

From Missoula, drive 24 miles south on Highway 93 to the Stevensville turnoff (Highway 269) and turn left (east). Continue 0.4 miles to the Stevensville River Park on the left, immediately after crossing the bridge over the Bitterroot River. Turn left and park on the left 0.1 mile ahead by the park sign.

From Hamilton, the Stevensville (Highway 269) turnoff is 19 miles north on Highway 93.

The hike

From the north end of the parking area, walk past the park sign on the footpath. Follow the east bank of the Bitterroot River downstream through a pine grove. At 0.15 miles is a junction. Begin the loop to the left, following the flow of the river. Sweeping views of the Bitterroot Range lie to the west. Pass a picnic table, a couple of riverfront benches, and a cut-across path for a shorter loop. Continue north, just inches from the river, to the trail's end at a fenced boundary. Return 80 yards to a trail split and veer left. Meander through the grasslands, scattered cottonwoods, and cattail-filled wetlands. At the south end of the loop, curve around a pond to the other trail access at the end of the park road. Continue a hundred yards straight ahead, completing the loop at the river. ■

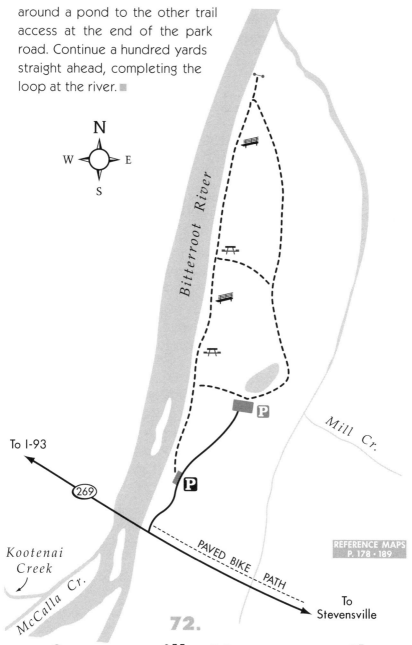

To I-93

269

Kootenai
Creek

McCalla Cr.

Bitterroot River

Mill Cr.

REFERENCE MAPS
P. 178 · 189

PAVED BIKE PATH

To
Stevensville

72.

Stevensville Nature Trail
STEVENSVILLE RIVER PARK

73. Willoughby Environmental Education Area

Hiking distance: 1-mile loop
Hiking time: 30 minutes
Elevation gain: 250 feet
Maps: U.S.G.S. Corley Gulch

The Willoughby Environmental Education Area lies in the foothills of the low and rounded Sapphire Mountains, located on the opposite side of the valley from the tall, jagged Bitterroot Mountains. The 40-acre reserve has an interpretive trail that passes through three distinct habitats: dry sagebrush on a plateau with wildflowers; timbered slopes with ponderosa pines; and a riparian valley bottom with an intermittent stream, cottonwoods, and apple trees. An interpretive brochure describes how the trees, rocks, soils, streams, animals, insects, weeds, fire, people, and surrounding landscape play a roll in this ecosystem. The brochure is available at the Lee Metcalf National Wildlife Refuge in Stevensville and the Stevensville Ranger Station.

To the trailhead

From Missoula, drive 30 miles south on Highway 93 to Bell Crossing, located 5.6 miles south of the Stevensville turnoff. Turn left (east) and go 2 miles to Eastside Highway. Cross through the intersection; the road then becomes Willoughby Lane. Continue 1.3 miles to South Sunset Road. Turn left and drive 4.4 miles to the posted trailhead parking lot on the right. The last two miles are on a dirt road.

From Hamilton, drive 13.5 miles north on Highway 93 to Bell Crossing on the right. Continue with the directions above.

The hike

Walk through the trailhead gate to the log picnic shelter. Begin the loop to the left. Head to the kiosk where the two paths from the parking lot merge. Cross the grasslands and descend into an open forest of ponderosa pines. Cross a gully and climb to the open sagebrush bench, with vistas of the Bitterroot Mountains, the Sapphire Range, and the adjacent irrigated ranchland. Curve right to the west boundary of the preserve, and descend to ephemeral Willoughby Creek amongst the cottonwood trees. Follow the creek downstream through riparian vegetation. Traverse the hillside slope through the pine forest, passing old wagon remains. With the aid of two switchbacks, the path returns to the bench and picnic shelter. ■

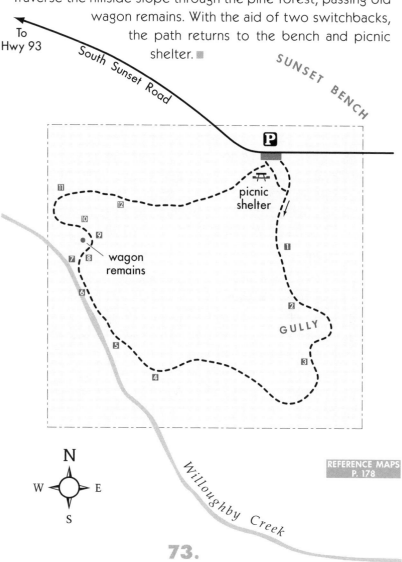

73.
Willoughby Environmental Education Area

74. Big Creek Trail

Hiking distance: 4 miles round trip
Hiking time: 2 hours
Elevation gain: 600 feet
Maps: U.S.G.S. Victor and Gash Point
U.S.F.S. Selway Bitterroot Wilderness
Beartooth Publishing: Missoula, Hamilton, Lost Trail Pass

Big Creek Trail is a popular hiking, fishing, and horsepacking trail to Big Creek Lake, the largest alpine lake in the Bitterroots. Big Creek flows down one of the widest drainages in this mountain range. The trail follows the creek for nine miles up to Big Creek Lake and dam at an elevation of 5,865 feet, gaining over 2,000 feet in elevation. This hike includes the first two miles of the trail to several white sand beaches near wide, slow moving sections of Big Creek. These streamside beaches are great locations for a picnic or for soaking your feet in the cool water.

To the trailhead

From Missoula, drive 30 miles south on Highway 93 to Bell Crossing West on the right, located 5.6 miles south of the Stevensville turnoff. Turn right (west) and continue 0.5 miles to Meridian Road. Turn right and follow the hiking trail signs for 2.8 miles to a road split just past the old mine pit. Take the right fork 1.2 miles downhill to the Big Creek trailhead parking area.

From Hamilton, drive 13.5 miles north on Highway 93 to Bell Crossing West on the left. Continue with the directions above.

The hike

The trailhead is at the far end of the parking lot by the Forest Service information board. The trail is immediately engulfed in the thick, shady forest. Bear to the left and cross the stream. Big Creek cascades down the canyon to the north of the trail. At one mile, enter the Selway-Bitterroot Wilderness, then descends a short distance to Big Creek and a bridge crossing. After crossing to the north side of the creek, continue up canyon 0.3 miles to the first in a series of sandy beaches. A side path on the left

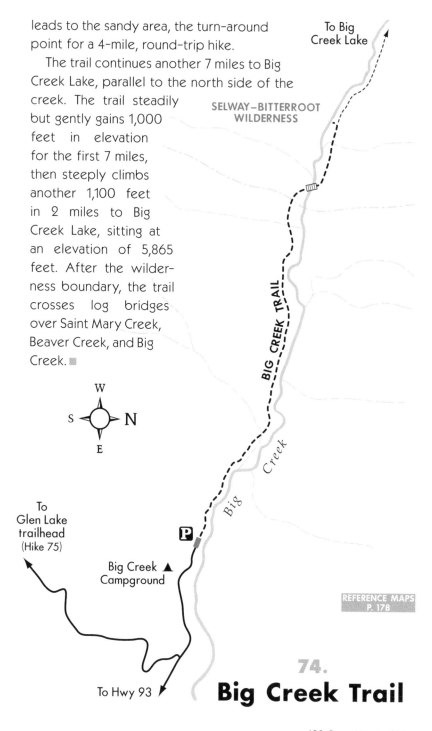

leads to the sandy area, the turn-around point for a 4-mile, round-trip hike.

The trail continues another 7 miles to Big Creek Lake, parallel to the north side of the creek. The trail steadily but gently gains 1,000 feet in elevation for the first 7 miles, then steeply climbs another 1,100 feet in 2 miles to Big Creek Lake, sitting at an elevation of 5,865 feet. After the wilderness boundary, the trail crosses log bridges over Saint Mary Creek, Beaver Creek, and Big Creek. ■

To Big Creek Lake

SELWAY–BITTERROOT WILDERNESS

BIG CREEK TRAIL

Big Creek

To Glen Lake trailhead (Hike 75)

P

Big Creek ▲ Campground

REFERENCE MAPS P. 178

To Hwy 93

74.
Big Creek Trail

75. Glen Lake

Hiking distance: 5 miles round trip
Hiking time: 2.5 hours
Elevation gain: 700 feet
Maps: U.S.G.S. Gash Point
      U.S.F.S. Selway Bitterroot Wilderness
      Beartooth Publishing: Missoula, Hamilton, Lost Trail Pass

Glen Lake is a beautiful high mountain lake surrounded by steep, serrated, bare-rock cliffs to the south and timbered slopes to the north. The eight-acre lake sits in a bowl below the towering mountains. The trail steadily climbs to Glen Lake, weaving through the remains of a small burn area. The trail enters the Selway-Bitterroot Wilderness and continues through a lichen-draped forest with larch, whitebark pine, and subalpine fir. En route to the lake are great views of the Bitterroot Valley and snow-capped Gash Point.

To the trailhead

From Missoula, drive 30 miles south on Highway 93 to Bell Crossing West on the right, located 5.6 miles south of the Stevensville turnoff. Turn right (west) and continue 0.5 miles to Meridian Road. Turn right and follow the hiking trail signs 2.8 miles to a road split just past the old Curlew Mine pit. Take the left fork 7.6 miles up several switchbacks to the trailhead parking pullouts on the right.

From Hamilton, drive 13.5 miles north on Highway 93 to Bell Crossing West on the left. Continue with the directions above.

The hike

The trailhead appears as though it is at the top of the mountain, but it is only near the top. Hike uphill past the trail sign, paralleling the Selway-Bitterroot Wilderness boundary north for 1.2 miles. The trail levels out in a small burn area, then curves west into the wilderness. Weave through the burn area from the 2006 Gash Creek Fire. Cross a saddle and descend to the southeast corner of Glen Lake. Paths lead around the shoreline in both directions. The lake cannot be encircled, as the mountains are too steep along the north side. Return along the same route.

To continue hiking from the east end of the lake, the trail climbs a quarter mile to two unnamed lakes connected by a stream and small waterfall. From there, the trail leads 2.5 miles northwest to Hidden Lake. The footpath is steep and vague. It is not recommended without topographic maps and good hiking skills. ■

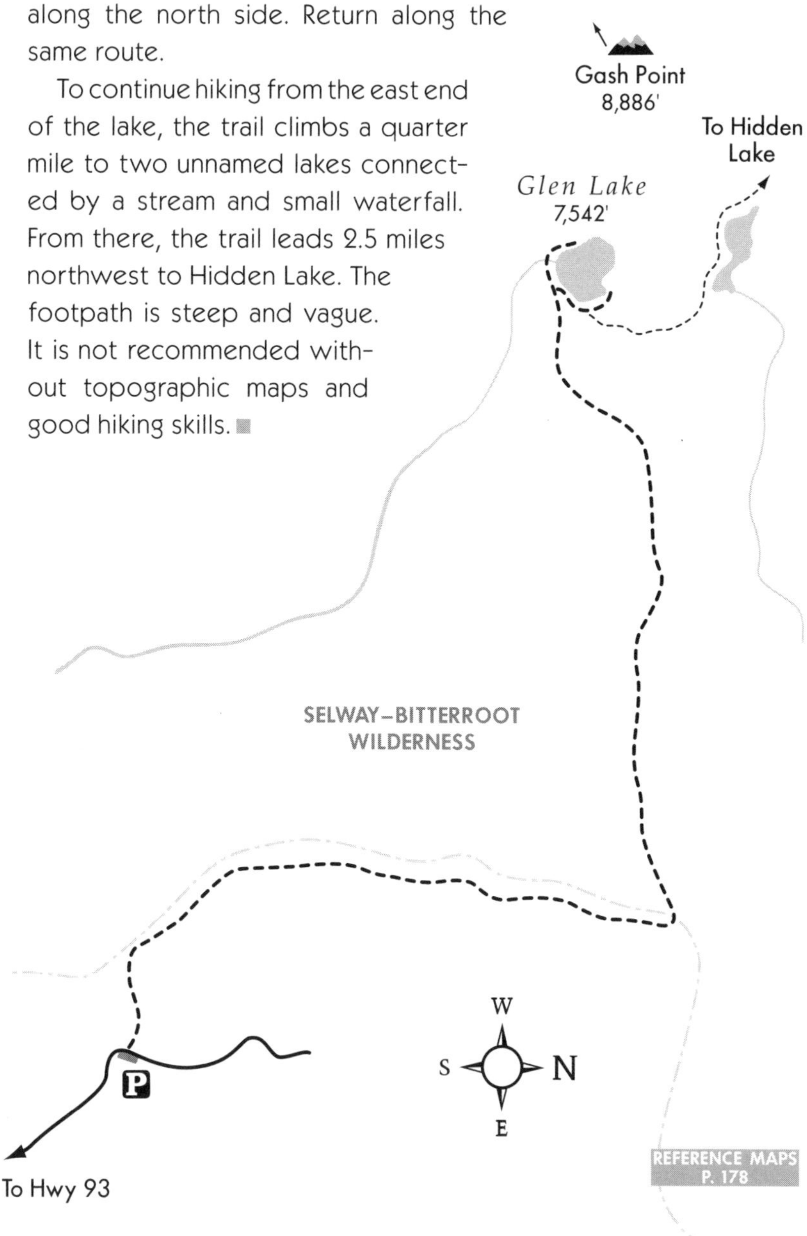

Gash Point
8,886'

To Hidden Lake

Glen Lake
7,542'

SELWAY–BITTERROOT
WILDERNESS

W

S ←○→ N

E

P

To Hwy 93

REFERENCE MAPS
P. 178

75.
Glen Lake

76. Bear Creek Trail to Bear Creek Falls

Hiking distance: 3 miles round trip
Hiking time: 1.5 hours
Elevation gain: 400 feet
Maps: U.S.G.S. Victor & Gash Point · U.S.F.S. Selway Bitterroot Wilderness
Beartooth Publishing: Missoula, Hamilton, Lost Trail Pass

The Bear Creek Trail is a long trail that branches into three drainages which emerge from the Bitterroots—the South Fork, Middle Fork, and North Fork. This hike follows the lower main drainage to a gorgeous waterfall a half mile shy of the Selway-Bitterroot Wilderness. The easy, well-defined path lies nestled between the forest, the steep canyon walls, and the creek, making a gradual ascent. The hike leads past pools in the smooth rock to Bear Creek Falls, which forms whirlpools, cascades, and water slides over a series of boulders. Terraced rock slabs offer flat areas for picnicking, sunbathing, and viewing the rocky cliffs. For a longer hike, trails continue up the three drainages to high alpine lakes atop the Bitterroot Range on the Montana–Idaho border.

To the trailhead

From Missoula, drive 35 miles south on Highway 93 to Bear Creek Road on the right (west). Turn right and continue 2.3 miles to Red Crow Road. Turn right and drive 0.7 miles to a road junction. Turn left and continue straight for 3.1 miles to the Bear Creek trailhead parking area.

From Hamilton, drive 8.5 miles north on Highway 93 to Bear Creek Road on the left. Continue with the directions above.

The hike

Take the clearly marked Bear Creek Trail at the far end of the parking lot. Bear Creek cascades down the canyon to the north of the trail, paralleling the creek through the forest. After crossing a boulder field, enter the forested canyon again. In a clearing just beyond the third boulder field is the cascade and falls. Bear Creek carves a beautiful whitewater mosaic through the rocks. Return along the same route.

To extend the hike, enter the Selway-Bitterroot Wilderness boundary at two miles and continue through a dense forest. The trail leads to an unmarked junction with the South Fork and Middle Fork Trails 1.5 miles from the wilderness boundary. The South Fork of Bear Creek follows the creek to Two Lakes along a poorly defined path. The Middle Fork of Bear Creek leads 7.7 miles to Bryan Lake in a glacial valley, continuing over Bear Creek Pass on the Bitterroot ridgeline. The North Fork of Bear Creek, 5.7 miles from the trailhead, leads 2.5 miles up to Bear Lake on another overgrown, poorly maintained trail, with a total gain of 2,400 feet. ■

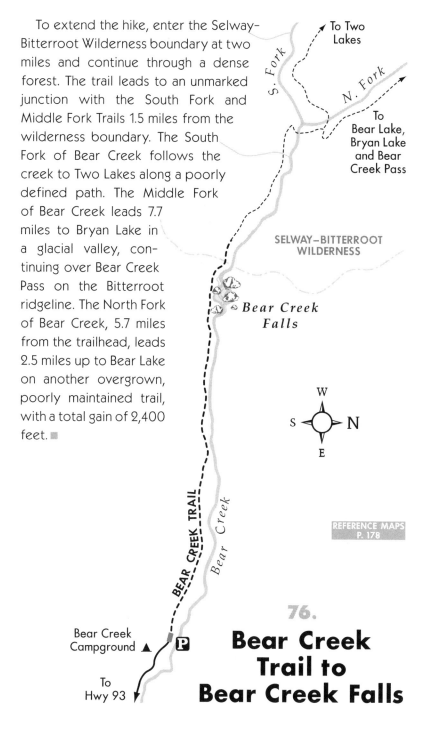

To Two Lakes

S. Fork

N. Fork

To Bear Lake, Bryan Lake and Bear Creek Pass

SELWAY–BITTERROOT WILDERNESS

Bear Creek Falls

W
S — ○ — N
E

REFERENCE MAPS P. 178

BEAR CREEK TRAIL

Bear Creek

Bear Creek Campground ▲ 🅿

To Hwy 93

76.

Bear Creek Trail to Bear Creek Falls

77. Mill Creek Trail to Mill Creek Falls

Hiking distance: 6 miles round trip
Hiking time: 3 hours
Elevation gain: 650 feet
Maps: U.S.G.S. Hamilton North and Printz Ridge
       U.S.F.S. Selway Bitterroot Wilderness
       Beartooth Publishing: Missoula, Hamilton, Lost Trail Pass

The headwaters of Mill Creek begin at Mill Lake at an elevation of 6,550 feet, 11 miles from the trailhead. The creek tumbles down the canyon in a continuous display of cascades, waterfalls, and pools. The Mill Creek Trail follows the rushing creek continuously to the lake, with soaring canyon walls towering over the trail. This hike includes the first three miles of the trail to a magnificent 60-foot waterfall and swimming hole at the base of the falls. Large boulders make perfect seats for viewing the falls and relaxing.

To the trailhead

From Missoula, drive 39 miles south on Highway 93 to Dutch Hill Road on the right, located 15 miles past Stevensville and 7.5 miles past Victor. The intersection has a flashing yellow light and a sign to Pinesdale and Corvallis. Turn right (west) and continue 2.4 miles to Bowman Road. Turn left and drive 0.3 miles to the road on the right with posted Mill Creek Trailhead. Turn right and drive 0.8 miles to the trailhead parking area at the road's end.

From Hamilton, drive 4 miles north on Highway 93 to Dutch Hill Road on the left. Continue with the directions above.

The hike

From the parking area, hike west past the information board. Parallel, then cross, a small stream. Mill Creek tumbles down canyon on the north side of the trail. At 0.5 miles, cross a bridge over Mill Creek, and head left up the narrow canyon. At one mile, the canyon widens, opening skyward to views of the towering rock cliffs. Enter the Selway-Bitterroot Wilderness at 2.2 miles. At 3 miles, cross a large, flat rock slab. Shortly beyond the slab is Mill Creek Falls. After enjoying the falls, return along the same trail.

To extend the hike, the trail continues 8 more miles along the north side
of Mill Creek, gaining 2,400
feet to Mill Lake just
below the ridgeline. ■

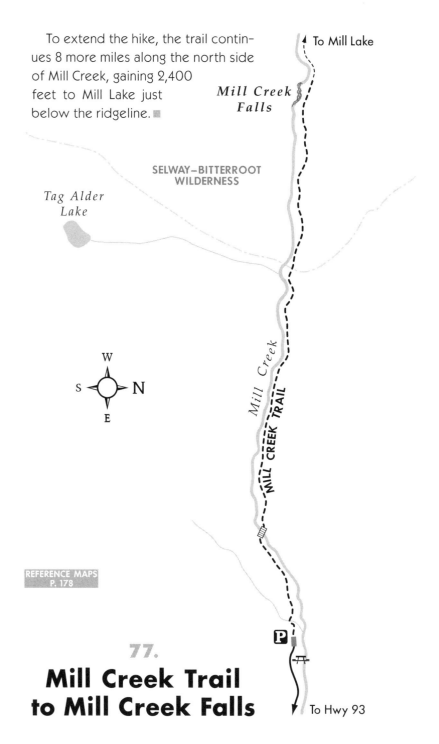

To Mill Lake

Mill Creek
Falls

SELWAY–BITTERROOT
WILDERNESS

Tag Alder
Lake

W
S — N
E

Mill Creek

MILL CREEK TRAIL

REFERENCE MAPS
P. 178

P

77.

Mill Creek Trail
to Mill Creek Falls

To Hwy 93

78. Teller Wildlife Refuge
Teller Trail
(406) 961-3507 · www.theteller.org

Hikng distance: 1.5-mile loop
Hiking time: 40 minutes
Elevation gain: level
Maps: U.S.G.S. Hamilton North
Teller Wildlife Refuge map

The Teller Wildlife Refuge is a private, 1,200-acre sanctuary located just north of Corvallis in the Bitterroot Valley. The refuge, established in 1987 by Otto Teller, is part of a non-profit organization promoting conservation, education, and recreation. The protected land spreads out along three miles of the 84-mile-long Bitterroot River. The area contains timbered river bottom, ponds, streams, wetlands, meadows, upland habitat, and agricultural land. Except for the Teller Trail, access to the main refuge is limited. Contact the office for additional public access information.

The dog-friendly Teller Trail is a 1.5-mile loop along the Bitterroot River floodplain. The trail weaves through the riparian habitat among cottonwoods, ponderosa pine, and willows. It is a popular birding and fishing area.

To the trailhead

From Missoula, drive 39 miles south on Highway 93 to Woodside Cutoff Road, located 15 miles past Stevensville and 7.5 miles past Victor. The intersection has a flashing yellow light and a sign to Pinesdale and Corvallis. Turn left (east) and continue 0.5 miles to the Woodside Bridge over the Bitterroot River. Just after crossing the river, turn left into the fishing access parking lot.

From Hamilton, drive 4 miles north to Woodside Cutoff Road on the right (east). Continue with the directions above.

The hike

Pass the trailhead gate by the Bitterroot River at the north end of the parking area. Follow the bank of the river downstream. Gradually curve away from the shoreline through grasslands and a forest of ponderosa pines, cottonwoods, and willows to a

Y-fork. Begin the loop to the left, staying closer to the river. At a rocky wash, stay to the left and continue through the natural area. The path returns to the river bank at the northern boundary. Curve right and loop around the north end. Follow the forested eastern perimeter and complete the loop at the Y-fork. Return to the left (south). ■

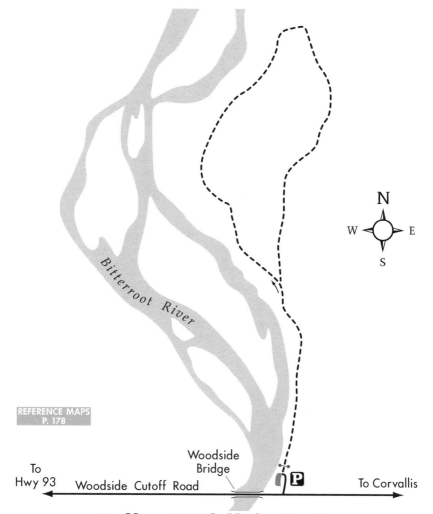

78. Teller Wildlife Refuge
TELLER WILDLIFE REFUGE

79. Calf Creek
Wildlife Management Area

Closed to public access: December 2–April 14
No dogs from October 15 – December 1

Hiking distance: 6.5-mile loop
Hiking time: 3 hours
Elevation gain: 800 feet
Maps: U.S.G.S. Corvallis and Willow Mountain
Montana Fish, Wildlife & Parks: Calf Creek Wildlife
Management Area map

The gently rounded hills of the Sapphire Range frame the east side of the Bitterroot Valley. Calf Creek Wildlife Management Area, established in 1960, encompasses 2,333 acres in the foothills of the Sapphire Mountains, eight miles east of Hamilton. The area is used to provide winter range for elk. It also offers access to hiking, biking, and equestrians.

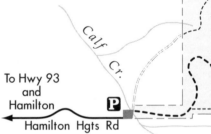

The rolling terrain is primarily a mix of sagebrush, native upland grasslands, ponderosa pine forest, and rocky outcrops. This hike loops through open foothills, up a ponderosa pine draw, and to viewpoints with sweeping vistas of the serrated Bitterroot Range.

To the trailhead

From Missoula, drive 39 miles south on Highway 93 to Woodside Cutoff Road, located 15 miles past

REFERENCE MAPS
P. 178

79.
Calf Creek
WILDLIFE MANAGEMENT AREA

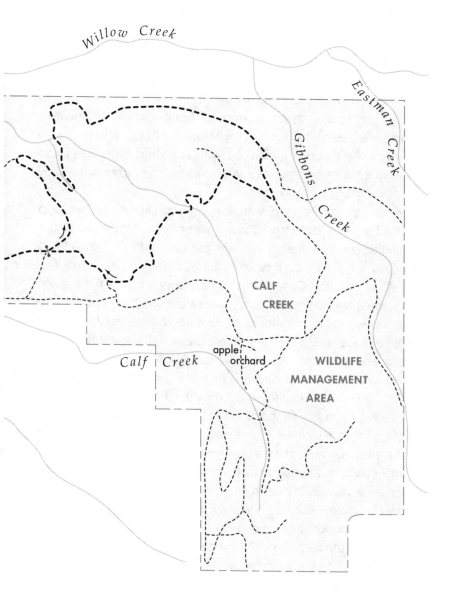

Willow Creek

Eastman Creek

Gibbons Creek

CALF CREEK

Calf Creek

apple orchard

WILDLIFE MANAGEMENT AREA

Stevensville and 7.5 miles past Victor. The intersection has a flashing yellow light and a sign to Pinesdale and Corvallis. Turn left (east) and continue 2 miles to the Eastside Highway (Highway 269) in Corvallis. Turn right and drive 2.5 miles south to Hamilton Heights Road. Turn left and go 5 miles east to the trailhead parking lot at the end of the road. The last half mile is on a dirt road.

From Hamilton, drive 4 miles north to Woodside Cutoff Road on the right (east). Continue with the directions above.

The hike

Pass the trailhead kiosk; walk through private land on a quarter-mile access road. Head east in the foothills of the Sapphire Mountains. At a huge granite outcrop, enter the Calf Creek Wildlife Management Area by a trail split. Veer left and head north through the open sagebrush and native grasslands with scattered outcrops. Loop around a hill with expansive vistas across the Bitterroot Valley and the Bitterroot Mountains.

At an open metal gate, leave the main trail and begin the loop to the left on a footpath. Follow a minor ridge with views of the rolling terrain and mountains. Skirt the east side of a knoll lined with ponderosa pines. Descend to a T-junction on the north-facing slope of Stuart Canyon. Bear right, directly across the canyon from a massive rock mountain. Traverse the south wall of the canyon, slowly losing elevation. Make a horseshoe left bend, and cross a seasonal tributary of Stuart Creek. Cross transient Stuart Creek, and climb through the pine-dotted grassland.

At the north boundary fence, curve right and parallel the north end of the wildlife area. Cross the flower-filled meadow with views into the Gibbons Creek drainage on the left. Gently curve right to a junction with a two-track trail. Bend to the right and walk a quarter mile to an unsigned footpath on the right. Bear sharply right and descend as the path fades in and out. Cross a draw to a distinct trail and bear left. Follow the slope of the draw to a two-track trail and stay to the left. Weave down the hill to a T-junction. Bear right and continue downhill, completing the loop by the metal gate. Follow the wide trail for a little under one mile back to the trailhead. ■

80. Hieronymus Park

Hiking distance: 1.5-mile loop plus 1.8-mile optional spur
Hiking time: 45 minutes to 1.5 hours
Elevation gain: level
Maps: U.S.G.S. Hamilton North
      City of Hamilton: Heironymus Park map

map
page 213

Heironymus Park sits at the northern edge of Hamilton along the Bitterroot River. The wetland park occupies 66 acres of floodplain along the east bank of the river, including 1,200 feet of river frontage. Within the park are grassy fields, lush riparian shrubs, and riverfront stands of ponderosa pine and cottonwoods. The Corvallis Canal, an old but active irrigation ditch, fronts the park. Across the canal on the southeast corner of the park is a six-acre pond. The loop trail mainly circumscribes the park. It follows the canal, circles the fishing pond, explores the river, and meanders through the wetlands. Bald eagles can be spotted perched in the riverfront cottonwoods. Along the trail are interpretive panels describing native wildlife and the area's history, including the Salish Indian culture and how they helped Lewis and Clark in the Bitterroot Valley.

To the trailhead

From Missoula, drive 23 miles south on Highway 93 to the north end of Hamilton. Turn right (west) on Bitterroot Plaza Drive by the Bitterroot River Inn. Go one block west to Hieronymus Park Drive. Turn left and drive 0.1 mile, passing the park entrance sign to the grassy parking area at the northeast corner of the park.

From Main Street in downtown Hamilton, drive 1.3 miles north on Highway 93 to Bitterroot Plaza Drive on the left (west). Continue with the directions above.

The hike

Walk south across the grassland to Corvallis Canal by the prominent lush vegetation. Follow the levee between the canal on the left and the grassy wetlands on the right. Pass a side path on the right that leads into the meadow, our return route. Continue upstream to a wooden bridge on the left, with great views of the Bitterroot Mountains to the west. Detour left and cross the bridge over Corvallis Canal to a large pond and a T-junction. Begin the loop around the pond to the right. Walk between the pond and the canal, crossing a plank bridge over the outlet stream. At the far end of the pond is a peninsula. A path leads out to two picnic tables on the point. The main path circles the pond, crossing a two-plank bridge over the inlet stream. Complete the loop and cross back over the bridge.

Bear left (south) and continue along the Corvallis Canal to a raised path by a metal culvert. Go to the right across the elevated path at the park's southern boundary. Enter a grove of cottonwoods, aspens, and scattered ponderosa pines along the banks of the Bitterroot River. Follow the river downstream, passing small pocket beaches and interpretive panels. Wooden posts and a trail junction mark the park's north boundary.

For an optional spur trail, the path along the river continues 0.9 miles beyond the park and follows the river to Silver Bridge, where Highway 93 crosses over the Bitterroot River. Or to stay within the park, take the footpath to the right into the riparian vegetation. Weave through the grassland, dodging the marshes, and return to Corvallis Canal to complete the loop. ■

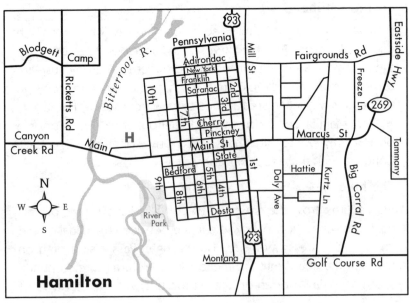

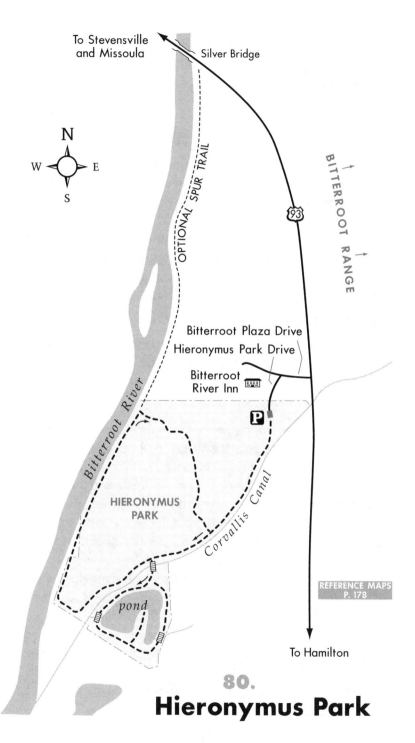

To Stevensville
and Missoula

Silver Bridge

N
W • E
S

OPTIONAL SPUR TRAIL

BITTERROOT RANGE

93

Bitterroot Plaza Drive
Hieronymus Park Drive

Bitterroot River

Bitterroot
River Inn

P

HIERONYMUS
PARK

Corvallis Canal

pond

REFERENCE MAPS
P. 178

To Hamilton

80.
Hieronymus Park

81. River Park

Hiking distance: 1.5 miles round trip
Hiking time: 45 minutes
Elevation gain: level
Maps: U.S.G.S. Hamilton South

River Park is located in the town of Hamilton along the Bitterroot River. The 65-acre park contains floodplain forest, riparian riverfront, quiet sloughs, and grasslands. Wide paved paths and narrow foot trails weave through the park, exploring the varied terrain, while sweeping views of the Bitterroot Mountains lie to the west. The park offers excellent bird watching, including nesting great horned owls and osprey. Moose are frequently seen in the park. During the summer, paths wander along the old oxbows at the southern end of the park.

To the trailhead

From Missoula, drive 24 miles south on Highway 93 to the town of Hamilton. Turn right on Main Street and drive 0.6 miles to 9th Street. Turn left and go 0.2 miles to the parking lot on the right.

The hike

Walk into the park on the paved path. Cross over a stream to a T-junction at a slough near the Bitterroot River. Bear left and parallel the slough to a trail fork. The paved path continues along the slough and wetlands, exiting the park at Desta and 8th Streets.

Return to the trail fork and take the dirt path. Cross the arched bridge over the creek to a trail split. Begin the loop to the left, and meander through cottonwoods, willows, and aspen. The path ends at a creek. Return 20 yards and go to the left to the Bitterroot River. Curve right and follow the river downstream, with a wide panorama of the Bitterroot Mountains. Curve right and weave through the forest back to the bridge.

Cross the bridge and return left to the first junction. Continue straight ahead on the paved path while following the course of the river. The pavement ends by wood posts at the park boundary. The dirt path continues along the river through the Fox property and leads to a parking lot on Main Street. ∎

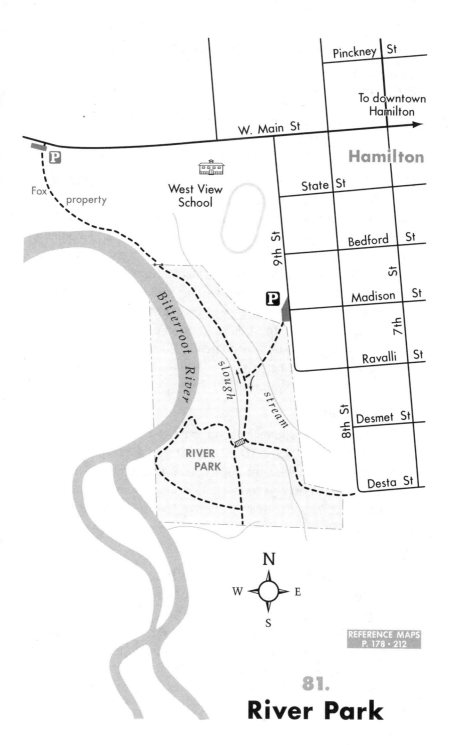

Pinckney St

To downtown
Hamilton

W. Main St

Hamilton

Fox property

West View
School

State St

9th St

Bedford St

7th St

Madison St

7th

Ravalli St

Bitterroot River

slough

stream

8th St

Desmet St

RIVER
PARK

Desta St

N

W ←◇→ E

S

REFERENCE MAPS
P. 178 · 212

81.
River Park

82. Blodgett Canyon to the waterfall

Hiking distance: 7 miles round trip
Hiking time: 3.5 hours
Elevation gain: 600 feet
Maps: U.S.G.S. Hamilton North and Printz Ridge
U.S.F.S. Selway Bitterroot Wilderness
Beartooth Publishing: Missoula, Hamilton, Lost Trail Pass

Blodgett Canyon is named for Joseph Blodgett, a settler who lived along the creek in the late 1860s. It is considered the most picturesque of the Bitterroot's many canyons. The vertical cliffs and jagged peaks of Printz Ridge to the north and Romney Ridge to the south rise nearly 4,000 feet from the canyon floor. Blodgett Creek snakes 19 miles through the deep, glacially carved canyon under stands of ponderosa pine, lodgepole pine, and fir. The creek alternates between wide, clear pools and turbulent whitewater cascades. The trail follows an easy elevation grade and is well-maintained. It winds nearly 20 miles up the canyon and into Idaho over Blodgett Pass. This hike includes the first 3.5 miles of the trail to a waterfall.

To the trailhead

From Missoula, drive 43 miles south on Highway 93 to the town of Hamilton. Turn right (west) on Main Street, and drive 1.2 miles to Ricketts Road on the right. Turn right and continue 0.5 miles to Blodgett Camp Road and turn left. Continue 2.4 miles to a junction with Road 736. Turn right and drive 1.5 miles to the Blodgett Creek trailhead parking area at road's end in the campground.

The hike

Walk back along the road, crossing Blodgett Creek to the trailhead on the right. Head west into the mouth of the canyon along the south side of the creek. The trail gently rises and dips, crossing talus slopes to a wide, clear pool at one mile. At 1.5 miles, views open to the sheer granite cliffs with jagged spires that reach three-quarters of a mile above the trail. The trail parallels Blodgett Creek upstream, and crosses a sturdy bridge over the creek at 2.5 miles. Along the way, Nez Perce Buttress, Blackfoot

Dome, Shoshone Spire, and Flathead Buttress tower over the canyon on the right. Continue heading west as the trail levels out and the canyon widens. One mile past the bridge, ascend a short hill to the waterfall and its deep pool. House-size boulders can be used to recline upon and relax. ■

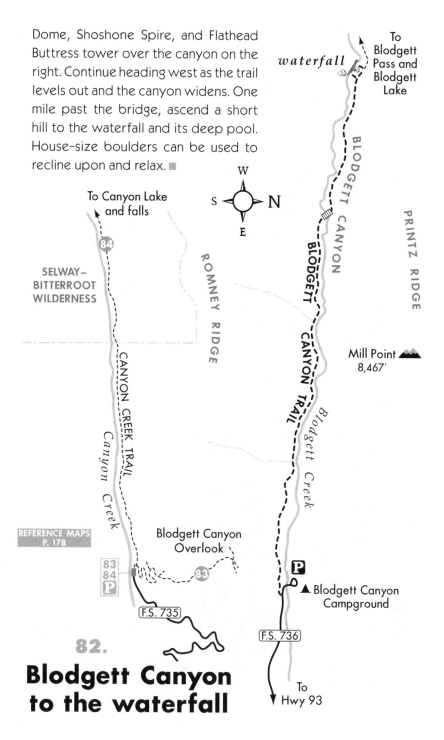

waterfall

To Blodgett Pass and Blodgett Lake

BLODGETT CANYON

PRINTZ RIDGE

W
S — N
E

To Canyon Lake and falls

84

SELWAY–
BITTERROOT
WILDERNESS

ROMNEY RIDGE

BLODGETT CANYON TRAIL

Mill Point ▲▲
8,467'

CANYON CREEK TRAIL

Canyon Creek

Blodgett Creek

REFERENCE MAPS
P. 178

Blodgett Canyon
Overlook

83

83
84
P

F.S. 735

P

▲ Blodgett Canyon
Campground

F.S. 736

82.

Blodgett Canyon
to the waterfall

To
Hwy 93

83. Blodgett Canyon Overlook
FIRE ECOLOGY INTERPRETIVE TRAIL

Hiking distance: 3 miles round trip
Hiking time: 1.5 hours
Elevation gain: 400 feet
Maps: U.S.G.S. Hamilton North
U.S.F.S. Selway Bitterroot Wilderness
Beartooth Publishing: Missoula, Hamilton, Lost Trail Pass

The Blodgett Canyon Overlook is a spectacular site on an exposed rocky ridge. The overlook includes awesome vistas into Blodgett Canyon, the massive vertical walls surrounding the canyon, the Canyon Creek drainage, the Bitterroot Valley, the town of Hamilton, and the Sapphire Mountains. All of these views are afforded with relatively little elevation gain. This stunning hike begins at Canyon Creek and leads north up to the overlook atop Romney Ridge, dividing Blodgett Canyon from Canyon Creek. Benches are provided at the various lookout points.

The Fire Ecology Interpretive Trail describes the effects of the Blodgett Fire of 2000. The fire burned 11,486 acres in Blodgett Canyon and the Canyon Creek drainage. An interpretive pamphlet is available at the Forest Service office, located at the north end of Hamilton on Highway 93.

To the trailhead

From Missoula, drive 43 miles south on Highway 93 to the town of Hamilton. Turn right (west) on Main Street and drive 1.2 miles to Ricketts Road on the right. Turn right and continue 0.5 miles to Blodgett Camp Road and turn left. Continue 2.4 miles to a junction with Road 735. Turn left and drive 2.8 miles to the Canyon Creek trailhead parking area at road's end.

The hike

From the parking area, head 25 yards west up the Canyon Creek Trail (Hike 84) to a junction. Take the signed right fork and head north. Follow the rock-lined path at a gradual uphill grade, with the cascading sounds of Canyon Creek below. Traverse

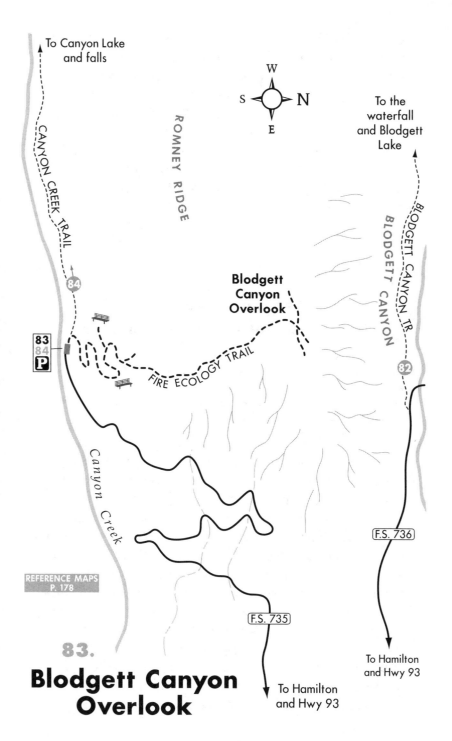

To Canyon Lake
and falls

W — N
S ✦ E

To the
waterfall
and Blodgett
Lake

ROMNEY RIDGE

CANYON CREEK TRAIL

84

83
84
P

Blodgett
Canyon
Overlook

FIRE ECOLOGY TRAIL

BLODGETT CANYON TR

BLODGETT CANYON

82

Canyon Creek

REFERENCE MAPS
P. 178

F.S. 736

F.S. 735

To Hamilton
and Hwy 93

83.
Blodgett Canyon
Overlook

To Hamilton
and Hwy 93

the southeast-facing canyon wall with the aid of switchbacks. Continue through a forest of ponderosa pines, with views up the Canyon Creek drainage. Pass a bench perched on cliffs at an overlook of the Bitterroot Valley and the Sapphire Mountains. At signpost 4 is a junction. Detour 20 yards to the left to an overlook of forested Canyon Creek. Back on the main route, the trail levels off and passes through the burn area from the Bitterroot fires of 2000. At 1.5 miles, the path reaches the cliffs atop Romney Ridge at the Blodgett Canyon Overlook. Benches are placed at overlooks along the way. At trail's end, there are many lookout points and ledges among the jagged peaks. Return along the same trail. ■

84. Canyon Creek Trail to Canyon Falls and Canyon Lake

Hiking distance: 7—9 miles round trip
Hiking time: 3.5 hours to pool; 4.5 hours to lake
Elevation gain: 1,400—2,400 feet
Maps: U.S.G.S. Hamilton North, Printz Ridge, Ward Mountain
U.S.F.S. Selway Bitterroot Wilderness map
Beartooth Publishing: Missoula, Hamilton, Lost Trail Pass

The headwaters of Canyon Creek form in the Bitterroots at Canyon Peak directly west of Hamilton. Three connecting lakes lie below Canyon Peak in a gorgeous glacial cirque beneath the shadow of the 9,153-foot peak. Just below the third lake, Canyon Creek drops 200 feet off the rocky cliffs in a spectacu-lar cascade called Canyon Falls. The Canyon Creek Trail follows the north side of the creek to the falls and continues to East Lake and Canyon Lake in the canyon's upper reaches, 5.5 miles from the trailhead. This hike includes the first four miles of the trail to an overlook of Canyon Falls. The creek can be heard through the deep, quiet forest but only approaches its banks occasionally. The trail moderately gains elevation along Canyon Creek until a half mile before the falls, where the path steeply climbs several hundred feet in elevation to the lake at 7,300 feet.

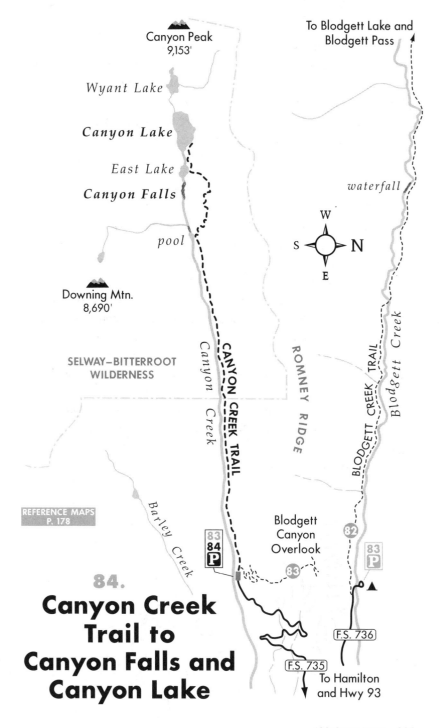

Canyon Peak
9,153'

To Blodgett Lake and
Blodgett Pass

Wyant Lake

Canyon Lake

East Lake

Canyon Falls

waterfall

pool

W
S ✦ N
E

Downing Mtn.
8,690'

Canyon Creek

CANYON CREEK TRAIL

ROMNEY RIDGE

BLODGETT CREEK TRAIL

Blodgett Creek

SELWAY–BITTERROOT
WILDERNESS

REFERENCE MAPS
P. 178

Barley Creek

83
84
P

Blodgett
Canyon
Overlook

83

82

83
P

84.
Canyon Creek
Trail to
Canyon Falls and
Canyon Lake

F.S. 736

F.S. 735

To Hamilton
and Hwy 93

To the trailhead

From Missoula, drive 43 miles south on Highway 93 to the town of Hamilton. Turn right (west) on Main Street and drive 1.2 miles to Ricketts Road on the right. Turn right and continue 0.5 miles to Blodgett Camp Road and turn left. Continue 2.4 miles to a junction with Road 735. Turn left and drive 2.8 miles to the Canyon Creek trailhead parking area at road's end.

The hike

Hike west past the Forest Service information board. In a few yards, pass the Blodgett Canyon Overlook Trail on the right (Hike 83). Stroll through the thick forest at a moderate grade. Thick tree roots reach across the trail along with stable, well-seated rocks. Enter the Selway–Bitterroot Wilderness at 1.8 miles and continue up canyon. At 3.5 miles, a side path on the left leads to a small but beautiful cascade with a clear pool. It is a wonderful spot to rest. The trail heads away from Canyon Creek and steeply climbs up several switchbacks for a half mile. The long cascade of Canyon Falls will become prominent as the clearing draws near. Although they are not visible from this elevation, East Lake and Canyon Lake sit above the falls.

To extend the hike, climb above the falls another half mile, skirting the north side of East Lake in a meadow. Follow the stream to the northwest shore of Canyon Lake in an alpine setting surrounded by steep rock walls. ■

85. Lake Como

Hiking distance: 8-mile loop
Hiking time: 4 hours
Elevation gain: 60 feet
Maps: U.S.G.S. Darby and Como Peaks
      Beartooth Publishing: Missoula, Hamilton, Lost Trail Pass

**map
page 225**

Lake Como is a premier recreation destination between Hamilton and Darby. The lake, the largest in the Bitterroots, was named by Father Ravalli for the Lake Como in his native country, Italy. The 906-acre, manmade lake lies in a gorgeous glacial basin at 4,245 feet beneath the stunning granite spires of Como Peaks. The lake area was a major trading and gathering site for the Salish, Kootenai, and Pend d'Oreilles Indians, who called it *In-Pa-Neh-T-Koo* (*Lake of the White Moose*). Rock Creek, Little Rock Creek, and several seasonal streams feed the earth-dammed lake, which supplies irrigation water to the Bitterroot Valley. Amenities include campgrounds, picnic areas, a protected swimming beach, a boat launch, and multi-use trails. This 8-mile loop combines a paved interpretive trail with a hiking-biking-equestrian route around the perimeter of the lake. At the far west end of the lake, a bridge crosses Rock Creek to Como Falls, a raging waterfall that empties into Lake Como. Just beyond the waterfall is the Selway-Bitterroot Wilderness.

To the trailhead

From Missoula, drive 56 miles south on Highway 93 to Lake Como Road/County Road 82. It is located 12.5 miles south of the town of Hamilton and 4 miles north of Darby. Turn right (south) and drive 2.8 miles to a road fork. Curve right on Forest Service Road 5623, and continue 0.9 miles to the parking lot on the left. Additional day-use parking lots are located 0.25 miles and 0.4 miles ahead on the left. A parking fee is required.

The hike

From the first parking lot and sandy beach, climb steps to an overlook of Lake Como and the Como Peaks. Head west along the north side of the lake, and follow the path through a picnic area, walking parallel to the park road. Enter the campground and a second day-use parking lot to the interpretive trail. Follow the paved path perched on the hillside above the lake, passing six interpretive panels about the natural history of the area. The National Recreation Trail #502 begins where the paved path ends. Take the dirt trail into the ponderosa pine forest. The views constantly change of the lake, canyons, and surrounding peaks. Across the lake, the waterfall and whitewater of Little Rock Creek can be seen cascading into the lake. Cross over a couple of seasonal streams, and enter a rock-strewn meadow with glacial erratics.

Near the west end of Lake Como, rock-hop over a stream by a small waterfall. Continue 250 yards to a posted junction. Rock Creek Trail #580 continues straight ahead and follows Rock Creek into the Selway-Bitterroot Wilderness to Elk Lake. Bear left and descend, crossing a wooden bridge over the raging whitewater of Rock Creek in a vertical rock gorge at the west tip of the lake. Climb a small slope, and detour 20 yards on a side path on the right to an overlook of Como Falls (also called Rock Creek Falls).

Return to the main trail, and cross a slab of exposed bedrock. Veer right onto the trail, overlooking the 3.2-mile length of Lake Como. Cross a series of trickling streams through a forest of young pines regenerated from the 1988 Little Rock Creek Fire that burned 2,400 acres. Curve around a small bay, and cross two single-log bridges over two forks of Little Rock Creek. Continue along the south shore, passing the trail to Little Rock Creek Lake. Weave in and out of the forest, with continual views of the lake and mountains. At the southeast corner of the lake, drop down to the boat launch area and dam. Cross the road to the dam, and follow the dirt path across the top of the dam. The overflow spillway exits below. Cross a bridge over the Rock Creek Spillway to the northeast shore, completing the loop. ∎

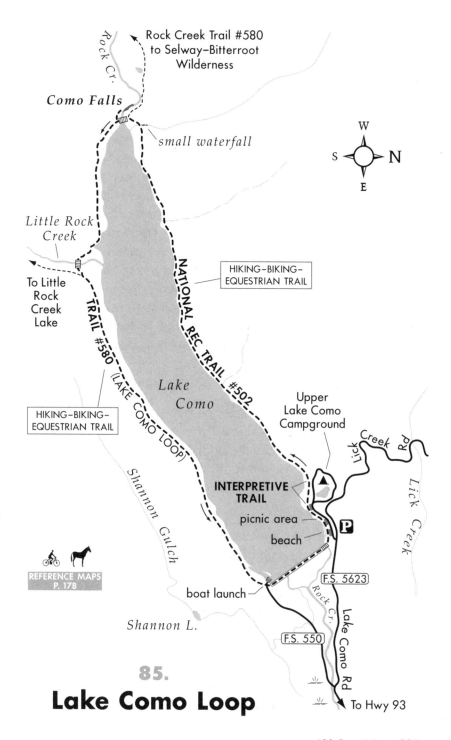

Rock Creek Trail #580
to Selway–Bitterroot
Wilderness

Rock Cr.

Como Falls

small waterfall

W
S   N
E

*Little Rock
Creek*

To Little
Rock
Creek
Lake

NATIONAL REC TRAIL #502

HIKING–BIKING–
EQUESTRIAN TRAIL

TRAIL #580 (LAKE COMO LOOP)

*Lake
Como*

HIKING–BIKING–
EQUESTRIAN TRAIL

Upper
Lake Como
Campground

Lick Creek Rd

Lick Creek

Shannon Gulch

INTERPRETIVE
TRAIL

picnic area

beach

P

REFERENCE MAPS
P. 178

boat launch

Shannon L.

F.S. 5623

Rock Cr.

Lake Como Rd

F.S. 550

To Hwy 93

85.
Lake Como Loop

86. Valley of the Moon Nature Trail

Hiking distance: 0.5-mile double loop
Hiking time: 40 minutes
Elevation gain: level
Maps: U.S.G.S. Iris Point

Rock Creek, a tributary of the Clark Fork River, flows out of the Welcome Creek Wilderness in the Sapphire Mountain Range. The creek flows 52 miles northwest through beautiful Rock Creek Valley amid rocky bluffs, green pastures, and mountain ranges rising up along both sides of the valley. Rock Creek offers blue ribbon trout fishing with healthy populations of browns, cutthroat, rainbow, and bull trout. The scenic valley also offers horseback riding, wildlife viewing, bird watching, and hiking. Valley of the Moon Nature Trail (formerly called Rock Creek Nature Trail) is a short interpretive trail with ten information stations. The panels describe the lush creekside habitat and wildlife. The hike weaves through the lush riparian area among cottonwoods, alders, willows, and hawthorns.

To the trailhead

From Missoula, drive 21 miles east on I-90 to Rock Creek Road/Exit 126. Turn right and continue 2.2 miles to the posted trailhead turnoff. Turn right and cross the bridge over Rock Creek. Drive a quarter mile and curve right to the trailhead parking lot on the right.

The hike

Cross the bridge over a wetland to the banks of a channel of Rock Creek. Bear left on a boardwalk and curve right, crossing another bridge over the creek to a junction. Begin the first loop on the right fork, leaving the boardwalk to a forested footpath. A side path on the right leads 20 yards to an overlook of the creek. The main trail curves left into a meadow with a bench. Pass the meadow into a cottonwood forest and a Y-fork. The right fork crosses a third bridge to another trail split, forming a loop. Veer right along the old slough where Rock Creek used to flow. Follow the slough to the west bank of Rock Creek. Go to the left along the creek, completing the loop at the bridge. Cross the bridge to the Y-fork and continue to the right. Curve left, completing the second loop at the bridge. ■

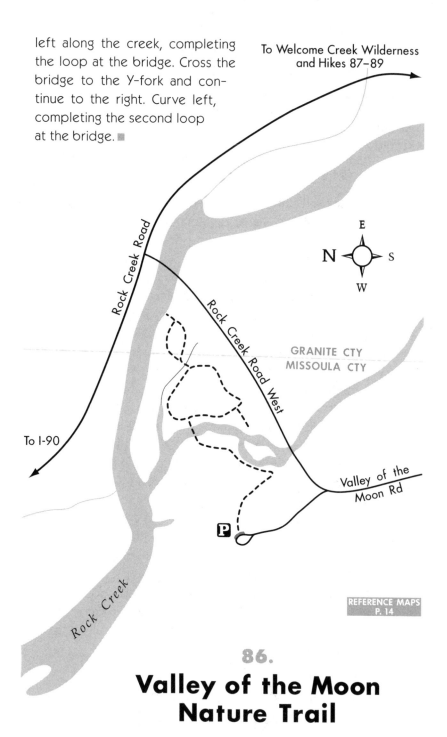

To Welcome Creek Wilderness and Hikes 87–89

Rock Creek Road

Rock Creek Road West

GRANITE CTY
MISSOULA CTY

To I-90

Valley of the Moon Rd

P

Rock Creek

REFERENCE MAPS
P. 14

86.
Valley of the Moon Nature Trail

87. Babcock Creek Trail to Mormon Spring

Hiking distance: 7 miles round trip to Mormon Spring
8 miles round trip to Burnt Mountain saddle
Hiking time: 4—5 hours
Elevation gain: 1,700 feet to Mormon Spring
2,100 feet to Burnt Mountain saddle
Maps: U.S.G.S. Iris Point and Ravenna

map
page 230

Babcock Creek, a tributary of Spring Creek, is located in the Rock Creek drainage of the Sapphire Mountains. The creek's headwaters begin at Mormon Spring and Horse Pasture Spring, then flow through a narrow canyon on the southern base of Babcock Mountain. The Babcock Creek Trail drops into Babcock Canyon and follows the creek up canyon through a conifer forest with riparian vegetation. The hike traverses talus slopes, crosses the creek numerous times, passes overlooks, and leads to Mormon Spring in a flower-filled meadow. From the spring, the trail climbs the west slope of Burnt Mountain to a ridge with far-reaching views of the Sapphire Range.

The Babcock Creek Trail actually begins on the Spring Creek Trail. The outdated USGS topo maps show the Spring Creek Trail zippering up the mountain from Spring Creek to the ridge, connecting with the Babcock Creek Trail. Unfortunately, the Spring Creek Trail no longer exists up the mountain, so this hike cannot be made into a loop.

The Babcock Creek Trail is closed from April 15 through June 7 to protect the bighorn sheep from human disturbance during the lambing season. In 1979, 26 bighorn sheep were transplanted from Flathead Lakes Wildhorse Island. Currently, the Lower Rock Creek herd of Bighorn sheep numbers about 150 animals. They roam across 8,000 acres, from Brewster Creek to the Clark Fork River, and can often be spotted from the trail along the rocky cliffs and grassy slopes.

To the trailhead

From Missoula, drive 21 miles east on I-90 to the Rock Creek Road/Exit 126. Turn right and continue 6.2 miles to the posted trailhead parking area on the left at mile marker 6. There is also a parking area on the right.

The hike

Head east, passing the bighorn sheep information kiosk. Walk through the open lodgepole pine forest on a private ranch land easement for a quarter mile. Climb a small rise to a meadow above the south bank of Spring Creek. Cross over the top of the creek to a signed fork at the mouth of Spring Creek Canyon. The right fork leads up Spring Creek Canyon, staying close to the creek. (For a side hike up Spring Creek, see the trail details below.)

For this hike, follow the "trail" sign to the left. Ascend the north canyon slope beneath vertical rock cliffs. Curve right and traverse the west-facing slope of the mountain while enjoying the great views of Rock Creek Canyon. Cross a few talus slopes, and drop into the Babcock Creek drainage. Head up the canyon bottom, following the south side of Babcock Creek. Cross over the creek, then steadily climb up the lush, forested drainage. Cross the creek a few more times as the canyon narrows. At 3 miles, the canyon and trail bend right (east). Follow the watercourse into a meadow to Mormon Spring on the right at 3.5 miles. The spring runs through a pipe into a watering trough. This is the turnaround spot for a 7-mile round-trip hike.

To continue, hike uphill and ascend the steep west slope of Burnt Mountain, gaining over 400 feet in the next 0.3 miles. Cross an old grass-covered road and continue ascending, passing side paths on the right. The main trail curves right and the steep grade eases up. Traverse the hillside to the ridge on a 5,914-foot saddle at 4 miles. The USGS map shows a trail continuing west across the ridge, skirting four knolls before descending into Spring Creek. This route no longer exists and is not recommended. Instead, return along the same route.

SIDE HIKE 1: The Spring Creek Trail has been abandoned and is difficult to locate. However, a segment of the path does continue from the junction with the Babcock Creek Trail and leads about one mile up Spring Creek Canyon along the drainage. The trail weaves along the canyon floor through lush riparian vegetation in a shaded canopy and across talus fields. En route are gorgeous multi-colored rock cliffs and talus slopes.

SIDE HIKE 2: Across Rock Creek Road, the Solomon Ridge Trail heads a quarter mile west to the banks of Rock Creek. The creek is wide and deep and is not safe to ford. The area is beautiful and fishermen paths meander through the forested meadows. Across the river, the Solomon Ridge Trail continues 9 miles to a junction with the Bitterroot Divide Trail. ■

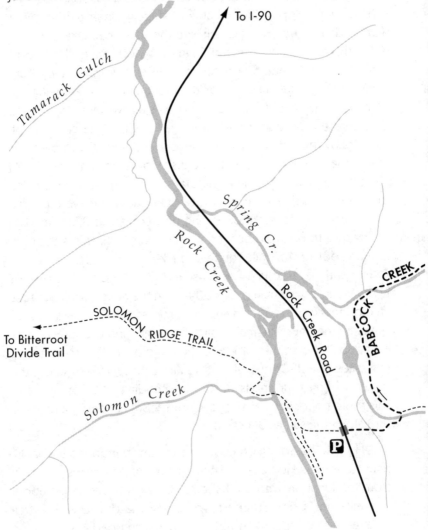

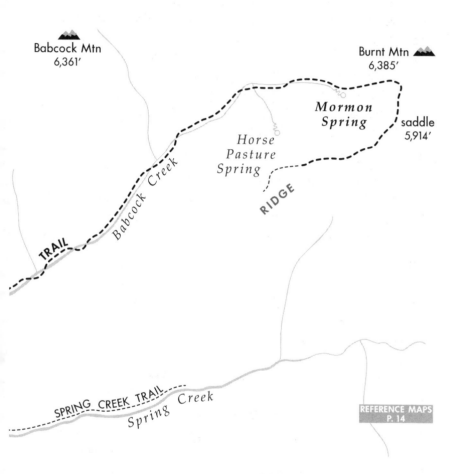

Babcock Mtn
6,361'

Burnt Mtn
6,385'

Mormon Spring

Horse Pasture Spring

saddle
5,914'

Babcock Creek

TRAIL

RIDGE

SPRING CREEK TRAIL

Spring Creek

REFERENCE MAPS
P. 14

87.
Babcock Creek Trail to Mormon Spring

88. Grizzly Creek Trail

Hiking distance: 6.4 miles round trip
Hiking time: 3 hours
Elevation gain: 1,000 feet
Maps: U.S.G.S. Grizzly Point and Spink Point
      U.S.F.S. Lolo National Forest

The Grizzly Creek Trail is a beautiful but seldom hiked trail with a deep wilderness atmosphere. The Grizzly Creek drainage is located southeast of Missoula adjacent to the 28,000-acre Welcome Creek Wilderness in the Sapphire Mountains, part of the Lolo National Forest. The remote creek is a tributary of Ranch Creek, which joins the tumbling waters of Rock Creek a mile down canyon. This trail begins at the base of Grizzly Point and heads into the canyon along Grizzly Creek.

To the trailhead

From Missoula, drive 21 miles east on I-90 to Rock Creek Road/ Exit 126. Turn right and continue 11.4 miles to the Ranch Creek Road junction on the left. Turn left and drive 0.8 miles to the Grizzly Creek trailhead parking area on the left.

The hike

Head east past the buck fence, and immediately enter the mouth of Grizzly Canyon. Grizzly Creek flows down canyon along the south side of the trail. The canyon begins to narrow at 0.5 miles. At 0.75 miles is the first of six creek crossings. There are no bridges, but the creek is narrow; wade or rock-hop across the creek. The second crossing is at one mile. The trail continues gently but steadily up the narrow canyon. At 2.6 miles, after the fifth creek crossing, Drake Gulch enters the canyon from the north. Thereafter, the gradient steepens. At 3.2 miles, the trail leaves the creek and climbs northeast up the mountainside between Spink Point and Sliderock Mountain. This is our turn-around point.

To extend the hike, the trail zigzags up the mountain to dirt roads which link several old mines on the southwest slope of Sliderock Mountain. ■

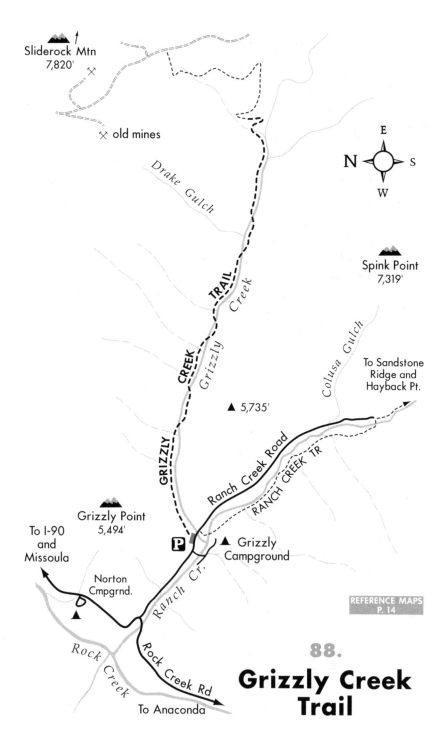

Sliderock Mtn
7,820'

✕ old mines

Drake Gulch

N E S W

Spink Point
7,319'

Grizzly Creek

GRIZZLY CREEK TRAIL

Colusa Gulch

To Sandstone
Ridge and
Hayback Pt.

▲ 5,735'

Ranch Creek Road

RANCH CREEK TR

Grizzly Point
5,494'

P

▲ Grizzly
Campground

To I-90
and
Missoula

Norton
Cmpgrnd.

Ranch Cr.

▲

Rock Creek

Rock Creek Rd

To Anaconda

REFERENCE MAPS
P. 14

88.
Grizzly Creek Trail

89. Welcome Creek Trail

Hiking distance: 5 miles round trip
Hiking time: 2.5 hours
Elevation gain: 500 feet
Maps: U.S.G.S. Grizzly Point and Cleveland Mountain
U.S.F.S. Lolo National Forest

The Welcome Creek Trail lies along the northern Sapphire Mountains in the 28,135-acre Welcome Creek Wilderness, the smallest designated wilderness area in Montana. The remote trail in the Rock Creek drainage enters a quiet, narrow canyon through an old-growth forest, passing 1900s-era gold mining ruins and abandoned log cabins. An Indiana Jones-style suspension bridge at the beginning of this hike makes the Welcome Creek Trail a hike long remembered. The suspension bridge crosses high over Rock Creek and a white sand beach below. The entire Welcome Creek Trail climbs 7.5 miles to the rocky divide near Cleveland Mountain. This hike takes in the first 2.5 miles to the confluence with Cinnabar Creek.

To the trailhead

From Missoula, drive 21 miles east on I-90 to Rock Creek Road/ Exit 126. Turn right and continue 14 miles to the Welcome Creek trailhead parking area on the right.

The hike

Cross the suspension bridge to the north side of Rock Creek, and head right. A short spur trail leads to the sandy beach at the base of the bridge. The trail follows Rock Creek a short distance downstream to a log bridge over Welcome Creek. After crossing, take the trail to the left (west), heading up canyon through groves of Douglas fir, spruce, and old-growth pines. Cross several boulder fields separated by dense forest. Watch for nettle plants, which cause exposed legs to tingle. At two miles, cross another log bridge over Welcome Creek. Just past the crossing is Cinnabar Cabin and Cinnabar Creek, the turn-around point.

To extend the hike, the trail continues another 5 miles to Cleveland Mountain at 7,200 feet and the Bitterroot Divide.

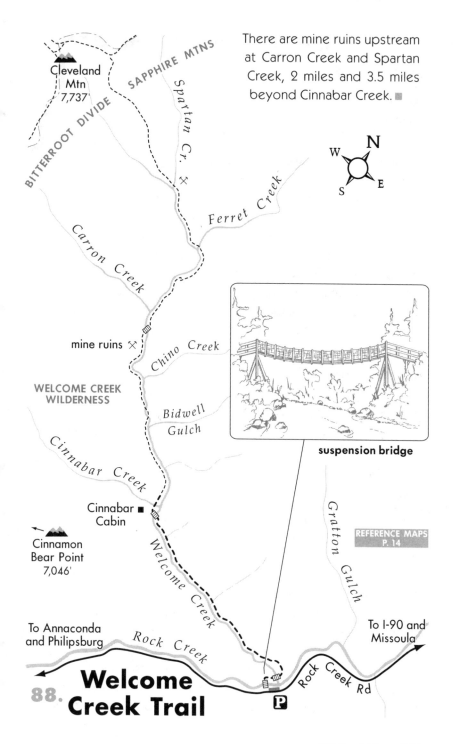

There are mine ruins upstream at Carron Creek and Spartan Creek, 2 miles and 3.5 miles beyond Cinnabar Creek. ■

Cleveland Mtn 7,737'

SAPPHIRE MTNS

BITTERROOT DIVIDE

Spartan Cr.

Ferret Creek

Carron Creek

N
W   E
S

mine ruins ✕

Chino Creek

WELCOME CREEK WILDERNESS

Bidwell Gulch

suspension bridge

Cinnabar Creek

Cinnabar Cabin

Cinnamon Bear Point 7,046'

Welcome Creek

Gratton Gulch

REFERENCE MAPS P. 14

To Annaconda and Philipsburg

Rock Creek

To I-90 and Missoula

Rock Creek Rd

88. **Welcome Creek Trail**

P

90. Beavertail Hill State Park

Hiking distance: 1-mile loop
Hiking time: 30 minutes
Elevation gain: level
Maps: U.S.G.S. Ravenna
       Beavertail Hill State Park Interpretive Trail map

Beavertail Hill State Park is a small 65-acre gem located 26 miles east of Missoula. The park fronts the Clark Fork River with camping and fishing sites. A one-mile, self-guided interpretive trail was developed by Montana Fish, Wildlife and Parks. The park was named after the hill to the west, which was originally shaped like a beaver. Interstate 90 was built, chopping off the tail of the formation. The trail weaves through forests, prairies, wetlands, and riparian habitats. An interpretive brochure describes the history of the area and its natural features, including wildlife, insects, and the surrounding vegetation. The area is also a spring and summer habitat for moose.

To the trailhead

From Missoula, drive 26 miles east on I-90 to Beavertail Road/ Exit 130. Turn right and continue 0.4 miles south to the posted state park entrance. Turn left and park in the pullouts on the right. There is additional parking 50 yards ahead by the information kiosk.

The hike

Take the posted trail on the left (north) through the grasslands dotted with cottonwoods and ponderosa pines. Head northeast on a historic Milwaukee Railroad bed built in 1883. Enter the campground and walk to the banks of the Clark Fork River. Continue downstream through the pine forest, curving away from the river through the campground. Cross the campground road, and pass through a trail gate to the banks of the river. Notice the conical-shaped beaver lodges along the riverbanks and the great blue heron nests high in the cottonwood trees. Follow the edge of the river and pass through a second gate, returning to the forest. Weave through the prairie, and pass a wetland area by a small waterway on the left, completing the loop at the trailhead. ■

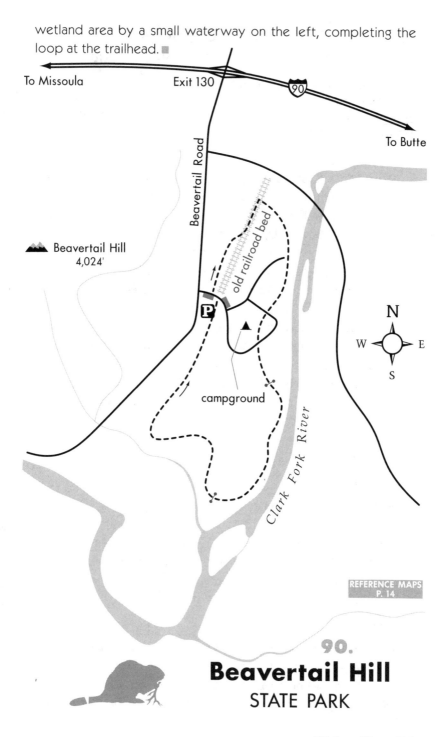

To Missoula

Exit 130

90

To Butte

Beavertail Road

Beavertail Hill
4,024'

old railroad bed

P

▲

campground

Clark Fork River

N
W ◆ E
S

REFERENCE MAPS
P. 14

90.
Beavertail Hill
STATE PARK

91. Whitaker Bridge to Belmont Creek
BLACKFOOT RIVER RECREATIONAL CORRIDOR

Hiking distance: 3.8 miles round trip
Hiking time: 2 hours
Elevation gain: level
Maps: U.S.G.S. Potomac

**map
page 240**

The Blackfoot River runs 130 miles, from the glaciated high-alpine meadows at the Continental Divide near Lincoln to its confluence with the Clark Fork River near the town of Bonner. For centuries, Native American trails paralleled the north bank of the river, followed by wagon roads and railroads. The Nez Perce, Salish, Kootenai, and Shoshone Indians used this valley as a route to hunt buffalo on the eastern plains. Meriwether Lewis and his party of nine men also used this route on their return trip from the Pacific Ocean in July 1806. In the early 1900s, the Big Blackfoot Railroad steamed up and down the canyon, hauling lumber to the mill in Bonner. This hike follows a portion of the abandoned railroad bed from Whitaker Bridge to Belmont Creek along the north side of the Blackfoot River. The creek is one of a few remaining tributaries of the Blackfoot River that still supports spawning bull trout. The trail passes through stands of old-growth ponderosa pine and pristine meadows with views of Red Rock Flat and Goose Rock Flat (Hike 92).

To the trailhead

From Missoula, drive 4 miles east on I-90 to Highway 200 East/Exit 109. Continue 12 miles to Johnsrud Park Road, signed for the Blackfoot Recreation Corridor. Turn left and continue 6.4 miles to Whitaker Bridge. Cross the bridge over the Blackfoot River and immediately turn left into the Whitaker Bridge Day Use Area parking lot.

The hike

Walk back down the road to Whitaker Bridge. Before crossing it, bear left on the footpath. Follow the forested path upstream along the north edge of the river. Curve left up the canyon amongst ponderosa pine and cottonwoods, following the watercourse. The footpath merges with a raised gravel road which was once a railroad bed. As the river makes a sweeping U-shaped bend, the road/trail veers away and out of view of the river. The river views soon emerge again. Across the river is Red Rock Flat, a large meadow surrounded by the forested mountains. Red Rock, a vertical multi-colored formation, rises from the shore of the river. At 0.6 miles, detour off the trail to the right to Red Rock Beach, a popular swimming area in the shadow of the gorgeous formation. Continue northeast on the elevated road, passing fractured red rock outcroppings. The views through the trees reveal Goose Rock Flat across the river. Curve away from the river in a prairie, returning back to the river at 1.6 miles. At the top of another U-shaped river bend, pass berms and descend to Belmont Creek, where the pilings from a washed out train trestle remain. This is our turn-around spot.

To extend the hike, rock-hop or wade across Belmont Creek. In high water, climb up to Johnsrud Park Road and detour around the creek. The trail continues 1.5 miles along the river to the River Bend Fishing Access. ∎

92. Whitaker Bridge to Red Rock Flat and Goose Rock Flat
BLACKFOOT RIVER RECREATIONAL CORRIDOR

Hiking distance: 6 miles round trip
Hiking time: 3 hours
Elevation gain: 150 feet
Maps: U.S.G.S. Potomac

map
page 240

The Blackfoot River Recreational Corridor follows the lower 26 miles of the river from Johnsrud Park to the Russell Gates Fishing Access. The recreational corridor was formed by a partnership between landowners, the Bureau of Land Management, and the Montana Department of Fish, Wildlife and Parks. The glacially carved river valley is known for its scenic beauty, trout fishing, and whitewater rafting. It is among the most popular recreational rivers in Montana, used for fishing, rafting, swimming, camping, and hiking. The Blackfoot River, a tributary of the Clark Fork River, was made famous by the book and movie *A River Runs Through It*. This hike follows the south side of the river, passing through Red Rock Flat and Goose Rock Flat. The trail leads to overlooks of the river and valley, ending in a pristine meadow.

To the trailhead From Missoula, drive 4 miles east on I-90 to Highway 200 East/Exit 109. Continue 12 miles to Johnsrud Park Road, signed for the Blackfoot Recreation Corridor. Turn left and continue 6.4 miles to Whitaker Bridge. Cross the bridge over the Blackfoot River and immediately turn left into the Whitaker Bridge Day Use Area parking lot.

The hike Walk back down the road to Whitaker Bridge. Cross the bridge over the Blackfoot River, and bear left around the vehicle gate. Head up the old dirt road, following the river upstream. Enter the evergreen forest and traverse the hillside high above the river. Steadily climb, passing fractured red rock outcroppings with mossy ledges. Top the slope to vistas of the surrounding mountains and the scenic river. Descend into Red Rock Flat, a lush riverfront plateau at 0.7 miles. The trail cuts away from the river and circles the perimeter of the

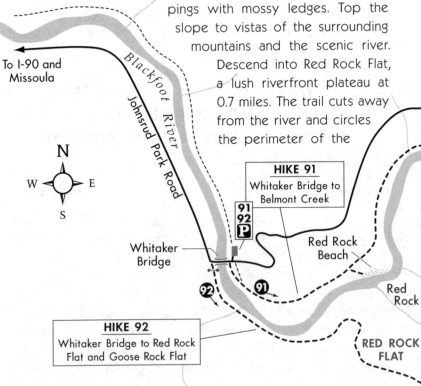

To I-90 and Missoula

Blackfoot River

Johnsrud Park Road

N
W · E
S

HIKE 91
Whitaker Bridge to Belmont Creek

91
92
P

Whitaker Bridge

Red Rock Beach

Red Rock

92

91

HIKE 92
Whitaker Bridge to Red Rock Flat and Goose Rock Flat

RED ROCK FLAT

plateau. A couple of animal/angler paths weave through the flat to the river. Loop around the mountain bowl, where the road is being reclaimed by grass. Stroll through a young pine forest with charred remains from an old fire. Curve left along the base of a mountain ridge separating Red Rock Flat from Goose Rock Flat. Bend around the mountain point, entering Goose Rock Flat at 1.7 miles. Cross the flat through the open forest, and drop down to an unsigned Y-fork at 2.5 miles. The right fork heads uphill and climbs the mountain. Veer left on the grass-covered road. Follow the tree-lined lane to an overlook of the Blackfoot River and Goose Rock. Gradually descend to a quiet meadow, where the trail fades away. Return by retracing your steps. ■

Belmont Creek

Johnsrud Park Road

Blackfoot River

To River Bend
Fishing Access

91

Goose
Rock

GOOSE
ROCK
FLAT

92

REFERENCE MAPS
P. 14

HIKES 91–92
Blackfoot River
Recreational Corridor

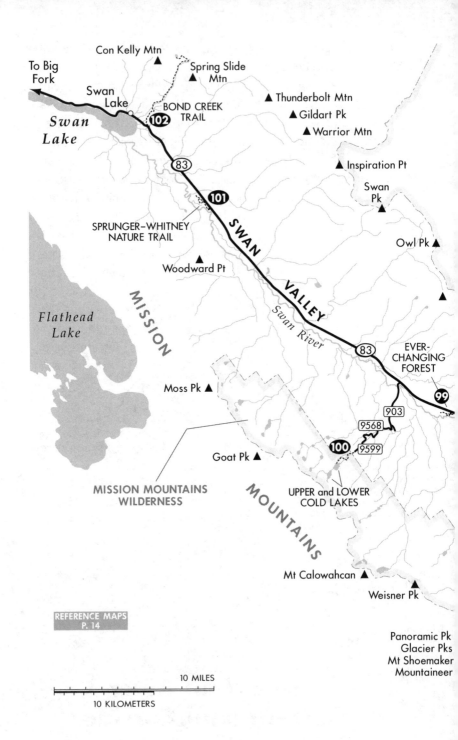

To Big Fork

Swan Lake

Con Kelly Mtn ▲

Spring Slide Mtn

▲ Thunderbolt Mtn

▲ Gildart Pk

▲ Warrior Mtn

Swan Lake

102

BOND CREEK TRAIL

83

101

▲ Inspiration Pt

Swan Pk ▲

SWAN

SPRUNGER–WHITNEY NATURE TRAIL

Woodward Pt ▲

Owl Pk ▲

▲

VALLEY

Swan River

Flathead Lake

MISSION

83

EVER-CHANGING FOREST

99

Moss Pk ▲

903

9568

100   **9599**

Goat Pk ▲

MISSION MOUNTAINS WILDERNESS

UPPER and LOWER COLD LAKES

MOUNTAINS

Mt Calowahcan ▲

▲ Weisner Pk

REFERENCE MAPS P. 14

Panoramic Pk
Glacier Pks
Mt Shoemaker
Mountaineer

10 MILES

10 KILOMETERS

Seeley–Swan Valley

HIGHWAY 83:
Seeley Lake to Swan Lake

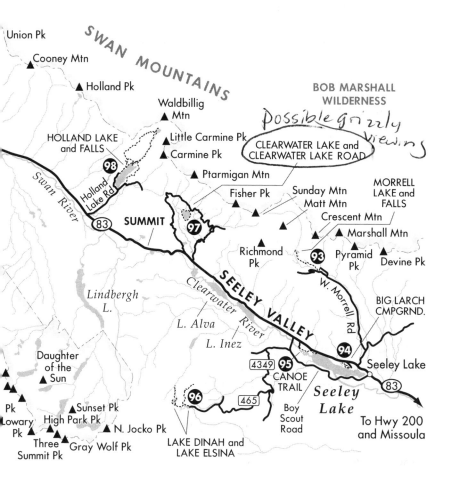

BOB MARSHALL
WILDERNESS

Union Pk

Cooney Mtn

SWAN MOUNTAINS

Holland Pk

Waldbillig
Mtn

BOB MARSHALL
WILDERNESS

Possible grizzly viewing

Little Carmine Pk

CLEARWATER LAKE and
CLEARWATER LAKE ROAD

HOLLAND LAKE
and FALLS

Carmine Pk

98

Ptarmigan Mtn

Holland Lake Rd

Fisher Pk

Sunday Mtn
Matt Mtn

MORRELL
LAKE and
FALLS

Swan River

97

Crescent Mtn

SUMMIT

83

Marshall Mtn

Richmond
Pk

93

Pyramid
Pk

Devine Pk

Lindbergh
L.

Clearwater River

SEELEY VALLEY

W. Morrell Rd

BIG LARCH
CMPGRND.

L. Alva

L. Inez

Daughter
of the
Sun

4349

95

94

Seeley Lake

CANOE
TRAIL

Seeley
Lake

83

Pk
Lowary
Pk

Sunset Pk
High Park Pk

96

465

Boy
Scout
Road

To Hwy 200
and Missoula

N. Jocko Pk

Three
Summit Pk

Gray Wolf Pk

LAKE DINAH and
LAKE ELSINA

93. Morrell Lake and Falls
MORRELL FALLS NATIONAL RECREATION TRAIL

Hiking distance: 5 miles round trip
Hiking time: 2.5 hours
Elevation gain: 250 feet
Maps: U.S.G.S. Morrell Lake · U.S.F.S. Lolo National Forest—Seeley Lake

The Morrell Falls National Recreation Trail is among the most popular trails in the Seeley Valley. Morrell Creek, formed in the Grizzly Basin, is located at the base of the Swan Mountain Range adjacent to the Bob Marshall Wilderness. The trail parallels Morrell Creek to Morrell Falls, a series of steep cascades and falls for a total 200-foot drop. The gently rolling terrain leads through an evergreen forest and passes 26-acre Morrell Lake, where Crescent Mountain rises sharply from the eastern shore. From the end of the trail and base of the falls is a stunning view of the 90-foot lower falls, the largest drop.

To the trailhead

From Missoula, drive 4 miles east on I-90 to Highway 200 East/ Exit 109. Continue 33 miles to Clearwater Junction at Highway 83 and turn left. Seeley Lake is 15 miles ahead. From the town of Seeley Lake, drive less than a half mile north to Morrell Creek Road (also known as Cottonwood Lakes Road) and turn right. Continue 1.1 miles to a signed junction. Turn left on West Morrell Road, and drive 5.6 miles to another posted junction and turn right. The trailhead parking area is 0.7 miles ahead, curving left en route.

The hike

Take the well-marked trail west from the end of the parking lot. After a short distance, curve right and head north. The rolling, forested terrain gains little elevation. At two miles, pass a pond and continue past the west shore of Morrell Lake. At the northern end of the lake is a trail fork. Take the left fork, leading away from Morrell Lake to a bridge that crosses the lake's outlet stream. From the bridge, the trail curves right to the base of Morrell Falls. Return along the same route. ■

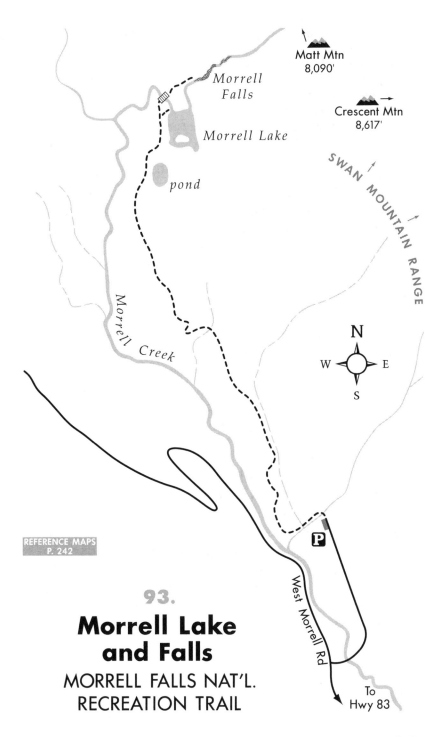

Matt Mtn
8,090'

Crescent Mtn
8,617'

Morrell Falls

Morrell Lake

pond

SWAN MOUNTAIN RANGE

Morrell Creek

N
W   E
S

REFERENCE MAPS
P. 242

P

West Morrell Rd

To
Hwy 83

93.

Morrell Lake and Falls
MORRELL FALLS NAT'L. RECREATION TRAIL

94. Big Larch Nature Trail

Hiking distance: 0.5-mile loop
Hiking time: 30 minutes
Elevation gain: level
Maps: U.S.G.S. Seeley Lake East
Lolo National Forest Big Larch Nature Trail map

The Big Larch Nature Trail borders the east shore of Seeley Lake adjacent to the Big Larch Campground just north of the town of Seeley Lake. The beachside path meanders along the lake through a mature stand of old larch trees and riparian vegetation. The trail returns through the woods with moist, rotting stumps and trees draped in lichen. A self-guided interpretive pamphlet (available at the trailhead) describes the tree species, flora, and wildlife.

To the trailhead

From Missoula, drive 4 miles east on I-90 to Highway 200 East/Exit 109. Continue 33 miles to Clearwater Junction at Highway 83 and turn left. Drive 15 miles north to the posted Big Larch Campground turnoff on the left, between mile markers 15 and 16, one mile north of the town of Seeley Lake. Turn left and drive 0.5 miles (entering the campground) to the first right turn. Turn right and park in the trailhead lot.

The hike

At the trailhead, the Big Larch Nature Trail takes off on the left. On the right is the posted Interpretive Trail, which leads 80 yards to a small seating area for campfire talks. Take the nature trail to the shoreline of Seeley Lake. To the left is a sandy beach. Curve right and follow the lakeshore through a large open grove of towering larch trees. Curve right, away from the lake, to a T-junction. The left fork continues north, weaving through the scenic larch grove. The right fork heads south, returning to the campground. Complete the loop to the right. ■

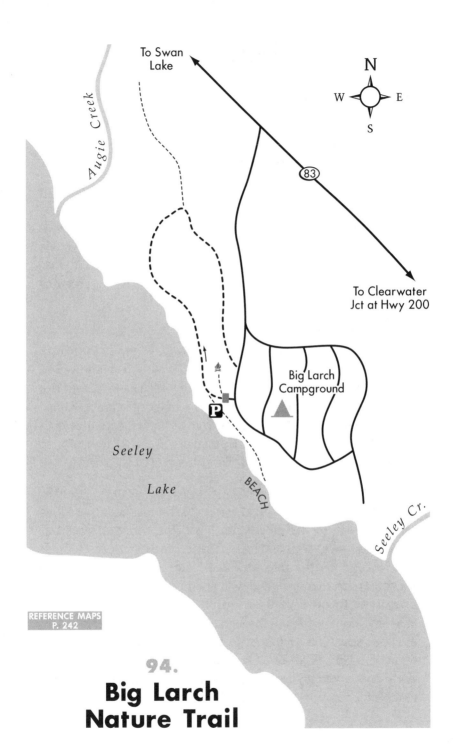

To Swan Lake

N
W E
S

Augie Creek

83

To Clearwater
Jct at Hwy 200

Big Larch
Campground

P

Seeley

Lake

BEACH

Seeley Cr.

REFERENCE MAPS
P. 242

94.
Big Larch
Nature Trail

95. Clearwater River Canoe Trail

Hiking distance: 3 miles round trip
Hiking time: 1.5 hours
Elevation gain: level
Maps: U.S.G.S. Seeley Lake West
      U.S.F.S. Lolo National Forest—Seeley Lake
      Lolo National Forest Clearwater Canoe Trail map

The Clearwater River Canoe Trail is used as a return route for canoeists on the slow-moving Clearwater River above Seeley Lake. The level trail is a wonderful path through forests and wetlands parallel to the serpentine river. The hike leads to a wildlife viewing blind overlooking a large marshy wetland. The riparian habitat along the river is the protected home to hundreds of animals, plants, waterfowl, and songbirds.

To the trailhead

From Missoula, drive 4 miles east on I-90 to Highway 200 East/ Exit 109. Continue 33 miles to Clearwater Junction at Highway 83 and turn left. Drive 17.7 miles to the Seeley Lake Ranger Station at the north end of Seeley Lake. From the ranger station, continue north on Highway 89 for 0.8 miles to the signed Clearwater River Canoe Trail turnoff, between mile markers 18 and 19. Turn left and drive 0.6 miles to the parking area at the end of the road.

The hike

Head south past the trailhead sign, crossing the meadows along the east bank of the Clearwater River. The trail alternates between open wetlands and mature aspen and pine forests. Cross the wetland on the dry, elevated path. At 1.2 miles, cross a footbridge to the wildlife viewing blind on the right. Follow the boardwalk to observe the wetland through the blind. On the main trail, continue south through the dense forest, bearing right at a trail split. Follow the edge of the wetland past the maintenance buildings. The trail arrives at the canoe takeout at the north end of Seeley Lake. A side path leads east to the Seeley Lake Ranger Station. Return along the same route. ■

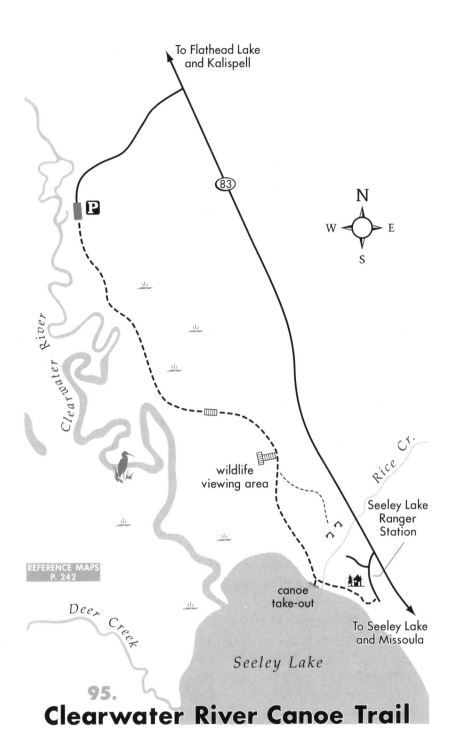

To Flathead Lake
and Kalispell

83

P

N

W ✦ E

S

Clearwater River

wildlife
viewing area

Rice Cr.

Seeley Lake
Ranger
Station

REFERENCE MAPS
P. 242

canoe
take-out

To Seeley Lake
and Missoula

Deer Creek

Seeley Lake

95.
Clearwater River Canoe Trail

96. Lake Dinah Trail from Lake Elsina

Hiking distance: 5 miles round trip
Hiking time: 2.5 hours
Elevation gain: 700 feet
Maps: U.S.G.S. Upper Jocko Lake and Lake Marshall
U.S.F.S. Lolo National Forest—Seeley Lake

Both Lake Dinah and Lake Elsina are gorgeous subalpine lakes in the high country basins of the Mission Mountains near the Clearwater-Jocko Divide. The lakes are partially covered with lily pads and surrounded by conifer forests. This trail begins at Lake Elsina and winds through lush undergrowth, dense forest, and grassy meadows to 36-acre Lake Dinah. The mosquitoes can be prolific, so bring insect repellent.

To the trailhead

From Missoula, drive 4 miles east on I-90 to Highway 200 East/Exit 109. Continue 33 miles to Clearwater Junction at Highway 83 and turn left. Drive 17.7 miles to the Seeley Lake Ranger Station at the north end of Seeley Lake. From the station, continue north on Highway 89 for 1.6 miles to the signed West Side Trail turnoff between mile markers 19 and 20. Turn left and take Boy Scout Road 0.8 miles to unpaved Forest Service Road 4349. Turn right and drive 5.5 miles to a signed road split. Bear right on Forest Service Road 465, and go 4.8 miles to a T-junction. Turn left and drive 2.1 miles to the parking area at the road's end by Lake Elsina.

The hike

Walk a few yards to Lake Elsina, and follow the eastern shoreline to the right (north). The path winds through the forest, leaving the shoreline. At the north end of the lake, cross logs over several inlet streams. Climb up a ridge and cross the flat meadow with stands of mature evergreens. At the head of the meadow, traverse the hillside over a second ridge. Watch for a junction as Lake Dinah and the Seeley Valley come into view on the right. The right fork descends to the southeastern edge of Lake Dinah. The left fork descends to the west side of the lake. Both routes are worth exploring. Return along the same path. ∎

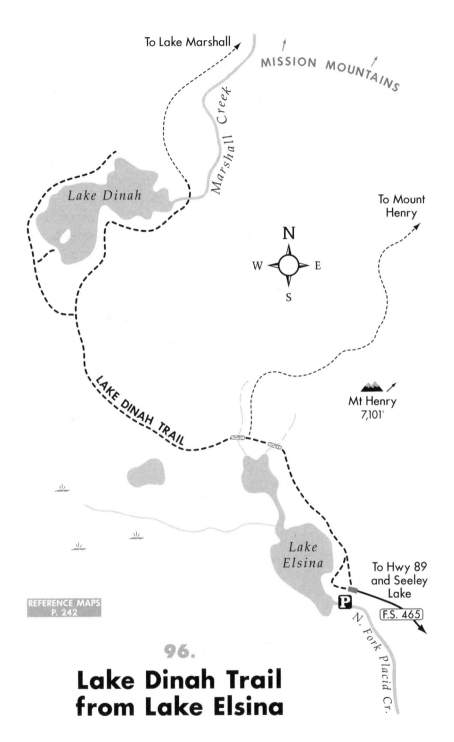

To Lake Marshall

MISSION MOUNTAINS

Marshall Creek

Lake Dinah

N
W E
S

To Mount Henry

LAKE DINAH TRAIL

Mt Henry
7,101'

Lake Elsina

To Hwy 89 and Seeley Lake

F.S. 465

REFERENCE MAPS
P. 242

P

N. Fork Placid Cr.

96.

Lake Dinah Trail from Lake Elsina

97. Clearwater Lake Loop

Hiking distance: 2.9-mile loop
Hiking time: 1.5 hours
Elevation gain: near level
Maps: U.S.G.S. Holland Lake
U.S.F.S. Lolo National Forest—Seeley Lake

Clearwater Lake reposes beneath Ptarmigan Mountain at the foot of the Swan Mountain Range. The 120-acre lake is completely surrounded by a lush, old-growth forest. The Swan Mountain Range looms to the east while the Mission Mountain Range stretches across the western horizon. This easy, level trail circles the perimeter of the lake, which lies a short distance from the headwaters of the Clearwater River. Ducks and loons are frequently spotted on the lake.

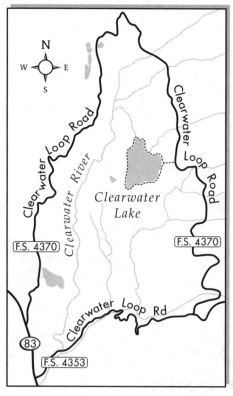

To the trailhead

From Missoula, drive 4 miles east on I-90 to Highway 200 East/Exit 109. Continue 33 miles to Clearwater Junction at Highway 83 and turn left. Seeley Lake is 15 miles ahead. From the town of Seeley Lake, continue north on Highway 89 for 13.6 miles to Clearwater Loop Road on the right, between mile markers 28 and 29. Turn right and continue 7 miles on the winding road to the Clearwater Lake trailhead parking area on the west side of the road.

After the hike, the drive can be continued along

the Clearwater Loop Road for another 6.2 miles. The road loops up and around, back to Highway 83. (See map on page 252.)

The hike

The trail heads west through the forest for a short quarter mile to Clearwater Lake. Choose either direction around the lake. The perimeter of Clearwater Lake is 2.4 miles; the trail stays close to the shoreline, with a few small dips and rises and several stream crossings. Throughout the hike are vistas of the Mission Mountains and the Swan Mountains. ■

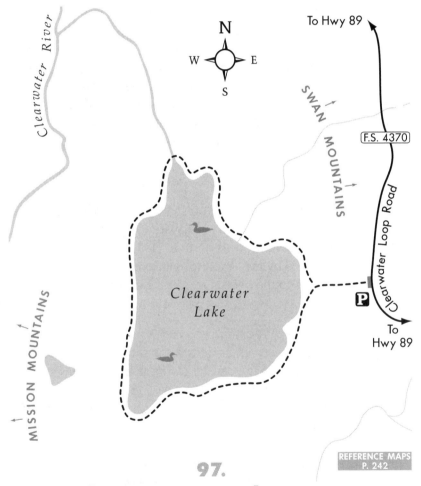

97.

Clearwater Lake Loop

98. Holland Lake and Falls

Hiking distance: 3 miles round trip
Hiking time: 2 hours
Elevation gain: 600 feet
Maps: U.S.G.S. Holland Lake · U.S.F.S. Lolo National Forest—Seeley Lake

Holland Lake is a large 416-acre lake that lies at the base of the Swan Mountains at an elevation of 4,031 feet. The lake is fed by Holland Creek, which forms in the upper reaches of Waldbillig Mountain on the edge of the Bob Marshall Wilderness. Holland Falls is a beautiful and majestic 84-foot waterfall at the far east end of the lake. The Holland Falls Trail parallels the northern shore of Holland Lake to the creek and falls. The trail passes through stands of evergreens and leads to rock ledges, natural coves, and resting areas ideal for viewing the falls. From the overlook are sweeping vistas across Holland Lake, the Swan Valley, and the Mission Mountains. The trail is a popular access route into the Bob Marshall Wilderness, passing Upper Holland Lake en route to the boundary.

To the trailhead

From Missoula, drive 4 miles east on I-90 to Highway 200 East/Exit 109. Continue 33 miles to Clearwater Junction at Highway 83 and turn left. Drive 35 miles north to Holland Lake Road, right after mile marker 35 by the large "Holland Lake" sign. Turn right and continue 3.8 miles to the parking area at the end of the road.

The hike

From the parking area, take the posted trail south toward the shore of Holland Lake. Twenty yards before the shoreline, the Holland Falls Trail heads east (left), parallel to the lake's northern shore. As the trail climbs and dips along the hillside, pass a beautifully forested island in Holland Lake. At the east end of the lake, curve around the shoreline to four log crossings over inlet streams. After crossing, ascend 400 feet up a series of switchbacks. As the trail climbs, magnificent views emerge of the lake, the expansive glacial valley, and the snow-streaked Mission Mountains. At 1.5 miles, the trail reaches the rocky ledges overlooking Holland

Falls. To return, retrace your steps, or continue around the lake on the Holland Gordon Trail for a 5.5-mile loop.

The Holland Gordon Trail continues along the creek for 5 miles to Upper Holland Lake, just below the wilderness boundary and Waldbillig Mountain. The trail gains another 1,750 feet to the upper lake. ■

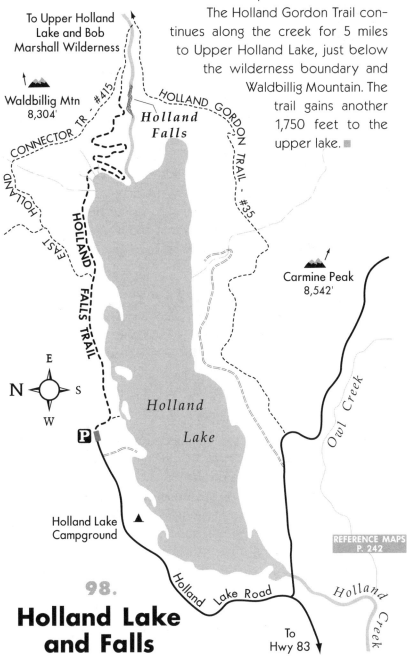

To Upper Holland Lake and Bob Marshall Wilderness

Waldbillig Mtn
8,304'

CONNECTOR TR. - #415

Holland Falls

HOLLAND GORDON TRAIL - #35

EAST HOLLAND

HOLLAND FALLS TRAIL

Carmine Peak
8,542'

N ← E / S / W

Holland Lake

P

Holland Lake Campground

Owl Creek

REFERENCE MAPS
P. 242

98.

Holland Lake and Falls

Holland Lake Road

Holland Creek

To Hwy 83

99. Everchanging Forest Nature Trail

Hiking distance: 1.2 miles round trip
Hiking time: 1 hour
Elevation gain: 50 feet
Maps: U.S.G.S. Condon
Swan Ecosystem Center Everchanging Forest Trail map

The Everchanging Forest Nature Trail borders the Swan River by the Condon Ranger Station in Upper Swan Valley. The trail follows a section of the original road through Swan Valley, abandoned in the late 1950s. The old roadbed leads through an evergreen forest on Smith Flats. A side path leads to a channel of the Swan River under towering cottonwoods. Another side path weaves through an old logging site. The self-guided interpretive trail describes the forces of nature in a forest and how insects, birds, and animals affect the decaying trees.

To the trailhead

From Missoula, drive 4 miles east on I-90 to Highway 200 East/ Exit 109. Continue 33 miles to Clearwater Junction at Highway 83 and turn left. Drive 42 miles north to the Condon Ranger Station and Swan Ecosystem Center on the left, between mile markers 42 and 43. Turn left and drive 0.1 mile, passing the ranger station and following the trail signs to the trailhead parking area.

The hike

Two trails depart from the trailhead. To the right is a short 0.15-mile Firewise Interpretive Trail. Begin on the left fork on the Everchanging Forest Nature Trail. A short distance ahead is a posted junction. Veer left on the Streamside Loop, and descend 22 steps into a cottonwood tree grove. The riparian vegetation includes tall reed canary grass, junipers, willows, alders, spruce, and dogwood. Stroll northwest along the river channel. Leave the streamside area and ascend the hill, returning to the Closed Canopy Connector Trail (the old road). Head north through a stand of ponderosa pine to the Open Ponderosa Loop on the right. Bear right and weave through the grove clockwise, passing interpretive panels around the loop. Return to the left on the old roadway. ■

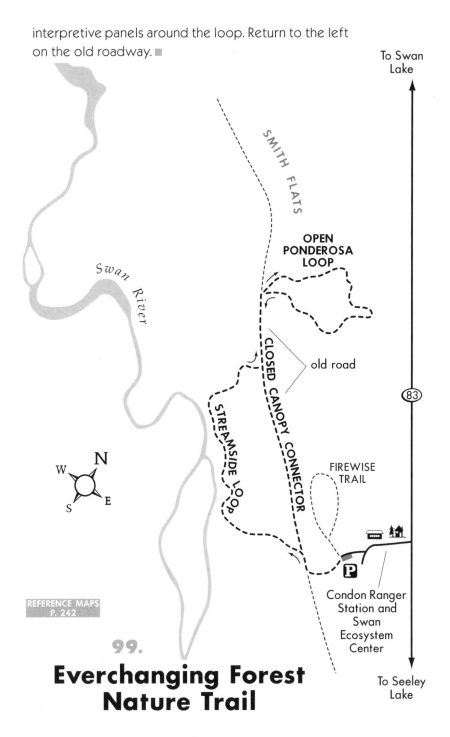

To Swan Lake

SMITH FLATS

OPEN PONDEROSA LOOP

Swan River

old road

CLOSED CANOPY CONNECTOR

STREAMSIDE LOOP

FIREWISE TRAIL

N
W   E
S

83

P

Condon Ranger Station and Swan Ecosystem Center

To Seeley Lake

REFERENCE MAPS P. 242

99.
Everchanging Forest Nature Trail

100. Lower Cold Lake

Hiking distance: 3.6 miles round trip
Hiking time: 2 hours
Elevation gain: 700 feet
Maps: U.S.G.S. Piper Crow Pass and Peck Lake
U.S.F.S. Lolo National Forest—Seeley Lake

Lower Cold Lake sits just below the crest of the Mission Range on a scenic 5,745-foot shelf in the Mission Mountains Wilderness. Rugged mountains to the south and west bound the beautiful tree-lined lake. The 80-acre lake is fed by the North Fork of Cold Creek and Upper Cold Lake, residing in a mountain cirque above. This hike follows the watercourse of the North Fork of Cold Creek through a mixed forest to the Lower Cold Lake shoreline. En route, the trail crosses tributary streams and log bridges over the creek.

To the trailhead

From Missoula, drive 4 miles east on I-90 to Highway 200 East/Exit 109. Continue 33 miles to Clearwater Junction at Highway 83 and turn left. Drive 46.7 miles north to posted Cold Creek Road #903 on the left, between mile markers 46 and 47. Turn left and drive 3 miles west to the signed Forest Service Road 9568. Veer right and drive 2.9 miles to a posted road fork. Turn left onto Forest Service Road 9599, and go 1.5 miles to the trailhead at the end of the road on a large grassy flat.

From the north, Cold Creek Road is located 23 miles south of Swan Lake.

The hike

Head west into the lush forest with an understory of huckleberries, thimbleberries, and beargrass. Enter the Mission Mountains Wilderness at a quarter mile, and cross a seasonal feeder stream, passing scattered moss-covered boulders. At 0.6 miles, cross a log bridge over the North Fork of Cold Creek, and climb a natural stone staircase. Cross another log bridge over a rocky creekbed and pass a fern-filled grotto. At one mile, cross the North Fork of Cold Creek once again on a large, single-log bridge.

Traverse the south edge of a tree-rimmed meadow, backed by the dramatic peaks along the ridge of the Mission Mountains. Pass a pond on the right, which evolves into a wet meadow late in the season. Continue uphill on a gentle grade to the northeast end of Lower Cold Lake at the base of the steep mountains. Return along the same route.

To extend the hike, walk along the north end of the lake to the inlet stream, and climb a quarter mile to Upper Cold Lake. This area does not have a trail and entails navigating over downfall. ■

MISSION MOUNTAINS

Upper Cold Lake

Lower Cold Lake

Cold Creek

North Fork

MISSION MOUNTAINS WILDERNESS

FLATHEAD NATIONAL FOREST

REFERENCE MAPS P. 242

P

F.S. 9599

To Hwy 83

100.
Lower Cold Lake

101. Sprunger—Whitney Nature Trail

Hiking distance: 2.1-mile loop
Hiking time: 1 hour
Elevation gain: 240 feet
Maps: U.S.G.S. Cilly Creek · Sprunger-Whitney Nature Trail map

The Sprunger—Whitney Nature Trail lies along the Swan River seven miles south of Swan Lake. The trail is named for Elmer Sprunger and Jack Whitney, long-time resident conservationists in the Swan Valley. The interpretive trail begins at the Point Pleasant Campground and follows a section of the Old Swan Highway, originally a Pend d'Oreilles and Bitterroot Salish Indian trail. It was also a portion of the route used by Lewis and Clark. The trail weaves through an old-growth riparian forest with a vast cross-section of trees. Interpretive panels describe the tree species, plants, life cycles, and the effects of insects and other natural forces.

To the trailhead

From Missoula, drive 4 miles east on I-90 to Highway 200 East/ Exit 109. Continue 33 miles to Clearwater Junction at Highway 83 and turn left. Drive 63 miles north to posted Point Pleasant Campground turnoff on the left, between mile markers 63 and 64. Turn left and drive 0.15 miles to the first turnoff on the right on a horseshoe bend in the road. Turn right and go 0.1 mile to the parking area on the right.

From the north, the Point Pleasant Campground turnoff is located 7 miles south of Swan Lake.

The hike

Pass the guardrail and follow the wide, grassy path (the old road-bed) through the open forest. Follow the gradual uphill slope, overlooking the meadow and the Mission Mountains to the west. At a quarter mile is a posted Y-fork. Begin the loop to the left. Gradually descend through a mosaic of trees, including a tree marred from a lightening strike at signpost 2. Quickly reach the valley floor down a series of five switchbacks. Weave through the fern-filled valley bottom on a spongy needle-covered path.

Cross a log bridge and meander through old-growth stands of western larch, passing a tree with scars from bear scratchings. Zigzag up the hillside, returning to the old road. Bear right on the old roadbed back to the trailhead. ■

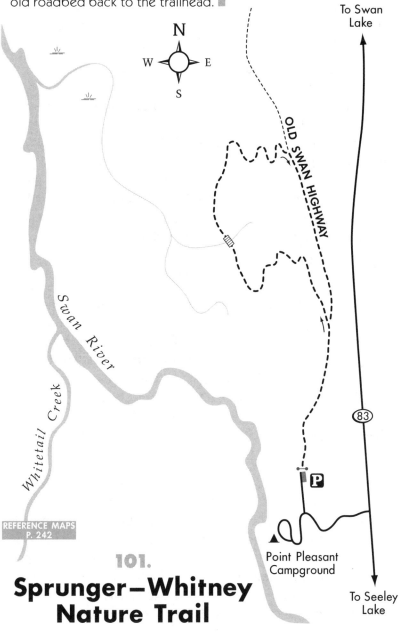

N
W E
S

To Swan
Lake

OLD SWAN HIGHWAY

Swan River

Whitetail Creek

83

REFERENCE MAPS
P. 242

101.
**Sprunger–Whitney
Nature Trail**

P

Point Pleasant
Campground

To Seeley
Lake

102. Bond Creek Trail at Swan Lake

Hiking distance: 3.5 miles round trip
Hiking time: 2 hours
Elevation gain: 300 feet
Maps: U.S.G.S. Swan Lake
U.S.F.S. Flathead National Forest

Bond Lake is nestled in a 5,400-foot mountain basin on the north flank of Spring Slide Mountain in the Swan Range. Bond Creek cascades out of the five-acre lake and tumbles six miles west, dropping 2,300 feet into Swan Lake. The Bond Creek Trail follows the course of the creek six miles to Bond Lake and continues another mile up to Trinkus Lake. This easy hike follows the lower end of the trail through a quiet, thick forest with birch trees, maples, and lichen-draped conifers. A thick riparian understory with ferns, thimbleberry, and Oregon grape blanket the ground. The trail leads to a large, single-log bridge over Bond Creek.

To the trailhead

From Missoula, drive 4 miles east on I-90 to Highway 200 East/ Exit 109. Continue 33 miles to Clearwater Junction at Highway 83 and turn left. Drive 69 miles north to the posted Bond Creek trailhead on the right (east) side of the road, between mile markers 69 and 70. Turn right on the gravel road, and park on the left at the base of the hill by the trailhead. The gravel road continues 0.1 mile to the upper stock trailhead parking area.

From the north, the trailhead is located 0.8 miles south of the Swan Lake post office.

The hike

Walk east into the dense conifer forest and lush understory. Merge with the stock trail from the upper trailhead in 100 yards, and cross a bridge over a feeder stream. At 1.2 miles is a T-junction with the north end of Forest Service Road 9507 on an open flat. Bear left and continue on the footpath, staying on the posted Bond Creek Trail. Follow the left side of a tributary stream, then cross it on a wooden bridge. Parallel the south edge of Bond Creek, and gradually descend to the creek at 1.7 miles.

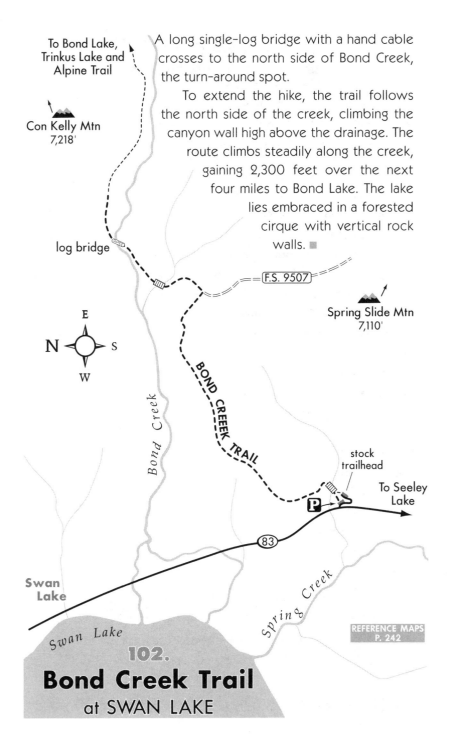

A long single-log bridge with a hand cable crosses to the north side of Bond Creek, the turn-around spot.

To extend the hike, the trail follows the north side of the creek, climbing the canyon wall high above the drainage. The route climbs steadily along the creek, gaining 2,300 feet over the next four miles to Bond Lake. The lake lies embraced in a forested cirque with vertical rock walls. ■

To Bond Lake, Trinkus Lake and Alpine Trail

Con Kelly Mtn
7,218'

log bridge

F.S. 9507

Spring Slide Mtn
7,110'

N E S W

Bond Creek

BOND CREEK TRAIL

stock trailhead

P

To Seeley Lake

83

Swan Lake

Swan Lake

Spring Creek

REFERENCE MAPS
P. 242

102.
Bond Creek Trail
at SWAN LAKE

DAY HIKE BOOKS

Day Hikes In Yellowstone National Park	978-1-57342-048-8	$12.95
Day Hikes In Grand Teton National Park	978-1-57342-046-4	11.95
Day Hikes In the Beartooth Mountains Billings to Red Lodge to Yellowstone N.P.	978-1-57342-064-8	15.95
Day Hikes Around Bozeman, Montana	978-1-57342-063-1	15.95
Day Hikes Around Missoula, Montana	978-1-57342-066-2	15.95
Day Hikes In Sequoia and Kings Canyon N.P.	978-1-57342-030-3	12.95
Day Hikes In Yosemite National Park	978-1-57342-059-4	13.95
Day Hikes On the California Central Coast	978-1-57342-058-7	17.95
Day Hikes On the California Southern Coast	978-1-57342-045-7	14.95
Day Hikes In the Santa Monica Mountains	978-1-57342-065-5	21.95
Day Hikes Around Sonoma County	978-1-57342-053-2	16.95
Day Hikes Around Napa Valley	978-1-57342-057-0	16.95
Day Hikes Around Monterey and Carmel	978-1-57342-067-9	19.95
Day Hikes Around Big Sur	978-1-57342-041-9	14.95
Day Hikes Around San Luis Obispo	978-1-57342-051-8	16.95
Day Hikes Around Santa Barbara	978-1-57342-060-0	17.95
Day Hikes Around Ventura County	978-1-57342-062-4	17.95
Day Hikes Around Los Angeles	978-1-57342-061-7	17.95
Day Hikes Around Orange County	978-1-57342-047-1	15.95
Day Hikes Around Sedona, Arizona	978-1-57342-049-5	14.95
Day Hikes On Oahu	978-1-57342-038-9	11.95
Day Hikes On Maui	978-1-57342-039-6	11.95
Day Hikes On Kauai	978-1-57342-040-2	11.95
Day Hikes In Hawaii	978-1-57342-050-1	16.95

These books may be purchased at your local bookstore or outdoor shop. Or, order them direct from the distributor:

The Globe Pequot Press

246 Goose Lane • P.O. Box 480 • Guilford, CT 06437-0480
on the web: www.globe-pequot.com

800-243-0495 DIRECT **800-820-2329** FAX

DAY HIKES IN
Yellowstone
NATIONAL PARK
82 GREAT HIKES
Robert Stone

DAY HIKES IN
Grand Teton
NATIONAL PARK
72 GREAT HIKES
Robert Stone

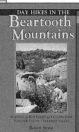
DAY HIKES IN THE
Beartooth Mountains
Robert Stone

DAY HIKES AROUND
Bozeman
MONTANA
Robert Stone

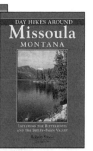
DAY HIKES AROUND
Missoula
MONTANA
Robert Stone

DAY HIKES IN
Sequoia & **Kings Canyon**
NATIONAL PARKS
Robert Stone

DAY HIKES IN
Yosemite
NATIONAL PARK
80 GREAT HIKES
Robert Stone

DAY HIKES ON THE
California Central Coast
120 COASTAL HIKES FROM SANTA CRUZ TO SANTA BARBARA
Robert Stone

DAY HIKES ON THE
California Southern Coast
100 GREAT HIKES
Robert Stone

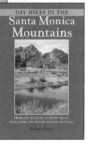
DAY HIKES IN THE
Santa Monica Mountains
FROM LOS ANGELES TO POINT MUGU INCLUDING THE ENTIRE BACKBONE TRAIL
Robert Stone

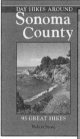
DAY HIKES AROUND
Sonoma County
95 GREAT HIKES
Robert Stone

DAY HIKES AROUND
Napa Valley
88 GREAT HIKES
Robert Stone

DAY HIKES AROUND
Monterey & Carmel
Robert Stone

DAY HIKES AROUND
Big Sur
80 GREAT HIKES
Robert Stone

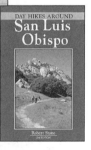
DAY HIKES AROUND
San Luis Obispo
Robert Stone

DAY HIKES AROUND
Santa Barbara
113 GREAT HIKES
Robert Stone

DAY HIKES AROUND
Ventura County
116 GREAT HIKES
Robert Stone

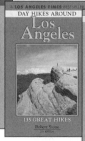
DAY HIKES AROUND
Los Angeles
135 GREAT HIKES
Robert Stone

DAY HIKES AROUND
Orange County
108 GREAT HIKES
Robert Stone

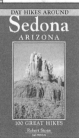
DAY HIKES AROUND
Sedona
ARIZONA
100 GREAT HIKES
Robert Stone

Day Hikes Around Bozeman, Montana

Bozeman, Montana is an amiable mountain community steeped in history and surrounded by stunning landscape. The city lies between the Gallatin and Yellowstone River valleys amidst several mountain ranges that run through the Continental Divide. The fantastic scenery combined with national forests, wilderness areas, and an outdoor-oriented community make the hiking in this area superb.

Day Hikes Around Bozeman, Montana has won awards from both the Northwest Outdoor Writers Association and the Rocky Mountain Outdoor Writers and Photographers. This guide book includes 110 of the best day hikes in a straight-forward, hassle-free guide aimed to get you on the trails. *Outside Bozeman Magazine* affirms, "This is a must-have book. Period."

320 pages • 110 hikes • 4th Edition 2011 • ISBN 978-1-57342-063-1

Day Hikes In Yellowstone National Park

Yellowstone National Park is a magnificent area with beautiful, dramatic scenery and incredible hydrothermal features. Within its 2.2-millions acres lies some of the earth's greatest natural treasures.

Day Hikes In Yellowstone National Park includes a thorough cross-section of 82 hikes throughout the park. Now in its fourth edition, the guide includes all of the park's most popular hikes as well as a wide assortment of secluded backcountry trails. Highlights include thundering waterfalls, unusual thermal features, expansive meadows, alpine lakes, quiet forest paths, the Grand Canyon of the Yellowstone, geysers, hot springs, and 360-degree vistas of the park.

184 pages • 82 hikes • 4th Edition 2005 • ISBN 978-1-57342-048-8

LINDA STONE

About the Author

Since 1991, Robert Stone has been writer, photographer, and publisher of Day Hike Books. He is a Los Angeles Times Best Selling Author and an award-winning journalist of Rocky Mountain Outdoor Writers and Photographers, the Outdoor Writers Association of California, the Northwest Outdoor Writers Association, the Outdoor Writers Association of America, and the Bay Area Travel Writers.

Robert has hiked every trail in the Day Hike Book series. With 24 hiking guides in the series, many in their fourth and fifth editions, he has hiked thousands of miles of trails throughout the western United States and Hawaii. When Robert is not hiking, he researches, writes, and maps the hikes before returning to the trails. He spends summers in the Rocky Mountains of Montana and winters on the California Central Coast.